# MANAGEMENT CONSULTING

# MANAGEMENT CONSULTING

## A COMPLETE GUIDE TO THE INDUSTRY

**Sugata Biswas** and **Daryl Twitchell**

### John Wiley & Sons, Inc.

New York • Chichester • Weinheim • Brisbane • Singapore • Toronto

Maura Rurak and Perri Capell (page 27) appear with permission from the *National Business Employment Weekly,* © Dow Jones & Co., Inc. All rights reserved.

Nina Munk and Suzanne Oliver (page 133) appear with permission from *Forbes.*

This book is printed on acid-free paper. ∞

This publication is designed to provide accurate and authoritative information in regard to the subject matter covered. It is sold with the understanding that the publisher is not engaged in rendering professional services. If professional advice or other expert assistance is required, the services of a competent professional person should be sought.

*Library of Congress Cataloging-in-Publication Data:*

Biswas, Sugata, 1967–
    Management consulting : a complete guide to the
industry / Sugata Biswas, Daryl Twitchell.
        p.      cm.
    Includes bibliographical references and index.
    ISBN 0-471-29352-0 (cloth : alk. paper)
    1. Business consultants.   2. Business consultants
—Vocational guidance.   I. Twitchell, Daryl, 1971–
II. Title.
HD69.C6B537   1999
001'.023'73—dc21                              98-30144

Printed in the United States of America.

10 9 8 7 6 5 4 3

# ACKNOWLEDGMENTS

**W**e want to express our sincere appreciation for all the assistance we received in writing this book. Over the past two years, we refined our approach to understanding the industry and our strategies for getting a job in consulting, by teaching and receiving feedback from hundreds of people. We thank all those who have contributed to the development of our concepts: practicing consultants and firm leaders, recognized business academics, professional recruiters, industry thought-leaders, and undergraduate and graduate students at Brown University, Cornell University, University of Pennsylvania, and Yale University. Because we have worked with such a wide range of industry leaders, candidates, and recruiters, our book encompasses a full range of perspectives.

In particular, we are grateful for the assistance of the following people: Lisa Adams, President of The Garamond Agency; Barry Nalebuff, Milton Steinbach Professor at Yale School of Management; Rena Henderson, Editor; and the editors at John Wiley & Sons, Inc.

Finally, we extend a special acknowledgment to Tim Bourgeois, Director of Research at Kennedy Information Research Group, for his generosity in granting us access to their consulting industry data. Kennedy Information is the leading information provider on the management consulting profession, and can claim more than 25 years of experience in this role. Through its two flagship publications,

## Acknowledgments

*Consultants News* and *The Directory of Management Consultants,* and its recently formed research group, Kennedy maintains an extensive database of the most up-to-date and comprehensive information available on management consulting.

S.B.
D.T.

# CONTENTS

# Chapter 3
## PERSPECTIVES ON CONSULTING    41

# Contents

# MANAGEMENT CONSULTING

# INTRODUCTION

**B**ecause you are interested in the field of management consulting, you probably already know that it is one of the most popular career choices for today's graduating students and career-changing professionals. The industry is growing fast, both in the demand from organizations seeking consulting services and in the supply of candidates seeking a consulting position. Although thousands of individuals receive offers every year, tens of thousands compete for those offers. In the face of such intense competition, applicants need all the help they can get.

Students, who especially like the accelerated professional track of consulting, have turned the field into one of the hottest choices for entry-level professionals. Approximately 40 percent of graduates in each MBA class attempt to enter the consulting industry, and between 30 and 35 percent of these candidates get an offer. Undergraduates, too, find the field incredibly attractive and often face the same intense competition to land a consulting job offer. Intrigued by the doors that consulting can open, even graduating JDs, MAs, MSs, PhDs, MPPs, MIAs, and MDs, to name but a few other degrees, have been applying for positions in increasing numbers. And even professionals with established careers look toward consulting for opportunities to accelerate their professional development, or to switch career directions entirely. As management consulting firms multiply and grow, the demand for experienced hires who can establish and build new practices will likewise grow. But once again, the number of candidates exceeds the available positions, making the competition fierce.

Firms, literally buried in resumes, have developed a highly stylized and occasionally mysterious tool to select the top candidates from the masses: the case interview. The most challenging hurdle to clear in the job search process is the abstract and often technical case question. Even if you are fortunate enough to be invited to interview, you might be quickly eliminated by a single case question such as "How much does a Boeing 747 jumbo jet weigh?" or, "How does Amtrak price a rail ticket from Boston to Washington, DC?"[1]

And even if you make it through the first case interview, you typically have to survive three to five more. The process closely resembles the old carrot and stick maneuver: As you successfully navigate each case interview, you feel another step closer to that elusive offer. Guess again. Yet another savvy consultant stands ready to challenge you with an additional case interview. Any one of these interviews has the power to eliminate you, even if you impressed the firm in previous interviews. Only those candidates who maintain the stamina and drive to succeed in each and every case interview will ultimately receive an offer.

The competition has become so severe that candidates now have to invest considerable time in researching firms and practicing cases. Just as test prep courses for standardized tests like the SAT or GMAT have helped people get higher scores, so too has interview training become the key to a successful consulting job search. You need all the help you can get to remain competitive with your peers, who are preparing for interviews at the same set of leading management consulting firms. Everything counts: knowing the firms in detail; understanding one's strengths and weaknesses and how to position them to a firm; being comfortable with the language of consulting and being able to think on one's feet; and appreciating the importance of organizational culture and "fit."

Are you completely discouraged? Don't be. By simply reading this far, you have already started your preparation and are that much ahead of your peers. *Management Consulting: A Complete Guide to the Industry* is the first consolidated resource containing information on every step of the management consulting job search. From the initial introspective stage of considering consulting as a career, to learning about the work and lifestyle from those who experience it every day, to interviewing and, finally, negotiating among offers, this book will help you stand apart from your competition. The chapters that follow cover each step of the consulting job search process in detail, providing valuable insider information on the work and lifestyle of the profession, as well as tools and techniques for successfully landing a job offer.

Chapters 1, 2, and 3, by painting an objective, candid picture of the industry, will help you decide whether management consulting is the career for you. After you have evaluated your interest in consulting and are ready to begin the job search, continue with Chapter 4 and learn how to get your foot in the door. Chapter 5 then teaches you a proven step-by-step method for successfully navigating case interviews, as you work your way to an offer. And finally, Chapter 6 teaches you how to negotiate among your offers for the most attractive package.

In addition, three unique appendixes provide critical information for a successful consulting job search. Appendix I lists 15 of the most common case frameworks to draw on when answering case questions. Even if you have a prior academic or professional business background, you can benefit from reviewing these business topics and learn to use them effectively during case interviews. When you are ready to practice interviewing, turn to Appendix II, where you will find 100 case questions and 10 sample answers. And for easy reference, Appendix III provides a directory of 50 consulting firms.

By arming yourself with knowledge of the industry and its firms, and by mastering your interview skills, you will be prepared to successfully navigate the consulting job search process. We believe you will find this book an invaluable investment in your future career as a management consultant.

# CHAPTER 1

## THE MANAGEMENT CONSULTING INDUSTRY

*Management consultants directly out of business school can earn over $100,000 a year. It is yours if you can estimate the number of gas stations in the United States.*

**S**tarting salaries in management consulting are among the highest available for entry-level professionals, rivaling the traditionally high earnings potential of investment banking, venture capital, and law. Whether changing career paths or graduating from school, candidates are inundating firms across the country with applications for a relatively few coveted jobs. In 1998, top business school graduates fortunate enough to land a management consulting job received starting salaries of approximately $92,500[1] plus signing bonuses up to $40,000, while undergraduates received base salaries of $40,000 to $45,000 plus a bonus of around $5,000.

But the potential to earn stratospheric salaries is only one of the attractions of consulting; candidates also recognize its power to accelerate a career. Former consultants are valued for their carefully trained analytical minds and for their presumed expertise at solving business problems. As a result, many who leave consulting are likely to enter companies at higher levels than their peers who have worked the same number of years, but in other fields. There is a strong and arguably justified perception that a stint as a management consultant is the key to future professional success.

5

Sounds great, but is the occupation right for you? Are you ready and willing to jump on the consulting bandwagon? With the information in this chapter, you can begin to develop a complete and candid picture of management consulting. We introduce you to the profession that has attracted such high interest and help you answer these and other questions as you explore your career goals. We describe several kinds of management consultants and what they do. We then examine the consulting product and explain some of the popular theories of strategy. We show you how to segment the wide range of consulting practices into categories to obtain a broad view of the industry. And finally, we look at the origins and development of the profession, and offer some perspectives on emerging trends in the industry. The rich and multifaceted story of management consulting is entertaining as well as helpful as you move toward becoming an industry expert.

# THE ROLE OF A MANAGEMENT CONSULTANT

The traditional professional titles of "lawyer," "architect," or "medical doctor" have widely recognized definitions. But when people hear the title "management consultant," they tend to define it either as (1) an extremely important, impressively bright individual, who deals only with the top management of large companies on critical matters; or (2) simply an unemployed individual who has resorted to selling time for a fee until a real job comes along. Neither description is entirely accurate.

To truly understand what a management consultant does, we need to analyze the role of a "consultant," a universal term for any professional who provides assistance to others, usually for a fee. Under this definition, we can imagine consultants operating in just about any industry—and indeed they do. Graphic design consultants, wedding consultants, fashion consultants, and career consultants are recognizable consulting roles, but other consultants with whom we deal all the time are college advisers, headhunters, travel agents, and even realtors. The list is almost infinite. Simply select an industry name or practice area, add the word "consulting," and you have identified yet another type. Management consulting is but one kind of consulting in the marketplace, and it is by no means the only trade referred to in that sense.

What, exactly, do management consultants do? Of their many responsibilities, perhaps the most common is the identification, diagnosis, and resolution of business issues. A company experiencing a severe decline in profits may hire a management consulting firm to develop a strategy for reversing the trend. Conversely, a company enjoying rapid growth and astoundingly high profitability may look to management consultants for a way to remain successful. Although the issues consultants examine are sometimes positive and sometimes negative, they all have significant implications for an organization's future. Management consultants are hired to predict these implications and to help a company seize control of its destiny.

In addition to working as business doctors, management consultants often fill a host of other roles: (1) officiating as experts in a given industry, operational function, or business situation; (2) serving as unbiased, external third parties to validate a concept or argument; (3) confirming a hypothesis or point of view through exhaustive analysis; (4) acting as conflict resolution mediators; (5) teaching organizations how to make decisions; (6) facilitating discussions to convert information into knowledge; and many more.

The list of roles is endless. New consulting firms offering unique specialties open every year, and continue to expand the competencies of the management consulting profession. Between 1980 and 1996, the demand for management consultants ballooned from less than $5 billion in total worldwide revenues to more than $60 billion, as is illustrated in Figure 1.1. And the industry is expected to grow at a similarly rapid pace, topping $100 billion by the year 2000.

## THE CONSULTING PRODUCT

What are consulting firms selling to generate such high revenues? The primary product is the intellectual capital of its consultants: quick and

**Figure 1.1**
**The Global Consulting Marketplace, 1980–2000**

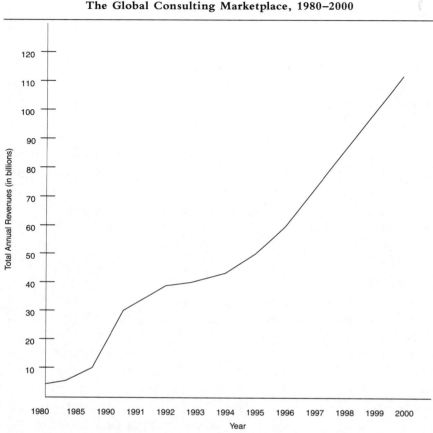

*Source: The Global Management Consulting Marketplace: Key Data, Forecasts & Trends, 1997 Edition.* Kennedy Information Research Group, 1998.

astute minds, proprietary business and organizational strategies, and an aptitude for managing relationships. Thus, the consulting product is actually a service that has an immensely valuable potential to bring about significant change. Because consultants are neither fortune-tellers nor magicians, they cannot guarantee a certain outcome from their work. They can only offer their best recommendation for success, stand prepared to respond to unexpected changes and road-blocks, and collaborate closely with their clients in developing a strategy to achieve a stated goal. Thus, the final outcome of a consultant's service is a goal rather than a certainty. Like teachers, who are compensated for helping others grow, consultants are paid for the objective of helping organizations improve. Therefore, the effectiveness of a consultant is only as good as the intellectual capital of the consulting team.

But when all firms claim to have the brightest and most astute consulting minds, how can a company know which to select? Consulting firms recognize this dilemma and attempt to attract companies by neatly packaging their intellectual capital under trademarked strategic frameworks, often derogatorily described as business buzzwords. A wide array of strategic frameworks have been promoted over the years; some of the most popular ones are presented in Table 1.1.

While some frameworks focus on growth and attempt to help organizations increase revenues and market share, others concentrate on cost-cutting initiatives to help organizations protect against losses. On the growth side, recent strategies include "Value Migration" by Corporate Decisions, Inc. (now Mercer Management Consulting), and "Value Engineering" by Booz•Allen & Hamilton. And to evaluate the competitive dynamics of an industry to identify an attractive market niche, Monitor Company promoted Michael E. Porter's "Five Forces," and The Boston Consulting Group touted its "Growth-Share Matrix," now famous for its use as a portfolio strategy tool. On the cost-cutting side, CSC Index achieved astounding success by promoting "Reengineering," and was soon followed by a host of other firms offering similar products under different names.

# THE RANGE OF CONSULTING FIRMS

Since consulting is generally considered a behind-the-scenes professional service, it rarely receives widespread press coverage—except, perhaps, from business publications. And since many consulting engagements involve unpleasant or not-so-glamorous issues (e.g., downsizing), companies undergoing such negative change do not

**Table 1.1**
**Selected Consulting Concepts**

| Concept | Year | Consultant | Organization |
|---|---|---|---|
| Portfolio Analysis | 1976 | Henderson | The Boston Consulting Group |
| Five Forces | 1980 | Porter | Monitor Company |
| Value Chain Analysis | 1985 | Porter | Monitor Company |
| Core Competencies | 1990 | Hamel & Prahalad | Harvard/Michigan/Strategos |
| Customer Retention | 1990 | Reichheld | Bain & Company |
| Cycle Time Reduction | 1990 | Stalk | The Boston Consulting Group |
| Mass Customization | 1992 | Pine | Strategic Horizons/Diamond Technology Partners |
| Reengineering | 1993 | Hammer & Champy | CSC |
| Shareholder Value Analysis/Economic Value Added (EVA) | 1993 | Stewart | Stern Stewart |
| Value Migration | 1996 | Slywotsky | Corporate Decisions, Inc. |
| Value Net | 1996 | Brandenburger & Nalebuff | Harvard and Yale |

*Source: The Global Management Consulting Marketplace: Key Data, Forecasts & Trends 1997 Edition.* Kennedy Information Research Group, 1998.

want their consultants to discuss projects with the press. However, some organizations can gain from actively publicizing their consulting engagements, especially if the organization's stakeholders (investors, customers, employees) are likely to react positively to a serious investment in change (i.e., hiring management consultants).

Still, most consulting firms are not household names, and you may be familiar with only a few—such as the largest forty management consulting firms presented in Table 1.2. It might be easy to assume that these firms represent the full spectrum of consulting practices. But such a narrow perception of the literally thousands of consulting firms could cause a candidate to overlook a potentially suitable

Table 1.2
Largest 40 Management Consulting Firms by 1996 Revenues

| Firm | 1996 Revenues ($M) | Firm | 1996 Revenues ($M) |
|---|---|---|---|
| Andersen Consulting | 4,720 | Aon Consulting | 473 |
| EDS/AT Kearney | 2,870 | Bain & Company | 450 |
| Computer Sciences Corporation (CSC) | 2,600 | American Management Systems | 440 |
| Ernst & Young | 2,100 | Woodrow Milliman | 350 |
| McKinsey & Company | 2,100 | PA Consulting | 326 |
| Cap Gemini Sogeti | 1,444 | Grant Thornton | 306 |
| Coopers & Lybrand | 1,422 | Roland Berger | 266 |
| KPMG Peat Marwick | 1,380 | Sedgwick Noble Lowndes | 262 |
| Arthur Andersen | 1,380 | Hay Group | 259 |
| Deloitte & Touche | 1,303 | Buck Consultants (Acquired) | 228 |
| Price Waterhouse | 1,200 | A Foster Higgins & Company (Acquired) | 208 |
| Mercer Consulting Group | 1,159 | Monitor Company | 181 |
| Booz•Allen & Hamilton | 980 | Mitchell Madison Group | 100 |
| Towers Perrin | 903 | Technology Solutions Company | 97 |
| Sema Group | 788 | Proudfoot | 96 |
| IBM Consulting | 730 | George S. May International | 91 |
| Watson Wyatt Worldwide | 656 | LEK Alcar | 90 |
| The Boston Consulting Group | 600 | The Segal Company | 88 |
| Arthur D. Little | 574 | Kurt Salmon Associates | 85 |
| Hewitt Associates | 568 | AT&T Solutions | 70 |

Note: Figures do not include outsourcing or nonconsulting revenues.
Source: The Global Management Consulting Marketplace: Key Data, Forecasts & Trends 1997 Edition. Kennedy Information Research Group, 1998. Individual firm information.

firm. To avoid that trap, the following sections explain the vast and varied aspects of the consulting industry.

# SEGMENTING THE INDUSTRY

As illustrated by Figure 1.2, firms in the consulting industry can be segmented according to four broad dimensions: (1) the industries consulted, (2) the functional types of consulting performed, (3) the sectors from which clients are drawn (private, public, nonprofit), and (4) the firm's affiliation with its clients (external firms or internal corporate strategic planning units).

First, consulting firms can be segmented by the industries that the firms serve. Although some firms intentionally specialize in a particular industry, others work with a mix of industries, but focus

**Figure 1.2**
**Segmenting the Consulting Industry**

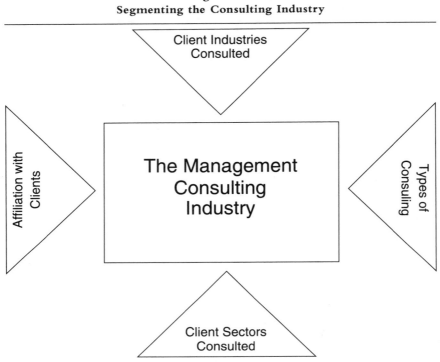

on a smaller subset. For example, The Wilkerson Group, an IBM company, APM (now part of CSC), and Hamilton KSA all focus on the healthcare industry. Other firms, such as McKinsey & Company, Gemini Consulting, and The Boston Consulting Group, consistently have engagements in the healthcare industry, but do not specialize in it. Depending on your personal interests and professional experiences, you may find certain firms more attractive than others. For example, a senior manager at a commercial bank wishing to enter the consulting industry should leverage his or her professional experience by targeting consulting firms serving or specializing in the financial services sector. But not all firms define industries using the same terminology—one firm's "electronic commerce" industry practice, for example, may be another firm's "technology" practice.

The second method of segmenting consulting firms is to consider the functional practice, or type of work, being performed. Although different firms define functional practices in different ways, the most common include corporate strategy, product strategy, operations management, information technology (IT) strategy, and systems implementation. Firms with functional practices usually seek engagements that span all industries, since companies in entirely different industries face many of the same issues. Corporate strategy, for example, is relevant to the management of just about every organization or entity.

The third method for segmenting firms is by the sector in which their clients operate: private, public, and nonprofit. As you might expect, almost all large firms have a strong focus on the private sector and derive the bulk of their revenues from for-profit corporations. Yet what may be surprising is that many of these same large firms also have healthy public-sector practices and increasingly seek clients in municipal, state, national, and international governments.

The firms that consult to nonprofit organizations are far fewer in number and generally smaller than firms operating in either of the other two sectors. Due to limited resources and earmarked contributions, nonprofits usually cannot afford to pay the high fees of private sector consulting firms. As a result, most of these firms can support only a few, experienced consultants, whose fees are generally less than those of their private sector peers. The small operating budgets of these firms limit their on-campus recruiting efforts, so it is up to graduating students to actively seek them out. Although some large private-sector firms do perform intermittent pro bono engagements for nonprofit organizations, their consultants obviously cannot work exclusively on no-fee projects. Therefore, candidates with a strong interest in nonprofit consulting may be better off finding a firm that explicitly consults to nonprofits for a fee, rather than working for a firm that consults primarily to the private sector and occasionally accepts pro bono engagements.

All three of these segmentations—by industry, by functional consulting practice, and by sector—are summarized in Table 1.3.

The final segmentation of the consulting industry is based on the affiliation of the consulting practice to the companies consulted: external or internal. Practices may be either independent of and external to the organizations they consult, or dependent on and internal to a specific company. Traditionally, management consultants have been thought of as independent, unaffiliated professionals who are retained temporarily by an organization for a project-based fee. However, this generalization excludes a growing circle of internal consultants who work for corporate strategic planning or business development groups. Figure 1.3 lists some of the major corporations that support internal consulting groups, and intend, through their investment in hiring consultants as full-time employees, to reduce expenditures on external management consultants. Many of these groups operate in Fortune 500 companies, which also traditionally spend the most on external management consultants.

Typically, internal consultants are permanent employees of a company whose roles are identical to those of external management consultants. Their work has the same scale and scope as that of external consultants, and the stages of project engagements are usually the same. Internal management consultants now frequently displace

**Table 1.3**
**Sample Segmentation Categories**

| Industry | Function | Sector |
|---|---|---|
| Communications | Corporate strategy | Nonprofit |
| Financial services | Human resources | Private |
| Health care | Information technology | Public |
| Insurance | Operations management | |
| Manufacturing | Reengineering | |
| Media and entertainment | | |
| Oil and gas | | |
| Retail | | |
| Transportation | | |

**Figure 1.3**
**Selected Companies with Internal Consulting Groups**

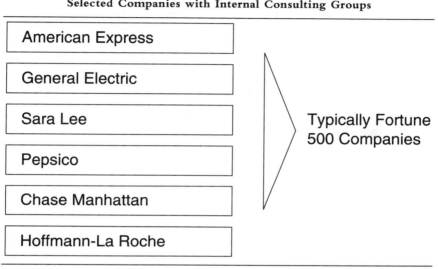

| American Express |
| General Electric |
| Sara Lee |
| Pepsico |
| Chase Manhattan |
| Hoffmann-La Roche |

Typically Fortune 500 Companies

external consultants and take on projects formerly handled only by external firms. Many internal consultants started their careers as external management consultants, but grew tired of adverse lifestyle requirements of external consultants, such as extensive travel. As internal consulting groups have grown, so too have their on–campus and headhunter recruiting efforts. Large internal corporate strategic planning groups now compete for the same student and professional candidates as external management consulting firms, and try to win the competitive recruiting game by promising a less demanding lifestyle, as well as the opportunity to interact daily with top management of Fortune 500 companies.

These four segmentations should help you make sense of the somewhat chaotic diversity of firms. With literally thousands of firms performing widely varied tasks for many clients, you can use this tool to identify the types of consulting practices that appeal to you most.

# THE EVOLUTION OF MANAGEMENT CONSULTING

So where did an industry with such rapid growth and huge candidate interest come from? How did the industry evolve into one of the hottest career paths available today? The answers lie in our earlier definition of a management consultant. Whether performing an economic analysis of a market, designing a new business, or justifying the release of 1,000 employees, management consultants perform a fundamental role: providing professional assistance to others, usually for a fee.

By this definition, consultants probably have been offering their services since the dawn of human civilization. Any person who used his or her competency or expertise to help someone else solve a problem could be thought of as an early consultant. In this sense, some American colonists could be considered consultants since they often extended their ideas and knowledge to others. Benjamin Franklin shared his knowledge of science, political philosophy, journalism, and diplomacy with others by forming the Philadelphia Library, the first public library in the United States that was established to bring "useful knowledge" to Americans across the colonies. And Thomas Jefferson, who was an architect, a gourmet cook, and an intellectual, used his skills as a statesman to help develop a system of government after the American Revolution.

Later, as a manufacturing economy took form during the industrial revolution, consultants with business and production acumen helped design and optimize assembly lines, build highway and transportation networks, standardize the size and shape of frequently used products to ensure universal compatibility, and so forth. Many specialists emerged, such as the engineer Frederick W. Taylor, who developed a system of production management and advanced the study of operations.

But the modern consulting firm did not exist until the mid-nineteenth century. Table 1.4 shows the founding dates of many recognized firms, going back to Foster Higgins in 1845, Sedgwick in 1858, and Arthur D. Little in 1886.

Many of these firms were founded by members of the engineering or accounting professions, who recognized the value of offering

**Table 1.4**
**Founding Dates of Selected Management Consulting Firms**

| Firm | Year Founded |
|------|-------------|
| Foster Higgins | 1845 |
| Sedgwick | 1858 |
| Arthur D. Little | 1886 |
| Arthur Andersen | 1913 |
| Booz•Allen & Hamilton | 1914 |
| Buck Consultants | 1916 |
| A.T. Kearney | 1926 |
| McKinsey & Company | 1926 |
| Towers Perrin | 1934 |
| Kurt Salmon Associates | 1935 |
| Hewitt Associates | 1940 |
| The Hay Group | 1943 |
| Watson Wyatt Worldwide | 1946 |
| The Boston Consulting Group | 1963 |
| The Wilkerson Group (now IBM Consulting) | 1967 |
| Cap Gemini Sogeti | 1968 |
| Index Group (now CSC) | 1969 |
| American Management Systems | 1970 |
| Mercer Management Consulting | 1970 |
| William M. Mercer | 1975 |
| Bain & Company | 1973 |
| Braxton Associates | 1977 |
| Marakon Associates | 1978 |
| Monitor Company | 1983 |
| Corporate Decisions, Inc. (now Mercer Management Consulting) | 1983 |
| The LEK Partnership | 1983 |
| CSC | 1988 |

*Source: The Global Management Consulting Marketplace: Key Data, Forecasts & Trends 1997 Edition.*
Kennedy Information Research Group, 1998. Individual firm information.

professional services on a project–fee basis. In 1926, A.T. Kearney was founded by Andrew Thomas Kearney to provide accounting and budgetary controls to corporations. During that same year, James O. McKinsey left a public accounting firm to found McKinsey & Company, a consulting firm originally committed to providing management and financial advice to senior corporate officers. Later, consulting firms branched out beyond accounting and engineering and started to sell industry management expertise. McKinsey & Company attracted professionals from a variety of industries who could provide expert advice based on their experience. Then when a lawyer named Marvin Bower joined McKinsey & Company in 1933, the firm began to recognize the untapped value of taking the raw intellectual talent of freshly graduated college and graduate students and professionally training them to use the consulting tool set. McKinsey & Company reputedly became the first to hire consultants directly out of graduate business schools, cementing the connection between management consulting and rapid career advancement.

The turn of the century saw rapid growth in the demand for consulting services. As in any free market where demand outpaces supply, the consulting industry afforded firms liberal opportunity for growth. And as corporations with broad geographic operations approached firms like Arthur D. Little, McKinsey & Company, and A.T. Kearney, the need for regional offices encouraged the consulting firms to expand nationwide.

Soon thereafter, the industry experienced rapid firm proliferation as partners from established practices acted on their entrepreneurial interests and founded their own firms. In 1963, Arthur D. Little saw Bruce Henderson leave the practice to work for the trust department of a Boston bank, where he created an internal consulting unit that later became The Boston Consulting Group (BCG). Ten years later, Bill Bain and a number of colleagues left BCG to found Bain & Company. Then, in the 1980s, several Bain professionals left to found their own practices, including Corporate Decisions, Inc. (CDI)[2] which, in the 1990s, saw one of its founding partners leave to form Vertex Partners. As a result, the industry has developed an extended and interrelated lineage, which continues to branch out to this day.

The recognized accounting firms—Arthur Andersen, PricewaterhouseCoopers, Deloitte & Touche, Ernst & Young, and KPMG Peat Marwick—fueled significant growth in the industry by opening their own consulting practices. Having deep and long-standing relationships with the entire Fortune 1000, the accounting firms were in an ideal position to cross-sell consulting services to their existing clients by touting "solutions" consulting. Because the accounting firms had direct access to their clients' financial information, they were in the best position (or so they claimed) to understand and develop a strategy to meet the needs of those companies.

The sales pitch worked, catapulting the accounting firms into the world of consulting. In terms of revenue, Andersen Consulting is now the world's largest management consulting practice, reporting worldwide 1996 figures of $4.72 billion and over 44,800 consultants.[3] In fact, the consulting groups of the accounting firms all are on the list of top 10 management consulting firms by revenue.[4] In 1996, the accounting firms collectively employed over 100,000 consultants.[5] Today, the consulting practices of the accounting firms continue to grow at some of the most rapid rates in the industry, offering services that run the gamut from high-level strategic consulting to more operational systems consulting. And consulting practices of the accounting firms now have turned to television and print advertising—traditionally considered taboo in the industry—to further accelerate their growth and attract customers outside their accounting base.

Finally, the globalization of business has emphasized the importance of international consulting projects. To meet the needs of multinational companies, management consulting firms have themselves become multinational with offices on other continents. And as businesses in emerging economies grow following deregulation and privatization, the demand for Western—and in particular—American consulting firms increases as well. Whether by acquiring a local consulting practice or sending a team of experienced consultants to open a new office, firms understand that they need scale to effectively compete for some of the most lucrative engagements. Not all management consulting firms have global aspirations, but all the large firms believe that global reach is a prerequisite to success.

Since 1990, overall revenues in management consulting have grown by more than 10 percent per year, and some firms have even reached 20 to 30 percent growth rate.[6] Although private sector engagements account for most of this growth, some consulting firms have made a substantial investment in servicing public and nonprofit organizations. In 1995, for example, KPMG Peat Marwick, Andersen Consulting, and Coopers & Lybrand collectively billed over $600 million to public sector clients.[7]

# CONTINUED GROWTH OF THE PROFESSION

Although the management consulting profession attracts new recruits seeking professional stature and stratospheric salaries, three other key drivers underlie the continued expansion of the industry. First, management consultants are in demand during all economic cycles. During times of recession or economic instability, consultants are needed for their reengineering, cost-cutting, and defensive strategy competencies. Conversely, during times of positive economic expansion, consultants help organizations retain or even accelerate their growth, capture additional market share from weaker competitors, and predict and prepare for emerging economic trends. Unlike almost all other industries, management consulting is relatively well protected from economic cycles.

Second, the profession has low barriers to entry since intellectual capital is the primary input into the product. The main material expenses of starting a small practice are the office space, the cost of accessing information, and the costs of communicating—telephone, computers, and, on occasion, travel, which is usually billed to clients separately. Although firms seeking high brand-name recognition must invest in sales and marketing, many consulting practices rely on the reputation of performing satisfactory work to capture clients.

Third, management consultants have attractive opportunities to exit the industry. Consultants are in high demand by organizations that are recruiting executive talent. Corporations that have hired consulting firms may seek to continue a relationship with members of the consulting team by extending full-time job offers to high-performing individuals. And most consultants are in frequent contact with headhunters, who routinely harvest top candidates for industry positions from consulting. Like most firms, McKinsey & Company is proud of its alumni placement record and promotes consulting as a career accelerator when recruiting candidates. McKinsey & Company alumni can be found in most, if not all, of the Fortune 500 companies, linking corporate America in an extended web. Many of the most respected CEOs and chairmen in the world were trained by McKinsey & Company including CEO Harvey Golub of American Express, CEO Louis Gerstner Jr. of IBM, CEO Michael Jordan of Westinghouse Electric, CEO Gary DiCamillo of Polaroid, CEO John Sawhill of The Nature Conservancy, CEO Leo Mullin of Delta Airlines, and CEO Joachim Vogt of Hugo Boss AG, to name but a few. With proven and attractive exit options, consulting has become—and is predicted to continue to be—a natural stepping-stone for young professionals seeking rapid career advancement.

# EMERGING TRENDS IN MANAGEMENT CONSULTING

Identifying general trends in an industry as diverse as consulting is extremely difficult, if not impossible. Simple characterizations are difficult to apply to the industry as a whole, since firms have different industry focuses, methodologies, and lifestyles, for example. Still, consulting firms appear to have identified and are heeding two drivers of change in the industry, one on the supply side, and one on the demand side. On the supply side, the desire to capture additional market share is leading to the development of a full range of consulting services, from high-level strategy to detailed systems and technology implementation work. On the demand side, customers are holding firms increasingly accountable for the quality of their work.

## Diversification of Consulting Services

Consulting firms have become aware that the key to sustained success is diversification. By varying the industries served, services offered, and geographic areas reached, firms are better able to serve the needs of their clients. Diversification builds additional intellectual capital and helps a firm capture a larger portion of the consulting pie. This quest for diversification, which has changed the face of consulting, is the driver behind three trends: (1) a substantial increase in firms acquiring or merging with other firms in a search for new competencies, (2) greater internationalization of firms seeking broader geographic reach to satisfy the needs of multinational corporations, and (3) the integration of information technology and strategy practices into individual firms.

First, firms seeking to diversify their services have dramatically increased mergers and acquisitions activity among consulting practices. As Table 1.5 shows, M&A activity since 1990 has involved firms of many sizes, functional practice areas, and industry focuses.[8]

But acquisition does not guarantee success. In 1989, for example, McKinsey & Company acquired Information Consulting from Saatchi & Saatchi, in an effort to develop information technology capabilities. The result was a textbook case of culture clash, and the expected benefits were never realized. When acquisitions succeed, however, the result can be a tremendous gain to both parties. CSC's 1995 purchase of DiBianca–Berkman successfully brought new skills in change management to the strong information technology firm.

Second, the need for diversification is encouraging firms to build an international presence. It has almost become a requirement for large consulting firms to have global offices to remain competitive in attracting companies that are either already multinational, or are seeking to penetrate emerging markets. Andersen Consulting has offices in six continents, and other firms have offices in five: McKinsey & Company, Booz•Allen & Hamilton, Arthur D. Little, and Watson Wyatt Worldwide, to name but a few. And firms that once concentrated on the United States, Western Europe, and Asia are now expanding into less saturated regions (e.g., Central Europe, the Middle East, and Africa).

Finally, the quest for diversification is motivating consulting firms to integrate information technology services with business strategy. Most corporations are unable to fully capture the added value offered by rapidly developing technology and, as a result, increasingly seek the help of IT consultants. Furthermore, when strategy projects end, the next steps often involve significant information systems work requiring the continued assistance of these consultants.

## Table 1.5
## Selected Consulting Firm Acquisitions since 1987

| Buyer | Acquiring Firm | Year | Size of Buyer ($M) | Size of Acquiree ($M) | Acquired Firm Specialty |
|---|---|---|---|---|---|
| Mercer Management Consulting | Corporate Decisions, Inc. (CDI) | 1997 | NA | NA | Customer-Driven Growth Strategy |
| CSC | APM | 1996 | 4,242 | 85 | Healthcare |
| IBM Consulting | The Wilkerson Group (TWG) | 1995 | 600 | NA | Pharmaceuticals & Medical Strategy |
| EDS | A.T. Kearney | 1995 | 8,600 | 346 | General Management Strategy in the Manufacturing Sector |
| The Boston Consulting Group | Canada Consulting Group | 1993 | 340 | 7 | Strategy & Organization; Focused on Canadian Market |
| LEK Consulting | Alcar Group | 1993 | 85 | | Valuation |
| Cap Gemini Sogeti | MAC Group | 1991 | 1,700 | 74 | Strategy |
| Staff Purchase | Hay Group | 1990 | Same | 188 | Compensation Studies |
| Marsh & McClennan | Strategic Planning Associates (SPA) | 1990 | 2,723 | 43 | General Management |
| McKinsey & Company | Information Consulting | 1989 | 635 | 20 | Information Technology |
| CSC | Index Group | 1988 | 1,150 | 25 | General Management & Reengineering |
| Staff Purchase | Arthur D. Little | 1988 | Same | 201 | NA |
| Marsh & McClennan | Temple Barker & Sloane (TBS) | 1987 | 2,147 | 52 | General Strategy Consulting |

*Source: Management Consulting Marketplace: Mergers & Acquisitions 1997 Edition.* Kennedy Information Research Group, 1998.

In 1996, worldwide information technology and systems–related consulting totaled more than $39.5 billion. It is expected to have the fastest growth rate in the consulting industry (18.6% per year through the year 2000) and is obviously an attractive pool that strategy consultants want to tap.[9] Many strategy firms that did not have the competency have actively sought to add information technology and systems practices, primarily through acquisition (e.g., McKinsey & Company, Booz•Allen & Hamilton, and Monitor Company). The enormous success of Andersen Consulting's IT practice has opened the eyes of many firms to the impact of information technology and has encouraged IT manufacturers (e.g., IBM), systems integrators (e.g., CSC), and telecommunications companies (e.g., AT&T) to introduce IT consulting practices of their own.

## Increased Firm Accountability

The second fundamental trend in the industry is the increased accountability of consulting firms for their services. This trend is driven largely by client dissatisfaction with the level of service and analysis received as well as by clients publicly voicing their complaints. In 1997, a client of Towers Perrin sued the firm on a charge that generic work was being peddled as unique analysis. And that same year, the former president of Club Med sued Bain & Company for alleged unsatisfactory work. These stories not only cast a dark shadow over the industry but also highlighted the growing doubt among many clients about the true value of hiring consultants. Other firms have also experienced the client backlash: The Boston Consulting Group was among a set of firms sued by the Cleveland-based conglomerate Figgie International for alleged overbilling and other errors, and Andersen Consulting was ordered by the British government to pay an $18 million penalty for not delivering a social security computer system on time.[10] The publication of books profiling client dissatisfaction, such as James O'Shea and Charles Madigan's *Dangerous Company: The Consulting Powerhouses and the Businesses They Save and Ruin* (New York: Random House, 1997), and Adrian Wooldridge and John Micklethwait's *The Witch Doctors: Making Sense of the Management Gurus* (New York: Random House, 1998), further reveals the growing determination of companies to hold consultants accountable for their work.

Partly in response to these client concerns, consulting firms have become more active in monitoring their own activities. They are placing greater emphasis on effective management of client relationships and on controlling client expectations. Today, some firms will not even accept a fee unless the client is completely satisfied with the work. And after completing projects, many firms now routinely follow up with clients to monitor their satisfaction and offer additional guidance without charge.

As pointed out earlier, these trends serve as predictions but are by no means prescriptions of events to come. In fact, they are at best only a limited set of predictions since each day brings a new perspective on the future of the industry. We chose to not highlight some popular predictions, including the rise of public sector consulting, and the increasing emphasis on capturing institutional knowledge within the firm through formalized processes and electronic libraries. Because the future is uncertain, we prefer to focus on the key drivers of change that have fundamentally influenced—and will continue to influence—the evolution of consulting: extended service diversification and increased consultant accountability.

# CHAPTER 2

## THE CONSULTANT'S WORK
## AND LIFESTYLE

*Consulting is a highly stimulating profession, allowing intelligent, confident professionals the chance to work with similarly bright specialists on cutting-edge ideas and technology.*

Maura Rurak and Perri Capell
National Business Employment Weekly

In this chapter, we profile the consultant's work and lifestyle and describe what it is like to be a management consultant, in terms of both the professional development opportunities, and the day-to-day balancing of work and private life. We begin by breaking down the organization of a typical consulting firm, examining the roles within its hierarchy and the keys to achieving success. Then, we will give you your first glimpse of the consultant's work style: how consultants interact with clients and with each other. The third part walks you through the steps of a typical consulting project, from its initial definition to the final presentation of recommendations. Once you have a full understanding of the way consultants work, we will give you two examples of the consulting lifestyle to compare with your own expectations.

## THE MANAGEMENT
## CONSULTING FIRM

Although highly variable in size, number of offices, and work performed, management consulting firms tend to follow a similar operating model. Most firms have an organizational structure of approximately six ranks, (see Figure 2.1): (1) Support Staff in the library, recruiting, and production departments; (2) Research Analysts or Associates, who hold undergraduate degrees; (3) Consultants, who most often have graduate business degrees as well as prior work experience; (4) Senior Consultants, who have from two to three years of post-MBA consulting experience; (5) Managers or Case Team Leaders, who usually have started with the firm as consultants prior to promotion; and (6) Partners, Directors, or Vice Presidents, who are also likely to have started with the firm at a lower rank and worked their way up. Firms may vary slightly in the number of levels in their hierarchy, but the vast majority are like this prototype.

Since consulting firms prefer to promote from within, they base the recognition and reward of their top performers on merit. Formal performance reviews, which usually occur twice a year, have a direct impact on a consultant's career progression and compensation. A firm

**Figure 2.1**
**Typical Consulting Firm Organizational Structure**

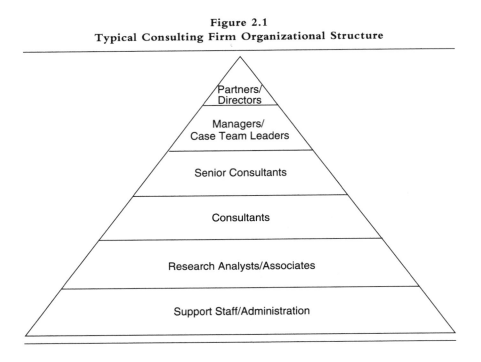

typically evaluates all its professionals using the same set of skill development criteria, such as analytics, teamwork, commitment and drive, presentation skills, time management, and people management. The list varies from firm to firm, but in all cases is designed to evaluate the key skills consultants need to lead people and manage work.

Different competencies are expected from consultants at different levels. Figure 2.2 illustrates the progression of skills by consulting position. Research analysts are expected to focus on their analytical and client communication skills. Once they master the basic consulting skill set, they learn how to assume the greater responsibilities of consultant and senior consultant: managing projects, and developing knowledge of industries and management functions. At the next professional level, managers take even greater responsibility and are expected to show aptitude for managing client relationships. At the highest professional level, partners generate new business and contribute to the growth and recognition of the firm through public speaking engagements, articles, and professional networking. Individual firms may diverge from this model. At smaller firms in particular,

**Figure 2.2**
**Typical Skill Progression of Consultants**

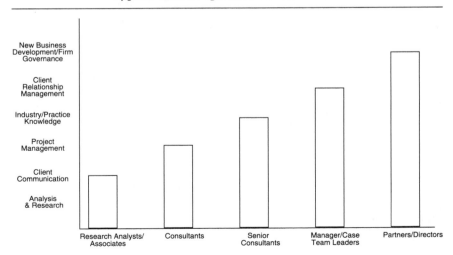

professional staff at each level may have greater responsibilities. Experienced senior consultants, for example, will probably participate in developing client relationships and selling new business.

Although the responsibility sets are usually clearly defined, the performance reviews based on them are, unfortunately, neither entirely objective nor scientifically performed. A subjective human element always creeps into such evaluations. Perception is reality, and individuals have to work diligently to manage the perceptions of their evaluators. The hard reality is that high-performing individuals can be perceived as poor performers if they never receive proper credit for their work. If taken too far, a meritocracy can produce a highly competitive atmosphere in which consultants vie for recognition or try to curry favor with the evaluators and senior members of the firm. In such a scenario, motivation comes from fear of failure, rather than from the prospect of reward. Our intent is not to undermine a system that works well for many firms and their employees, but rather to give you a complete picture of the structure you may encounter.

Most consulting firms prefer to hire consultants at junior levels and promote them through the ranks. Research analysts are commonly promoted to MBA-level consultant positions, and those who continue to be high performers may advance all the way up to the most senior partner levels. Instead of recruiting only established professionals who are recognized experts in specific fields, consulting firms have made a conscious decision to hire individuals who bring a fresh, can-do perspective. As a result, most firms rely on on-campus recruiting to fill their ranks, and invest significant time and resources to recruit top talent. In fact, some firms try to hold on to their top talent by paying for high-performing research analysts to attend business school, with the understanding that they will return to the firm after graduation.

Research analysts are usually hired during their senior year of college, while still working toward their bachelor's degrees. Although consulting firms are naturally attracted to students of Economics, Engineering, Business, and other quantitative majors, most firms also respect subjects such as History, International Relations, Psychology, and English, which require intensive research and writing. Research analysts generally have limited prior full-time work experience, but are likely to have held summer internships in business-related fields. They are recognized leaders in their schools, with strong records of academic achievement.

Consultant-level professionals are also hired through on-campus recruiting, primarily at graduate business schools. Since consultants at most firms are expected to supervise research analysts and manage projects, firms prefer candidates with academic and professional preparation that has taught them people and project management skills. And some firms actively seek candidates from the nation's top law and graduate programs, believing that these programs also develop high-caliber management competencies.

# THE CONSULTING WORK STYLE

Management consultants love teams. Whether performing client work or working on internal office projects, consultants prefer to apply the collective minds of a group to a problem. Even though team members are drawn from various ranks in the firm, the work style is collaborative and tends to downplay hierarchical relationships. Teams can range from 2 to 15 people, depending on the scale and scope of a project. However, most teams comprise 5 to 7 people, with a partner, a manager, 2 or 3 consultants, and 2 or 3 research analysts. Roles can vary dramatically depending on the size of the firm, and responsibilities can cross the lines of professional titles. But a common model in many recognized firms compartmentalizes roles by professional title in the following way: most data collection is performed by research analysts, who work closely with consultants and senior consultants to generate learnings; these three levels present their work to managers, who are primarily responsible for synthesizing team analyses into key lessons and next-step recommendations, and for leading presentations to the client. Partners are the primary liaison with clients, although all team members are likely to have client contact over the duration of a project.

At the same time, the client is likely to have created its own team to work closely with the consulting team throughout the project, with anywhere from 2 to more than 20 individuals from senior management.

Client teams commonly serve four purposes: (1) to provide information to the consultants as needed; (2) to serve as collaborative problem solvers with the consultants; (3) to absorb and retain knowledge from the project; and (4) to supervise the consultants in a way that ensures timely and effective delivery of the promised goal. Companies recognize that an effective consulting engagement is not one in which a large report is delivered after a number of months of behind-the-scenes work. Rather, it is one in which consultants and company executives work closely together in a continuous learning arrangement.

Although most consulting firms use the same team structure, these teams interface with the client in two essentially different ways: either on-site at the client's offices for the entire duration of a project, or off-site at the consultant's offices with periodic visits to the client. Each of these models has positive and negative features, depending on the project. Consulting firms disagree on which model is better, as do companies hiring consultants. However, individual firms have migrated over time to one or the other model and have developed reputations as prototypical "on-site" or "off-site" practices.

## On-Site Consulting

On-site firms are likely to argue that working in proximity to the client, surrounded by the people who the project directly influences, holds great value. On-site consultants can walk though manufacturing plants, view product testing and research facilities, speak with employees of all ranks, tap directly into corporate information systems, and observe day-to-day management and operation practices. On-site arrangements are more common for systems and information technology projects, as well as for implementation stages of work, each of which requires frequent and close contact with the company. Many companies prefer the on-site model since they can observe the daily work of the consultants and monitor their productivity. Furthermore, company employees are more likely to respect visibly hardworking consultants who interact with them every day. In contrast, consultants who work in their own offices and appear at the client site once a month may not develop these close working relationships and thus may not be as effective.

Still, the on-site model has significant drawbacks. Consultants are inconveniently distanced from essential library resources located in their home offices. They are separated from the presentation production assistants and have to rely on phone, fax, mail, and e-mail channels to communicate with the department when producing a presentation. Support services may be difficult to use from a remote location, and consultants can be hard to reach when they constantly change phone numbers. Worse still, many consultants find it difficult to think creatively and out-of-the-box when under constant surveillance by the client. Thus, on-site consultants may become risk-averse and fail to explore ideas simply because the client sees little value in them or wants to avoid them.

## Off-Site Consulting

The second model, working off-site at the consultant's home office, avoids most of the disadvantages of the first model: library, production, and support resources are within easy reach, and the client is usually not smothering the consulting team. Working away from the client site may facilitate creative thinking and even enable consultants to share ideas with and receive feedback from colleagues who are working on other projects. Companies that hire off-site consultants may also prefer the model, especially for sensitive projects that involve mergers and acquisitions, layoffs, or reengineering. Because privacy can be an advantage in these cases, it makes sense to use off-site consultants. Company employees then have minimal contact with the projects, and little or no reason to become uneasy.

But, like the on-site model, the off-site model has disadvantages. Clients may have difficulty following analyses if they cannot observe and participate in each step of the work. As a result, companies may question whether their consultants are working hard and can justify their high fees. Still worse, companies may become defensive when hearing conclusions and recommendations that do not appear to be well thought out. To avoid these pitfalls, off-site consultants need to have frequent contact with clients to keep them abreast of progress and may have to hold more frequent interim presentations than their on-site counterparts do.

## STEPS IN A CONSULTING ENGAGEMENT

Consultants use the term "engagement" to refer to the multistep process of helping a company achieve certain objectives. Although the particular process used depends on the help a client needs, a prototypical consulting engagement can be dissected into four broad workflow steps: (1) problem identification and definition, (2) analysis, (3) synthesis, and (4) presentation. This process, however, is not universally applicable to all projects. A consulting team may repeat steps before moving on to the next one, or even cycle through the entire four-step process multiple times before concluding an engagement. Still, this model makes two important points: each step is critical to the overall success of the engagement, and a consultant needs a variety of skills to be successful. Figure 2.3 outlines a typical work plan for an engagement.

**Figure 2.3**
**Typical Consulting Work Plan for an Engagement**

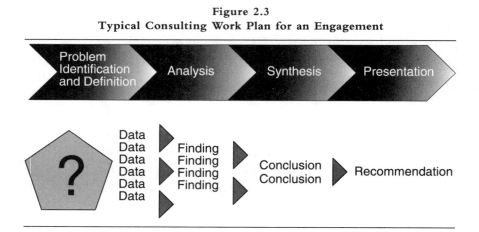

## Step 1. Problem Identification and Definition

The first step involves identifying and clarifying the business issues the client faces, outlining the engagement's specific objectives, determining the deliverables to be turned in at the end of the engagement, and scheduling the timeline for completion. Here, consultants need to differentiate between what clients are asking for and what they truly need, since clients who are stuck with their old habits may not be able to look at a situation objectively. Sometimes, clients are so involved in daily activities that they lack the perspective to identify the central issues behind their business problem. For example, is the client's problem a misalignment of its information technology with its business strategies or, more simply, the lack of a business strategy in the first place? Consultants must bring a certain degree of skepticism to an engagement to question the client's perception of the problem and not simply accept an obvious answer. A consultant's ability to listen well, to consider the whole picture, and to draw on industry and business experience is critical to the success of this step.

## Step 2. Analysis

The second step involves the gathering of primary and secondary data, building models and conceptual frameworks, soliciting feedback to ideas from experts and others with relevant perspectives, and analyzing the results of this research. Information may be gathered from surveys, telephone interviews, on–line searches, focus groups, and published materials. Models are workable abstractions of reality, ranging from highly quantitative financial models to qualitative assessments of public opinion. The challenge in building effective models and conceptual frameworks is balancing the need for abstraction with the need for complexity: they must be abstract enough to be useful, yet complex enough to be meaningful. And the analysis resulting from the synthesis of all the collected information should yield a set of alternative options based on a set of assumption-based scenarios. The consultant's ability to think in the abstract is crucial to success.

## Step 3. Synthesis

As the name suggests, synthesis involves combining the individual conclusions into a single set of findings, from which recommendations are then formulated. Developing a cohesive set of findings may be more difficult than it sounds if some of the information collected over the course of the engagement is contradictory, or if the models and conceptual frameworks do not adequately capture the complexity of the issues. In this phase, a consultant must remain objective and levelheaded to understand the underlying issues and construct appropriate and actionable recommendations.

## Step 4. Presentation

The engagement usually concludes with a presentation of the findings and recommendations to the client. All the work done previously is useless unless the consultant can communicate the message effectively, enabling the client to learn from the process. If the consultant does not provide the client with an understanding of the critical issues and the appropriate next steps, then the project will have no impact, regardless of how much work went into the first three steps. But when the consultant makes the key lessons and recommendations clear, the client should retain enough of the analysis to facilitate the decision-making process.

Although a typical engagement runs through these four steps, the final presentation does not necessarily mark the end of the project. Consultants may be retained for a second phase of work, which may involve additional analysis or even implementation of the recommended solution. Most consulting firms work diligently to extend projects, usually beginning to talk with the client about additional work as early as the second or third step of an engagement.

Through this four-step process, the client hopes to learn enough to make decisions that will bring the ultimate goal to fruition. And, admittedly, the consulting firm hopes to develop a deep and wide-reaching relationship with the client that creates a long-lasting revenue stream.

# THE CONSULTING LIFESTYLE

So, how do the different operating models—on-site and off-site—affect the lives of the consultants who must work under them? To answer this question, we will first describe a typical week in the life of an on-site consultant. After spending the weekend at home, the consultant flies back to the client site on either Sunday night or Monday morning, depending on the distance traveled. She lives in either a hotel room or a fully furnished executive apartment for the next four days. Then, on Thursday night or Friday morning, she returns home, since on-site consulting firms usually try to bring their professionals back to the office one day a week.

From Monday through Thursday, the consultant works in her temporary office at the client site, adjacent to the offices of full-time employees. She probably has her own portable laptop computer from which she can dial in to her consulting firm's e-mail and intranet system. She also remains connected to her firm through her home office voice mail system, and her temporary phone line at the client site. Most of her consulting team, as well as the designated client team, are located in offices near hers. Her days are generally busy, and frequently long, since she spends only four weekdays on-site. She has been provided with a rental car to drive between the airport, her hotel or apartment, and her office, and typically has a daily expense budget, which should cover all meal, taxi, and telephone expenses. And her firm may reimburse other expenses, such as dry cleaning and team dinners. Her weeks on the project proceed in this fashion for the duration of the project.

Many on-site consultants enjoy this lifestyle. With constant client contact, they can continuously receive feedback and recognition. And the "high life" of business travel and on-site work can be exciting. On-site consultants may also benefit financially since meals are usually paid for, and the combined mileage of the flights, rental cars, and hotels can quickly add up to free vacations. But separation from family and friends for extended periods may prove difficult for some people, not to mention the physical toll of frequent travel and life out of a suitcase.

Now we will look at a typical week in the life of an off-site consultant. Unlike the on-site consultant, who has a routine travel schedule, our off-site consultant makes fewer trips for a shorter duration. On average, he travels one or two days a week, often returning late at night on the same day he flies out. He has a permanent desk in his firm's office, with a single phone and voice mail number. He spends most of his time in his firm's office, using the library and production resources, conducting interviews over the phone, or meeting with members of the client team who have traveled to visit the firm. His primary means of contact with the client is the telephone, with occasional face-to-face contact at the client site during meetings and presentations.

Off-site consultants would rarely trade their lifestyle for that of on-site consultants. They return to their own homes each night and spend more time with family and friends, especially on weeknights. These consultants may collect fewer frequent flyer miles than their on-site peers, but the reward of free trips, they argue, is not worth the cost of being away from home and family. Still, there are some negatives to off-site work. These consultants may complain about a lack of client contact and feedback, and as a result, feel less reward from their hard work than their on-site peers. Long work hours may go unrecognized by the client, perhaps leaving consultants feeling underappreciated.

Whether off-site or on-site, all consultants share several lifestyle similarities. In addition to their professional responsibilities, consultants are expected to participate in internal firm development activities, such as recruiting, interviewing, staff training and development, and preparation of annual off-site events. Work weeks average between 50 and 80 hours, not including travel time, with peaks occurring prior to presentations and due dates, and valleys for a short time thereafter. Consultants have typically lived by the motto, "work hard, play hard," although firms are now downplaying this theme in favor of promoting a "balanced lifestyle." The industry as a whole suffers from a high turnover rate among junior staff, but it is better at retaining senior management.

Firms that do a good job of rewarding their consultants and providing flexible work arrangements have average tenures that exceed the industry average. Other firms, however, are notorious for employee burnout, and struggle to retain some consultants for more than a year. Still others are rumored to have an "up-or-out" policy, whereby consultants who are underperforming their peers must either improve within a specific time, or leave the firm.

But, regardless of a firm's working model or attitude toward long hours, certain people are just not built for the work and lifestyle of a consultant. Only those who can thrive under the pressure of hard work, can perform multiple tasks simultaneously, can cope with ambiguity and uncertainty, and can remain calm and collected when stressed or tired will be able to maintain a positive perspective on consulting and stick with it.

# CHAPTER 3

## PERSPECTIVES ON CONSULTING

**N**ow that you have a good understanding of the consulting industry, its multiple firms and practice areas, and the work and lifestyle, it is time to hear from some of the leading consultants and strategy academics themselves. The following insider perspectives on the industry were individually written by the people who are leading consulting into the next millennium. They offer unique insights into the future of consulting, are illustrated with case studies of actual consulting engagements, and are filled with personal anecdotes.

These essays will provide you with some of the latest thinking on the industry and will give you a rare insider's perspective into some of the industry's most respected consulting firms. Many of the essays touch on the same issues. Whether or not the editorialized comments that accompany each of these issues agree, their emphasis indicates they are the most widespread issues facing consultants today. For example, a common issue is whether a firm should specialize in an individual industry, or deliberately diversify its client mix to span several industries. L. John Wilkerson, chairman of The Wilkerson Group, argue in favor of firms that focus on a single industry, whereas Paul Smith, Director and Vice President of Bain & Company, takes a different position by promoting the generalist perspective, arguing that consultants are more effective when they observe patterns across industries. The perspectives of the essays are varied, and the opinions diversified. But each comes directly from a person who is influencing the future of consulting.

As you read through, note the reasons our contributors chose the field of consulting, and what they consider to be the risks and rewards of their work. As you read about specific industry and practice areas of consulting, try to envision yourself as a member of each one, and monitor your level of interest and enthusiasm. This will help you determine the area of consulting that is right for you and enable you to focus—and more efficiently complete—your consulting job search.

# Business Strategy and Consulting: A Theorist's View of Practice and a Practical View of Theory

BARRY NALEBUFF
YALE SCHOOL OF MANAGEMENT

I believe that a theory of business will prove useful, perhaps even invaluable, to you. As a professor, what matters more than anything else is discovering truth. But that is not the way it works in the "real world." As a consultant, it is not enough to discover the right answer—the answer also has to get implemented. I am a game theorist and I apply game theory to business strategy. But right now, I am writing about your future as a consultant and therefore better take heed of my own words. I recognize that my ideas, even if correct, do not count if you do not implement them. So now I must convince you.

# A THEORY OF BUSINESS

Harvard Business School Professor Adam Brandenburger likes to say, "There's nothing so practical as a good theory." A good theory confirms the conventional wisdom that less is more: less because it does not tell people what to do; but at the same time more, because it helps people organize what they know and uncover what they do not know.

And there is no better way to get someone to implement your ideas than for you to help them discover these ideas by themselves, so they think they came up with the ideas on their own.

*Co-opetition* (New York: Doubleday, 1996), the book I coauthored with Adam Brandenburger, develops a theory of business. It is a way to think about creating and capturing value. There is a fundamental duality here; whereas creating value is an inherently cooperative process, capturing value is inherently competitive. To create value, people cannot act in isolation. They have to recognize their interdependence. To create value, a business needs to align itself with customers, suppliers, employees, and many others. That is the way to develop new markets and expand existing ones.

But along with expanding the size of a pie, there is the issue of dividing it up. This is competition. Just as businesses compete with one another for market share, customers and suppliers are also looking out for their slice of the pie. Creating value that you can capture is the essence of business. To understand this duality, we use one of the key concepts of game theory, the idea of added value.

Added value =
Total value created with you in the game
minus
Total value created without you in the game.

Game theory says that if competition is unfettered, no player will get more than his or her added value in a game. Thus, added value allows us to characterize who has power and who does not. It allows us to understand how a pie is created and how it is divided up. If truth be told, this one equation seems simple, perhaps even too simple. But its simplicity is deceptive.

The first thing to note is that added value is an allocentric concept ("Allo" means others and is the reverse of "ego" or self). Instead of asking what you can get on your own, it requires you to ask what others will lose if you go away. It forces you to imagine a world without you—not a pleasant task—and understand just what you bring to others.[1]

What is your added value? Where does it come from? And how can you make it bigger, much bigger? Doing something better or cheaper than others is an important source of added value, but it is not the only one.

Take Microsoft. Whether or not it does things better or cheaper than others is somewhat beside the point. A key reason for Microsoft's enormous added value is the existence of Intel and the complementarity between their products. The existence of complements will be a key determinant of whether the network computer, electric cars, DVD players, digital cameras, and a host of other new technology products succeed or fail.

# COMPLEMENTORS

A complement to one product is any other product that makes the first one more, rather than less, attractive. Computer hardware and software are complements. So are hot dogs and mustard, cars and car loans, cable television and *TV Guide*, the Internet and high-capacity digital phone lines, catalogs and overnight delivery services—even red wine and dry cleaners, or Siskel and Ebert.

Traditionally, business strategy has largely focused on competition—Coke versus Pepsi—and in the process has underplayed complements. There has not even been a word to describe providers of complementary products. So we created one: "complementor," the natural counterpart to "competitor."

In new markets, paying attention to complements is a necessity. Without key complements, the market may never take off. In established markets, attending to complements has less dramatic but still valuable results. Here, complements most likely exist, but you can make your product more attractive by making the complements better, more plentiful, and less expensive.

Although your clients will probably know all about their competitors, chances are they will have thought less about their complementors. More to the point, which complementors are missing? Even a great product can sit on a shelf until key complements are developed.

One cannot assume that the essential complements to a business are going to be there. And if the complements are missing, you cannot assume that the market will solve the problem. The company will have to work with others to create the complements, or create them itself.

Companies involved in today's information revolution are prime candidates for this focus on complements. A new system of creating and sharing information is evolving, and it has many complementary parts. It is not enough to invent one part of the new system; one has to pay attention to all the parts at once.

Intel understands this idea, and provides a lesson for every business. The company's engineers have done a brilliant job of developing increasingly powerful computer chips. But the chip is only part of a larger system, and most of us already have more processing power than we need to run our favorite applications. Thus, outpacing competing chip makers is not enough—Intel must also engineer demand for its next-generation chips. So Intel is on the lookout for complementors: video games on PCs, desktop video-conferencing, and more. As I write this in 1998, look for voice recognition as the next technology that soaks up processing cycles and bet that Intel will take an active role in bringing that technology to the market.

Added value can also be tied to some of the best-known concepts in business strategy. Consider, for example. Michael Porter's concept of "competitive advantage." This is typically understood to mean some activity or set of activities that one organization can do better or cheaper than others. If you can do some things better or cheaper than others, then without you in the game, the total pie would indeed shrink.

Added value also fits nicely with Hamel and Prahalad's concept of "core competence." You can think of a core competence as a source of added value. Would value be lost if you, along with that competency, were out of the game? How well can others fill in? How much value would be lost?

Added value offers a different way of looking at the world. Conventional economics takes the structure of markets as fixed. People are thought of as simple stimulus-response machines. Sellers and buyers assume that products and prices are fixed, and they optimize production and consumption accordingly. Conventional economics has its place in describing the operation of established, mature markets, but it does not capture people's creativity in finding new ways of interacting with one another.

## CONCLUSION

In game theory, nothing is fixed. The economy is dynamic and evolving. The players create new markets and take on multiple roles. They innovate. No one takes products or prices as given. If this sounds like the free-form and rapidly transforming marketplace, that is why added value and game theory may be the kernel of a new economics for the new economy. You can say I told you so.

———— • • • ————

## *The Work of Consulting*

GARY NEILSON
BOOZ·ALLEN & HAMILTON

While I was earning my MBA at Columbia, I was attracted to consulting because it sounded like a continuation of business school—the chance to work on an assortment of the hardest, most critical business and organizational problems. But there would be a fundamental difference: as a consultant, I would be working "live" with real companies. The stakes and the pressure would be higher—these cases would involve real people and real capital—but so would the intellectual and financial rewards. Eighteen years later, my essential attraction to the profession has not dimmed.

This is a period of dramatic change. Call it the age of globalization, the age of information or the age of knowledge, the business world cannot sit back and let history define it for us. Too much hangs in the balance. Someone has to find ways of translating these overwhelming forces into coherent ways of thinking and practical courses of action. That line between theory and action is where the consultant's work begins.

## CONSULTANTS ARE PROBLEM SOLVERS

Companies do not bring in consultants for mundane problems. Although the consultant is an anonymous practitioner, there is glory in seeing your work in the second column of *The Wall Street Journal*, which is devoted to companies that are undertaking major initiatives. The visibility of your clients only adds to the stimulation.

We are outsiders. We are expensive, and we do not provide value if we are doing things that corporate staff members could do themselves, or if we are there to rubber-stamp management preconceptions. We have to know what we are talking about, we need the conviction to speak our minds, and we must be able to bring our experience to bear on client problems quickly and effectively. Our frameworks and platforms give us a ready-made set of standards to apply to each new situation and assess it expeditiously. We have established ways of proceeding and a conception of best practices.

This is not the much maligned cookie-cutter approach. We customize our work. However, while every situation is unique in its particulars, in broad terms it may have much in common with many other cases. Yet, the model is dynamic. Each engagement teaches us more. We are constantly refining our capabilities, improving our tools, and enhancing our practice.

Clients hire consultants who have seen problems before and understand the frameworks for solving them in as short a time as they responsibly can. The days are past when a company can afford to be smug about its own culture or its way of doing things. The competition is too intense.

When you are trying to merge one airline's routes, for example, into those of another airline by an announced date just a few months later, you do not want to reinvent the airplane—you want to get the job done. An engagement like this requires a vision that is both strategic and eminently practical. It needs to be done in a way that works. This involves tactical logistical thinking, such as ticketing, and making sure that the planes are available when the people are ready to depart. But it also requires ensuring organizational capabilities, such as scheduling, marketing, staffing, operations, and maintenance. Clients have all these capabilities in abundance, but extending them seamlessly across a much larger organization requires specialists who have seen it all before and know how it is done. That is what consultants can provide.

# THE CHANGING ROLE OF CONSULTANTS

The center of gravity in my work has shifted as I have matured professionally. Early in my career, I was engaged primarily in analysis and the requisite fact gathering. The product of my work was typically a rigorous formal presentation of data and analysis, at the end of which was a recommendation about what management should do. These meetings were often contentious and intellectually stimulating. The more vociferous the argument, the more successful the presentation was, in my view, because it meant we were really disturbing the universe.

Of course, implementation was another matter. If your recommendations entail justifying major capital investments or a radical change in management style and methodology, the client must marshal the capital and will to effect the change. The disconnection between what to do and how to do it may account for the failures of so many efforts at corporate restructuring.

Today, fact gathering and analysis are still critical to consulting. But the work involves much more collaboration with the client throughout the engagement. We work with company teams specially chosen by senior management to arrive not only at a plan of action and a rationale, but a plan for implementation. The ultimate product is not our presentation; it is their presentation. The program is backed not only by our opinions as "outside experts," but by the mandate of insiders as well.

The best consultants, in my mind, help clients do things. They guide, they brainstorm, but above all, they coach them to think about their business and solve problems for themselves. Consultants believe that you should teach a man to fish rather than give the man a fish to eat.

## THE CHANGING STRUCTURE OF COMPANIES

This mode of consulting ideally matches the needs of the emerging corporation, with a thin staff that bears scant resemblance to the corporations we knew years ago. In the new corporation, senior management must justify its existence by adding value every bit as much as the lines of business. Management is more likely to look outside to meet its needs—through outsourcing, strategic alliances, or vendor partnerships—than it is to create a new corporate department. Management consultants fit comfortably within that vision.

Keeping pace with this business takes a great deal of flexibility. You have to be temperamentally inclined toward a job-shop view of work—solid theoretical and methodological grounding, combined with an open mind. Alarms go off in my head when I interview a student who says he or she wants to be a partner. I ask myself, "How do they know? How can they be so sure?" I did not have that clear a vision of my future when I began. I wanted to learn as much as I could and have the chance to revisit my options. It turned out that I did become a partner, but only because this is a field where the challenges and opportunities constantly renew themselves. The field has changed, and I like to think I have grown.

## CONCLUSION

I would like to end on a personal note. When I started out, I worked 15 hours a day, six or seven days a week. Then I met the woman whom I later married. I had the choice of continuing to work that hard or

49

reengineering my own schedule so that I could have a life of my own. You would be surprised how efficient your own work processes can become when the incentives change. It is not that you do not occasionally work that hard or spend a great deal of time traveling. But weekends are much more clearly delineated on my calendar than they once were, and 6 P.M. on Friday is a more meaningful time.

Let me also mention that in the early days, before I began to limit my own hours, I much preferred working for people who had lives outside consulting than for those who worked as hard as I did. Lifestyle balance is not just a question of personal preference; it is a business necessity. If you work too hard, creativity and productivity begin to wane; and what is true for the individual is true for the firm. You cannot build teams or intellectual depth if you burn out each successive class of associates or partners. Any firm whose business is helping clients learn and change has to have the ability to learn about itself.

This is not an age for conventional thinking and closed minds. It is a time for learning, imagination, and perseverance. Our client companies and the people who depend on them deserve no less. Business history, like any other aspect of history, looks neat or inevitable only in hindsight. When we do our best, we help shape it for the better. That is the consultant's job.

— • • •

## *Can Consulting Be a Career?*

BILL MATASSONI
McKINSEY & COMPANY

Management consulting can be an ideal starting point for young professionals, but the reality is that most people who join consulting firms leave in a few years and take jobs outside consulting. Only a few stay long enough to receive more than one promotion, and even fewer are asked to become owners of their firms. Consulting gives professionals experience—lots of it, fast—and flexibility. It is an ideal professional development opportunity, but it is hardly a career.

# A PROFESSIONAL TRAINING GROUND

If management consulting is a professional development opportunity rather than a career, then ask yourself this question: as you think about consulting in general and about individual consulting firms in particular, what kind of development would be good for you, and where are you likely to get it? To find your answers, consider the three elements that enable firms to help their clients: knowledge, skills, and people.

For some consulting firms, knowledge is their dominant source of value added. They may have a comprehensive database that is key to helping clients with purchasing problems, or they may know the software industry backward and forward—or at least the current key success factors. Knowledge can also be a combination of theory and methodology, such as with EVA (economic value analysis) that helps managers think more rigorously about actions that will increase their companies' market capitalization.

Skills can vary as much as knowledge. Skills may be simply relevant to a particular problem-solving approach. After running clients through a reengineering process 20 times, you get fairly skilled at it. But consultants need other skills, too: communications skills, project management skills, people development skills and, at the higher levels, skills for interacting with senior management and keeping them involved in projects.

People, the last ingredient in this formula for a consultant's value added, is the hardest to pin down. People can be a synonym for leadership, values, commitment, professionalism, and trustworthiness. These are nice concepts, and all of us probably aspire to possess these attributes, but they may not always be required to have an impact on your client. A well-wrought combination of skills and knowledge,

51

alone, may be enough to have an impact with your client. You are the expert, the gunslinger who comes in to solve the problem, and then moves on.

But most consultants who aspire to work on a client's key problems—whether organizational, strategic or operational—understand that consulting is a very personal profession. You have to care about your clients, institutionally and individually, and they have to care about and trust you. There are many of us who believe that, even though our value to clients is delivered through a combination of people, skills and knowledge, the quality of our people is, in the end, what really matters. The mission statements of most consulting firms emphasize not only their aspiration to have impact, but also to attract the best people and really help them grow. That is the case at McKinsey & Company, for example, where we have a saying, "At first you are known for what you do, then for what you know, and finally for who you are."

The implications for someone considering consulting are straightforward. If you are interested in developing a knowledge spike, look for consulting firms that have track records in practice development and research. Check out how often they publish and who gets to publish. If you want to develop analytical or people skills, consider their approach to training and how they do their day-to-day work. Is the emphasis on process or problem solving? How extensively are teams used, and are clients on them? What kinds of formal development systems do they have? To get a really good picture of which skills really matter, ask to see the complete list of new partners from the previous year (not just the "poster" partners in the recruiting literature), and see what kinds of background they bring and experiences they have had.

As for the people dimension, assess whether or not there will be real leadership opportunities for you early on. What kinds of roles do you get to play with clients? What kinds of clients are served, and what criteria are applied when considering the personal characteristics of prospective clients? Put more simply, will you get to work with real leaders? And have newcomers been involved in starting new practices and offices? These can be great opportunities for personal development because of their entrepreneurial nature. Or maybe the litmus test for assessing how well a firm develops its people is what its consultants do when they leave their firms. Do they go on to top positions in business, government, or academia?

# AN AGENT OF CHANGE

Many consulting firms deliver on one or more of these dimensions of development, and that is what makes consulting so attractive. In fact, there has been a backlash in recent years because so many people find it attractive. Some critics have worried that with so much talent from business and other graduate schools going into consulting, American business and society are not being well served. That's not a fair argument. Indeed, consulting prepares many people to be successful, high-impact leaders. But some observers disagree, arguing that consultants do not implement anything, that they study things, give theoretical answers, and then leave. So, they argue, consulting does not prepare them for the real world. But what do these observers mean by implement?

- Do they mean developing a detailed plan regarding structure, systems, staff, and other key organizational changes, as well as a timetable for getting them done? Consultants do that.
- Do they mean giving top management real insight and conviction about what will create value in the future? Consultants do that.
- Do they mean experimenting on the front line with new approaches or prototyping new business models? Consultants do that.
- Do they mean marching people through a change process regardless of the situation? Some consultants do that, but it may not be right to do that.
- Do they mean running a client's business for them or usurping management's responsibilities? Consultants do not, or should not, do that.

The bottom line is that consultants do implement in many ways, and the best consultants, like their clients, cannot afford to just step back and study the situation. Russell Ackoff, a great thinker on strategy, once wrote:

> Managers are not confronted with problems that are independent of each other, but with dynamic situations that consist of complex systems of changing problems that interact with each other. I call such situations messes. Problems are abstractions extracted from messes by analysis; they are to messes as atoms are to tables and charts. Managers do not solve problems; they manage messes.[2]

Management consultants confront messes, too. And in the ambiguity and turmoil of these messes are the real opportunities to help your clients and develop yourself. This is not to say that consultants have not, at times, been guilty of favoring elegant and theoretical solutions rather than practical answers. Writing about operations research, Ackoff lamented that it had become identified with techniques, mathematical models, and algorithms, rather than with "the ability to formulate management problems, solve them, and implement and maintain their solutions in turbulent environments."[3] Consulting in the 1980s could have been similarly criticized, but think about the challenges managers face today. Situations are fluid and problems are interconnected, and it is hard to determine cause and effect with certainty over time. What is needed under these conditions is what Schön and Ackoff described as the "active synthetic skill" of "designing a desirable future and inventing ways of bringing it about."[4]

# A PERSONAL COMMITMENT

Helping clients design and invent—that is what consulting, at its best, is. It is not good enough to be right—your goal is to win. Your determination to help your client succeed goes beyond a professional obligation and becomes a personal commitment. As such, consulting can have a noble and admirable purpose, whatever the specific assignment and goal. It can mean helping a client develop and sell a terrific new product worldwide. It can mean helping a company in Kansas or Irkutsk stay independent and competitive. It can mean helping Glasgow renew its economy. It can mean helping a country's politicians understand how to create jobs.

Whatever the challenge, if you feel this sense of purpose when you consult, then the leadership, trust, skills, and knowledge that you aim to develop will all naturally result. And each year, when you ask yourself, "Should I keep doing this?" you will say, "Yes." But if that sense of purpose is absent, you have probably learned enough after a few years, and your answer should be, "No." It is time to move on.

———— • • • ————

## *Customer-Driven Growth Strategy*

CHARLES P. HOBAN
MERCER MANAGEMENT CONSULTING

Management consulting is not a homogeneous industry. The issues addressed, the analytical processes employed, and the day-to-day activities of the project team can vary widely from one type of consulting to another. As you face the challenge of choosing your career path within the consulting industry, you have to dig beneath the surface of the recruiting pitches and ask yourself: What kind of consulting do I want to do?

# CUSTOMER-DRIVEN GROWTH STRATEGY

If you were the CEO of a company in the 1970s, the rules were pretty simple. The number of things that you had to concern yourself with were relatively limited. It was a hard job because competition was fierce, but you knew how you were competing. You knew your competitors. You could count on certain economic rules applying. You wanted to gain high market share because that allowed you to advance down the experience curve. You wanted to get down the curve because that gave you a cost (and, therefore, profit) advantage. With that profit advantage, you could invest in the activities that allowed you to gain share. Your job as CEO was to lay out a plan to win at that game.

The consulting industry that grew up in the 1970s supported that task. Consulting was about experience curves, about relative cost positions, about pushing an organization to be more effective at that game. Even the 1980s' "paradigms"—total quality management, time-based competition, process reengineering—were all about making companies more competitive. In this world, "strategy" was sort of an academic exercise. Most companies knew where they were trying to go; they just needed help getting there.

Business has changed. Today, the number of strategic challenges facing a CEO is exploding. The amount of information available as input to decisions now seems infinite. The set of competitors is constantly changing. The traditional economic rules of the game do not seem to apply. Companies that got very good at competing in the old game may or may not be equipped to succeed as the game has changed. Too many companies have spent the past 20 years "getting competitive," only to find themselves looking up from that task to ask, "What am I competing for?" "Where am I trying to go?"

A client in a technology industry had long been successful by having the best products. They had invested in a product development capability that was world-class. They continued an unparalleled record of new product introductions, layering on new features at a startling pace. They were the market leader. In a matter of months, however, things began to shift. After years of impressive growth, three quarters in a row were disappointing. They were not getting the same kind of sales lift out of each new product. Something had changed, and they were just not sure what it was.

## CUSTOMER-DRIVEN GROWTH STRATEGY

The client hired Mercer to help them develop a Customer-Driven Growth Strategy. While there were lots of theories within the management team about what was wrong, no one could prove any of their hunches. The internal processes all seemed to be working fine—quality was up, customer satisfaction was high, product development was hitting every milestone. But sales were slipping. The stock market was beginning to notice. The growth stock suddenly had stopped growing.

Setting strategic direction in this new environment requires a fundamentally different approach. You need to have a much more thorough and dynamic understanding of the external environment, and work "outside-in." While most of your effort has been focused on benchmarking competitors, now your focus must shift to the edges of the radar screen, to new and nontraditional competitors who may have more effective business designs than any of the incumbents. Similarly, customer understanding used to be the task of market research—gauging satisfaction, testing new products. Today, customer understanding is a complex task of analyzing the customer's decision-making process and environment. It involves a detailed understanding of decision economics, of trade-offs among factors, and of the effect of changing conditions on future behavior.

The scope of options and strategic implications of this dynamic environment has also exploded. Businesses are considering an increasingly diverse range of strategic moves. New business models—new ways of competing—are sprouting up every day. Our clients face bigger decisions, with bigger stakes, than ever before.

Mercer's case team initially focused on understanding how the external environment had changed. A particularly useful approach was identifying a set of new, very different companies that were growing rapidly. While they looked nothing like our client (they were not on the client's list of competitors), they were succeeding by offering a subset of the product bundle in a dramatically simpler way. These companies were changing the rules. They used different channels and had very different cost structures. And they were winning customers.

The case team then focused on identifying the business models that would be successful in the future. The new competitors were successful today, and they gave us early clues, but to respond to them directly would only put our client further behind the changing market. To anticipate the best moves to make, we worked to understand how customers were using the products. Our analysis focused on detailing the systems economics of the customer.

This changing environment has created a new kind of need for consultants. It has opened a new era of strategy. Strategy, no longer merely an academic question for a company's planning department, has moved to the top of the corporate agenda. Strategy now requires new approaches and new frameworks that allow a senior management team to sort through the flood of information to find the optimal value growth opportunities. The task is complex. That makes this an exciting time to be in the strategy consulting business.

Our analysis identified a series of business design moves for our client to consider. Ranging from adjustments to resource allocation and channel structure in the existing business, to entirely new businesses that anticipated the next wave of market changes, the client had to reinvent the way they did business. The old rules, the foundation of success, were no longer valid. Together with management, we designed an implementation program to begin the process of reinvention.

The change program is ongoing. The rules continue to change. Reinvention is now part of the management process.

It is an incredibly challenging time to be in the strategy consulting business. If all the old rules are no longer valid, consultants can no longer depend on traditional benchmarks and frameworks. We can no longer safely extrapolate the future from the past. Success depends on developing new and innovative ways of looking at dynamic markets and identifying new opportunities to create value. At the same time, the pace of change is accelerating. At Mercer, we have focused on developing and applying innovative frameworks that help our clients interpret the chaos surrounding them.

# WHAT KIND OF CONSULTING DO YOU WANT TO DO?

My experience in the strategy consulting business has been extremely rewarding. I am as excited and challenged by the work today as I was when I started with Corporate Decisions, Inc. in 1990 (we merged with Mercer in 1997). Along with the many other attractions of consulting— rapid pace, smart people, learning about a variety of industries and issues—the content of the work has kept me motivated.

As a potential consultant, it is important to recognize the type of work that you like to do, that you are good at, and that will get you out of bed in the morning. Consulting of all types is demanding—clients expect excellence, energy, and a "pull out all the stops" approach. For that reason, you need to get a charge out of what you do. While many factors will determine the firm you want to join, the most important is the type of work they do.

The Customer-Driven Growth Strategy work that I have described is not for everyone. Understanding the external environment is, by definition, a boundless task. You never have "all" the information. Clients often ask you to deal with chaos and to put a structure on that chaos. You have to develop hypotheses and test them with the available information. Your research techniques must be creative. And you have to be willing to adjust your perspectives as you learn more about a situation.

By contrast, internally oriented consulting deals with more self-contained problems. The finiteness of the data leads to a different approach, and the process uses a different type of creativity for trying to find the right answer.

Take the time to understand the content of the work at the companies you are considering. Match that with the way that you think, the way you learn. The right match can be incredibly exciting.

———— • • • ————

# The Generalist Approach to Consulting: The Strategic Value of Breaking Industry Barriers

PAUL SMITH
BAIN & COMPANY

When I joined Bain & Company out of Harvard Business School in 1984, I planned to do consulting for a couple years, then get a job at Microsoft or Intel, three or four rungs up the product manager ladder from where I had left the high-tech industry. Born in Australia and raised in South Africa, I earned a degree in mathematics and computer science from UCLA. I moved first to Raytheon and then on to Burroughs to design computers. When Burroughs and Sperry merged to create Unisys, I took that opportunity to go to business school. As an R&D guy, I had very little exposure to the strategic aspect of the business. But I was intrigued by the consulting presentations I saw on campus. I saw that as a fairly junior consultant I could participate in many functional areas across multiple industries and have a lot of input into the most critical issues facing a company. The whole *results* pitch to develop practical strategic solutions that are implementable—which at the time no one else made—sold me on Bain & Company.

Within the context of Bain's generalist approach to consulting in a range of industries and functional areas, my high-tech experience and diverse geographic background have proved to be unexpected resources. I came expecting technology to be useless. But the true value of a well-run generalist firm is the ability to leverage knowledge. So, I find myself applying technology paradigms to nontech industries, and nontech modes of thought to our high-tech clients.

One significant—and unexpectedly positive—contrast with my background was doing something different every three to six months. The computer I designed at Burroughs took three years of my life and still did not come to market until three years after I left. In contrast, during the past 14 years I have worked on probably 100+ engagements:

from pricing strategy and redeployment in the banking industry to product line profitability and sales force management in healthcare distribution; from business unit strategy and mergers and acquisitions for a software firm to divestment analysis for the airlines; from purchasing strategy for a conglomerate to turnaround on a major computer manufacturer; and even corporate strategy in women's undergarments.

# A GENERALIST APPROACH TO FUNDAMENTAL STRATEGIC ISSUES

The generalist approach to strategy consulting is unusual in an industry of heavy specialization. Strategy consultants focus on issues that are of fundamental strategic importance to a business, unlike functional or systems consultants, who focus on operational, rather than strategic, issues. For example, if a business has run out of warehouse space and needs assistance in optimizing new warehouse locations or distribution points, a consultant specializing in logistics would be an appropriate choice. Systems or IT consultants would be required if the business has outgrown its current inventory tracking systems and needs a better solution. But if the real issue at stake is how the business should configure its distribution to attain maximum competitive advantage, whether to use direct or indirect distribution, or whether to use a single-tier or a double-tier system, then a strategy consultant is called for. At Bain, we define strategy as the science of allocating scarce resources, and strategy consulting as the art of helping our clients make the right decisions to capture and create value from those resources.

Our greatest "grand slams" in strategic decision making have usually been situations in which we have brought experience across an industry boundary. For example, our teams have taken loyalty work in financial services and applied it to the airlines. Using insights from completely different industries, we showed a major American automobile manufacturer how to think about product configuration and complexity. We constantly break traditional thought processes and work outside the barriers of industry paradigms. Because generalists are always learning, they ask questions that "industry experts" would never ask.

# CHALLENGING ORTHODOXIES

Individuals are not expected to spend their careers in any single industry. While this approach may seem harder, our clients benefit immensely from the fresh perspective, and we learn a lot in the process. This insistence on challenging orthodoxies and searching out strategic innovations requires that, as a firm, we leverage knowledge across the board. The real value generalists bring to a company is the experience of making change happen, of working through each case from the very beginning, without relying on preconceived notions about industry norms that would prohibit the genesis of breakthrough ideas.

Off-the-shelf solutions simply do not allow clients to distinguish themselves from their competitors. As generalists, we benefit from being able to start from a strong base of industry knowledge but go beyond the cookie-cutter answers. Instead, we value superior analytic thinking that treats each client as the unique organization that it is. We work from the perspective of the CEO, and unlike industry gurus, we think the way a new general manager thrown into the client's firm would think.

# STRATEGIC INSIGHT

The results of drawing on multi-industry experience are impressive. The following case study began with the question: "Why do we want to be in this business?"

The CEO of a $9 billion company came to us and said, "I have a division that is number 5 in this business worldwide, and I'm not even breaking even. I know number 5 businesses never survive. So why shouldn't I sell this thing tomorrow?" The division, at a little over $1B, was supposed to be a growth business, but wasn't making money. This CEO, a believer in the Jack Welch philosophy that "if a business is not number 1 or number 2, get out of it," asked us to validate that this business was a dead end and figure out how to exit it.

But our answer surprised the CEO: "Not only do you want to be in this business, but you should also invest in it!" Our work defied conventional wisdom and helped turn the division around to become a star performer in the company's portfolio.

We helped management understand how to target and capture the highest value customers in their market, how to take hundreds of millions of dollars out of the cost structure, gain market share to drive this multibillion dollar industrial products business from number 5 to number 3, and improve returns from –2 percent to 8 percent. The market cap of the parent has gone through the roof, and analysts and the press attribute much of this to the turnaround of the division.

So, what was the strategic insight? For the answer, we drew on our work in other industries, such as high-technology computer and software firms, in which the size and loyalty of the customer base drives the economics. What matters in an installed-base industry is how many people are using a particular product, not how many are sold every year—repeat purchase rates are the critical success factor. Historically, the company had been doing a strong business in North America and Europe, with developing markets in Eastern Europe, South America, and Asia. We decided we needed to understand how customer decisions were made in each of those markets, how pricing was done in each, and what it cost to serve customers across these markets.

By analyzing the customer base, we came up with an insight we often see in our work with clients in the financial services industry. The company would be more profitable if it focused on serving existing customers instead of engaging in dogfights over new customers in emerging markets. Our client was losing its shirt by offering huge discounts to new customers in Kazakhstan and Mexico rather than profitably capturing the next order from existing customers in Europe. It was a straightforward issue of customer retention. As in the insurance and credit card businesses, where customers are only profitable after many years, it was important for our client to understand how to run the business differently in areas where customers were already committed to them. The opportunity we identified for the client was to focus on servicing, follow-on sales, and adding the next set of features to a product, not just chasing new customers. We moved the best salespeople from new to existing accounts, helped change the sales and pricing incentives, and focused the business on where the profits lay.

Crossing not only industry boundaries, but also geographic lines, multioffice Bain teams throughout Asia-Pacific, Russia, Europe, and the Americas worked to customize strategies across the different markets for this client, as we rolled out the new strategy globally with management. For this particular client, the implementation of this strategy was a case in itself.

Within 12 months after our recommendation to stay in the business, the division had achieved 80 percent of its goal of a 10 percent return on sales, while continuing to accelerate its growth and removing hundreds of millions of dollars from the cost structure. Our work drew on our dealings with analogous situations of installed-base management in high-technology companies, retention in financial services clients, global competition in a consumer products client, and, of course, cost reduction in other industrial companies. And the end result was *results*.

# REALIZING BUSINESS OBJECTIVES

This is precisely what clients care about: *results*. Success, in our clients' eyes, requires the achievement of tangible results according to specific business criteria that we determine together at the onset of a case. To achieve the goals developed by both the client and our consulting team, we have to maintain a clear and consistent interaction with the client organization at all levels, not just the ear of the CEO or senior management. "Perfect solutions" that cannot be implemented throughout the organization have no value—the end product is simply a hefty report, not true results. If nothing changes, nothing was accomplished.

I was drawn to generalist consulting because I wanted to learn more and get involved in creating new solutions. What I found is that it is all about results—it is the only yardstick at the end of the day that matters.

And 14 years later (rather than the two years I expected to stay at Bain), this focus on results still has me captivated.

———— • • • ————

# Building a Healthcare-Focused Consulting Firm

L. JOHN WILKERSON, HARRI V. TARANTO,
AND MELISSA SABINO
THE WILKERSON GROUP

The founders of The Wilkerson Group (TWG) had the foresight, or perhaps luck, to establish an industry-focused consulting firm at the dawn of great prosperity for the healthcare industry. National health expenditures were reaching critical mass, initially in the United States and later worldwide. By 1967, the year of TWG's founding, health expenditures in the United States had passed $50 billion, more than double their amount in 1960. Healthcare was the beneficiary of materials, microprocessors, and other technologies coming out of the space program and defense industry. And, the unique American seed and venture financing system capitalized on these trends, creating a plethora of new medical products and high-growth companies.

TWG capitalized on this confluence of change in medicine, technology, and finance. The firm was the first to provide corporations and investors with objective perspectives on the commercial outlook for a seemingly endless stream of new medical technologies, products, and companies. The medical industry lends itself well to industry-focused, expertise-based consulting. Our engagements require not only a substantial understanding of scientific and clinical content, but also expertise in a fragmented marketplace characterized by different products, technologies, decision makers, distributors, and competitors.

Furthermore, clinical decision making and product selection in the healthcare industry has historically been difficult to codify; it is more art than science. All in all, this is an ideal market for experts capable of combining perspective and experience with facts to help clients see around corners. Today, we augment this core capability with greatly expanded skills to create business and information technology strategy.

It is not too surprising that TWG, like so many industry-focused firms, found it easier to satisfy clients than to master its internal organization. For example, we recognized early on that the linchpin of a quality firm was attracting and retaining superior team members to provide better-than-advertised services. We did this well, but we procrastinated in building infrastructure and systems. And, while praising the value of rainmakers and client problem solvers, we were slow to recognize our critical consulting support team. Once we confronted our mistakes, we grew steadily into a 150-person firm with a strong culture, loyal clients, an enviable franchise, and a highly skilled team.

The numerous forces affecting the worldwide healthcare industry made it necessary to continuously reinvent our firm. In the early days of the firm, assignments were plentiful, but they were often only $50,000 in scope, with short, 8- to 12-week deadlines. Not surprisingly, our hectic lives often made us feel like caged squirrels running on a wheel. Even though we were growing, and client feedback was more than encouraging, a number of our top producers went through periods of introspection: "Should I be an investment banker since I know more about this industry than they ever will?" "Why don't I go get a real job where we manufacture products that go out the backdoor every day?" Most of our team struggled with these questions, but, in the end, chose to stay and build their firm.

## STAGES OF EVOLUTION

As The Wilkerson Group evolved over more than 20 years, all facets of its business changed, including the industry segments served, its clients and competitors, and its organization. In retrospect, there have been three main stages of evolution for TWG: (1) the "go-go" years, from founding until the early 1980s; (2) the post-government-intervention years, from 1983 until about 1993; and (3) the rational medicine era of today.

We often described the firm in its early years as being in the happiness containment business: it seemed clients had the traditional five Ws of "who, why, when, where, and what" confused with "wow, whoopee, whew, wahoo, and why not." Fee-for-service was king, cost containment essentially nonexistent, and the focus was on disseminating new technologies as widely and rapidly as possible. The typical engagement involved helping the client decide which of the many fast-growing opportunities to pursue. In 1980, TWG was small, with billings under $1 million per year and a total staff of eight, almost entirely U.S.-focused, and driven by the skills and interests of its senior partners. The firm, then called Channing, Weinberg, was still run by its founders, but their interests had drifted away from consulting to venture capital. John Wilkerson, with industry and healthcare security analysis experience, was brought in to run the consulting practice in 1980.

Initially, TWG worked solely in the medical device and equipment market, where the founders had knowledge and contacts. As each new partner brought expertise to the firm, our client base broadened to diagnostics, biotechnology, pharmaceuticals, and for-profit healthcare services. It would be comforting to say each area was added for all the right reasons and also in a timely fashion. But the truth is, we made several changes because our client base was reeling from real or perceived threatening governmental initiatives.

In 1983, as a result of U.S. government-mandated billing guidelines, cost containment became the watchword in the hospital market, and the go-go years for hospitals came to an end. But the 1980s also ushered in the biotechnology revolution, marked by extraordinarily successful IPOs (initial public offerings) for companies like Amgen, Cetus, and Genentech. It was a time of rapid global growth for the pharmaceutical industry, with numerous new drug introductions and ongoing price increases. These changes prompted TWG to transition into pharmaceuticals and, consequently, shifted the demand for

TWG's consulting services from an entirely domestic to an increasingly international clientele.

Then, in the mid-1980s, two pivotal internal events occurred: The five senior partners acquired the firm from the two founders, who were, by then, entrenched in venture capital. Burdened by what seemed at the time an enormous bank debt, the partners realized that we needed change in order to succeed; we had to share ownership, institutionalize the firm via codification of research methodology, organize our world-class information base, and build a more extensive service line. One partner recently commented that buyout debt served to bring partners' interest in line—better than dynamic leadership and all the planning sessions we ever had.

By the early 1990s, it was evident that spending for healthcare was a lightning rod for payors and particularly the Clinton presidency. Within large pharmaceutical companies, it was glaringly obvious that technology and management needed to be focused on creating bigger and better drugs much faster. The biotechnology field responded to this mandate, and company formation reached the astonishing level of three per week. Formation of European biotechnology companies was about to take off. The growing European interest in biotech and almost all other areas of the medical products industry, along with our need to respond to our clients' global issues, drove our decision to open our first European office in London.

All these changes were positive for our consulting business, but two new issues emerged: healthcare had attracted many consulting powerhouses; and our clients needed new services we did not offer. One significant unmet need was the use of information as a strategic weapon. We initially sought a strategic investor-partner to augment our service offering, but, ultimately, we decided to join IBM Consulting because its information technology expertise had great depth and its new management placed a premium on consulting as a solutions provider to the healthcare industry.

Our union with IBM Consulting has resulted in an additional set of clients: hospitals and payors. The firm now has intellectual capital in the areas of providing services to healthcare product manufacturers, providers, and payors. Increasingly, winning strategies for any of our clients require integrating in-depth knowledge of all three dimensions.

Today, the bulk of our revenues are from ongoing relationships with the top 100 healthcare manufacturers and a client list of top-tier payors and providers. Instead of helping clients understand a new market about which they know very little, our firm now works in our clients' own backyard, joining their teams to devise creative strategies for their own markets.

## THOUGHTS ON CULTURE

Throughout these periods of change, the firm's culture has remained constant. To the extent it is possible to articulate culture, ours is about commitment and caring—about the right things. The firm developed a culture based on attracting people who, first and foremost, love healthcare; the opportunity to help medical professionals enhance worldwide healthcare is a fundamental driver of most who join TWG and, certainly, anyone who stays. We also have gone to great lengths to ensure that the people we seek out and invite to join our firm would pass the airport test—would they make a long delay at an airport enjoyable? This hiring requirement is important because it contributes to a collaborative environment where independent thinking strengthens the client deliverable.

A unique and most important other dimension of our culture is our appreciation of industry expertise. Rainmakers and process consultants are critical for our success, but our core competency is in knowing what we are talking about in technology, products, markets, and companies. Industry expertise is lauded at TWG and we encourage professionals to know more about relevant subjects than anyone else in the world.

## CONCLUSION

In thinking back about how we created our coveted industry franchise, it is clear we did a number of things right. We were fortunate to have focused on a rapidly growing and, as important, changing industry. We shied away from prospective clients who referred to consultants as vendors, and we shifted our energies from one-time descriptive studies to senior executives seeking industry-focused counseling.

Although it has been challenging to continuously reinvent our firm, our willingness to do so has resulted in a highly motivated firm comprising exceptional colleagues who work in arguably the most dynamic and worthwhile industry today. Expertise in all facets of this industry is our core competitive advantage.

———— • • • ————

## *Innovation in Consulting*

GEORGE STALK JR.
THE BOSTON CONSULTING GROUP

I was originally attracted to The Boston Consulting Group (BCG) because of its reputation for innovation. BCG's history is one of continuous innovation, including classics such as experience-based strategies, portfolio, stalemate, and average costing, and new wave strategies such as time-based competition, capabilities-based competition, and breaking compromises. And today, we pursue strategies based on the new economics of information. We are constantly searching for ways to compete that are not generally accepted, or that are overlooked, dismissed, or misunderstood.

## THE COMPANY AS A LABORATORY

We have enormous opportunity to innovate in the consulting business because our clients represent an almost limitless laboratory. In helping our clients find solutions to the challenges they face—be they growth, turnaround, or repositioning—patterns emerge. These patterns enable us to understand cause and effect. Once cause and effect are clear, we are just a step away from identifying a strategy innovation. And once we identify the innovation, we can transplant it from one industry to another.

For example, almost all factories can be made flexible for faster throughput by just-in-time processes. But factories are just a collection of machines operated by a human organization. Should not all human organizations be amenable to being made flexible? The answer is yes. Just-in-time works in insurance companies and in the back office processes of a securities firm. In another example, the strategies for strengthening brands in consumer goods companies are very often just as effective for strengthening brands in financial service and industrial companies.

# AN INNOVATION: TIME-BASED COMPETITION

Our work in making factories and other organizations flexible led us to time-based competition. The concept is simple: companies that meet the needs of their customers more rapidly than competitors do grow faster and are more profitable than others in their industries. We observed a pattern of faster throughput across a wide variety of factories that were made flexible. We incorporated speed into our strategy because we believe that time is the decade's most powerful competitive weapon and management tool.

And our beliefs were proven true. Companies of all sorts and sizes became or are becoming time-based competitors. By inspecting their processes and organizations through the lens of time, these companies found and are finding new ways to operate, satisfy their customers, compete, grow, improve quality, and invigorate themselves.

Time-based competition was directly lifted and applied to the management of hospitals. Karolinska Hospital, a leading research hospital in Stockholm, Sweden, used time-based competition to respond to reductions in government subsidies at a time when demand was growing. If people could get through the hospital faster, capacity could be freed up and costs reduced. At Karolinska, doctors were, at first, skeptical of the concept. How could they save time without risking quality, thereby imperiling patient care? In fact, they found that poor coordination and scheduling problems were not only reducing efficiency and inflating costs, but also causing patients unnecessary delay, inconvenience, anxiety and, sometimes, health complications.

By redesigning operating procedures and staffing patterns, Karolinska cut the time required for preoperative testing from months to days. By compressing the operating room cycle from admission through operation, to intensive care, and out, the hospital was able to close 2 of 15 operating rooms and still increase the number of operations per day by 30 percent. Doctors could schedule operations in weeks rather than months. The result: better service for patients with no loss of quality (indeed, faster care is better care), less overhead, and more growth.

# THE EXCITEMENT OF CONSULTING

The excitement of consulting is knowing that the patterns are out there to be observed, discovered, interpreted, and then transplanted. This excitement keeps many of us in consulting much longer than we anticipated when we first joined the profession.

Now, as a senior officer of BCG, I am extremely gratified to watch the progress of the bright, young people who enter consulting each year. As they develop tenure, their ability to innovate strengthens. First, experience brings stronger skills for faster pattern recognition and interpretation. Second, working with a client and an industry for a considerable period results in enhanced innovation. Clients do not keep consultants around to help with the same challenges over and over again. The bar keeps rising, and consultants must continually strive to hurdle it.

For example, I have been working as a consultant for an automotive OEM (original equipment manufacturer) since 1982. I have worked in component manufacturing, vehicle assembly, product development, and parts and services, and am now deeply involved in the distribution and retail end of the business. As I reflect on my years as a consultant, I realize that my tasks have become progressively more challenging.

This is frustrating and exciting at the same time. The frustration is that the job is not getting easier. The excitement is that the next request is always a more interesting and demanding challenge that will require innovation. Indeed, today we are questioning the fundamental structure of the automotive industry and how it will be affected by the forces of change, including the opening of markets, the restructuring of the supply base, electronic commerce, advances in technologies, changes in consumer behaviors, and changes in distribution and retail.

## BUILDING LONG-TERM CLIENT RELATIONSHIPS

I know it is through innovation that we will be able to deliver the assistance and the value our clients seek. I also know that value will accrue to BCG since innovation in the client environment strengthens our firm. Indeed, many things we have done along the value chain of the automotive industry were precursors to changes in other industries, such as consumer goods, insurance, and banking. For example, the notion that growth opportunities are hidden in compromises that companies impose on consumers arose from trying to make dealers "customer friendly." Now, the notion of breaking compromises to release value and to grow is spreading through many industries.

When we review our largest, and longest, client relationships, we are always struck by how these relationships began with the client adopting an innovation and then seeking additional help, either in dealing with the ramifications of that innovation or in seeking other innovations. Innovation is important for getting impact because, in many companies, it is hard to achieve significant change by simply improving existing strategies. Another result of innovation is that we gain our clients' trust, which, in turn, allows us to help with their more difficult problems. This is a virtuous cycle that strengthens the consultant-client relationship and provides us with the laboratory we need to stay ahead in the game of innovation.

• • •

## *Selecting a Small versus a Large Firm*

ELLEN MCGEENEY
VERTEX PARTNERS

When choosing among myriad opportunities, many prospective consultants look to firm size as a metric to narrow the field. After all, large firms provide a stable opportunity, brand recognition, formal training, and access to a worldwide organization, whereas small firms offer collegial atmosphere, good growth opportunities, and less politics and bureaucracy. Right?

Well, not exactly. Although firm size can impact the work experience, not all important differences among firms are predictably correlated with size. In fact, the size of the firm is a relatively good indicator of only two attributes: brand recognition and your ability to have an impact on the firm. Small firms typically cannot offer the same blue-chip aura as the largest firms, but the brand-conscious should beware of the "brand value trap." Brand name alone will not do much beyond opening the front door, and the richness of your consulting experiences will count for more than the name on your resume.

If leaving your imprint is important to you, you should know that, while your impact is likely to be greater at a small firm, there is no guarantee. Entrepreneurial pockets can exist within large firms seeking fresh ideas and leaders to steer future direction. And, although small firms typically move more quickly and seek out those with entrepreneurial energy, they can lack the leadership or processes to channel that energy effectively.

Beyond brand recognition and your impact within the firm, size does interact with other characteristics to create the firm of your dreams or nightmares. When evaluating which firm to choose, you should explore four essential topics: the firm's growth trajectory, the project work, the people, and the culture.

# GROWTH: GROWTH IS GOOD

Whether the firm you are considering is small or large, you must understand its growth trajectory to assess the opportunity. Senior consultants should be able to consistently and clearly articulate a compelling strategy for growth, and cite evidence to support the firm's progress toward achieving its growth goals. The firm's growth rate affects the risk profile of the opportunity, your career trajectory, and the balance between an exciting versus a stressful challenge.

People often look to firm size as a way to minimize risk and maximize reward, assuming that the stable option exists within the large firm. Just like any other high growth, competitive, and innovation-driven industry, however, consulting can be turbulent. Both large and small firms face layoff-generating hiccups in the revenue stream, and growth projections can be tough to meet at any firm, regardless of size. Adding to this risk, large firms can be plagued by greater political intrigues, leading to uncertainty for those whose careers are tied to specific partners. In comparison, a small firm with a strong growth strategy may provide greater upside potential for financial and personal reward.

The bottom line is slow growth can be a rate-limiting factor for your career. No matter how good you are, if the firm is not growing, your promotion track will be slow. This will frustrate you while you are at the firm and will not look good if you seek a job elsewhere. In contrast, too much unmanaged growth can wreak havoc on the worker bees (that means you). High turnover amidst growth is a sure sign of trouble and can quickly shift a challenging career into stressful overdrive.

# PROJECTS: A PASSION FOR THE WORK INEVITABLY BREEDS SUCCESS

Ask most consultants who have remained in the field why they are still there. We love the work. We need to—after all, other careers offer comparable return for less stress and fewer hours. To see whether you will be able to sustain a passion for consulting, you must answer four questions about the work: (1) What mix of industries and client problems is the firm's practice based on? (2) At what level in the organization does the firm typically work? (3) At which stage in the problem-solving process does the firm do its work? (4) How are consultants assigned to projects?

Most candidates emphasize the firm's industry focus (e.g., healthcare, financial services) over the mix of client problems addressed (e.g., merger and acquisition strategy, reengineering, sales-force design and strategy). Industry focus should drive your decision if consulting is a transition to specializing in a particular industry. Otherwise, being exposed to a variety of client problems is far more interesting and valuable than ensuring that each case is in a new industry. Be wary of being pegged as operations-focused, for example, if you want to do strategy work.

The second factor to investigate is the level in the organization at which the firm typically works. Engagements that operate below the level of CEO or senior VPs who head major functional areas tend to attract minimal client interest, receive inadequate client commitment, and, as a result, can have limited impact. Problems that are frankly of minor importance to the client are far less interesting to work on, and may challenge and teach you less than you expect.

The third question, the stage of problem solving the firm focuses on, often determines several important aspects of the work: how much client interaction you have, how much number crunching you do, how much impact you are able to see, and the intellectual challenge you face. Most firms focus either on the strategy development or on the implementation phase of problem solving. And most prospective consultants I have spoken to are initially enamored with strategy work. However, CEOs increasingly value strategies that *work* over the big idea that they know will require a struggle for their organization to implement. In addition, it can be frustrating to repeatedly work hard on strategies that end up as reports, collecting dust on the CEO's bookshelf. What is more, pure strategy cases often involve lots of lonely analysis, with only the most senior members of the team having significant client interaction. Unless you enjoy computers more than people, you may want to ensure that your work will combine some measure of implementation with the strategy.

The final question you should investigate is how project staffing decisions are made. In theory, small firm size limits the variety of projects available to you, but in many firms, large and small, you quickly become tied to specific partners, and your project options are limited to the work they sell. Thus, the process of assigning projects is more important than firm size: find out whether the firm uses the "free market" or the "central clearinghouse" system. The free market system requires you to be proactive to ensure that you are in the running for the project you want. How effectively you market your skills can make or break your career. In contrast, the central clearinghouse system usually employs a full-time staffing coordinator whose job is to make sure that individuals' needs and interests are balanced with client and firm requirements in the staffing process. Most firms use a combination of the two approaches, but it is useful to understand which method dominates and which best suits your professional demeanor.

# PEOPLE: THEY HAD BETTER PASS THE "AIRPORT TEST"

You will want to like and respect the people with whom you will be spending the majority of your time. Meet as many consultants as possible and give them the "airport test": if you got stuck in an airport with this person for five hours (it happens!), would you enjoy his or her company? Try to get a feel for whether or not your potential coworkers are happy with and challenged by their work.

In addition, look around for possible role models and ask people at different levels about the degree of interaction they have with partners or other senior mentors. Smaller firms may offer a more intimate and informal environment for building mentor relationships with senior partners, but larger firms can offer a bigger pool of mentors. In particular, if you are a woman or a minority member, check into how many others have made it to the top. If there are only a few, you may want to consider how great your desire is for blazing new trails. No matter who you are, make special note of those who have been successful. If you relate better to the people at the bottom than to those at the top, this may not bode well for your long-term prospects at the firm.

# CULTURE: IT IS THE SUM OF ALL THE LITTLE THINGS

Here lies a frequently neglected aspect of candidates' decisions. People do not know how to evaluate culture, so they avoid the topic. But, as you will soon learn in your new consulting job, all things *can* be measured. Look for evidence of the culture you are seeking. It matters.

For example, if being in a learning organization is important to you, find out about both formal and informal training. Again, size is not a great indicator of the learning organization. Investigate how the firm manages and shares knowledge. How much publishing and speaking do people do? Are promotions and bonuses influenced by contributions to the firm's intellectual capital? How strong is the mentoring program? Which partners are most admired—the smart ones or the rainmakers?

If you are concerned at all about lifestyle, try to garner insight into whether face time or efficiency is more highly valued. At Vertex, we track hours closely, talk to individuals who are working too many hours to understand why, and pressure case managers to stick to time budgets. Another good lifestyle indicator is the firm's philosophy toward the professionals' time. Does the firm see consultants as a fixed cost investment with 24 hours of capacity that should be used however necessary to get the job done? Or, are consultants viewed as having a variable cost component that shows up in increased turnover and reduced quality? A firm's culture is the sum of many small things that add up to an environment that can foster your strengths or produce endless frustration. You ignore it at your peril.

## CONCLUSION

Size matters far less than other characteristics of the firm. Although size can affect your work experience, you should not rely too heavily on it as the metric for the qualities you seek. You need to scratch beneath the surface to understand the opportunity the firm is offering. You have invested a tremendous amount of time and money into your education, so be equally thoughtful about your career decision.

— • • • —

## *The Internal Consulting Practice of Strategic Planning*

CATHERINE ARNOLD
HOFFMAN-LA ROCHE INC.

You may be surprised to learn that careers in consulting and strategic planning do not differ that much, particularly in terms of work content. Instead, the differences lie with the culture, lifestyle, variability, and predictability of the job issues. In fact, strategic planning can be thought of as a segment within the consulting profession.

## CORPORATE STRATEGIC PLANNERS VERSUS EXTERNAL CONSULTANTS

Corporate strategic planners are a department or group of company employees responsible for ensuring that an organization's strategy is established, and that a plan to implement the strategy is executed. The strategy is usually developed through the interactions of strategic planners with the management team—the "client." Once the strategy is defined, strategic planners must see that it is effectively communicated throughout the organization. This communication is essential for promoting the client's use of the strategy in making decisions. If the client consistently considers the defined strategy when making short-, medium-, and long-term decisions, the strategy is more likely to be achieved.

Strategic planners know the organizational strategy intimately because of their role in developing it and supporting its execution. For this reason, they may also have responsibilities that require its intensive consideration, including corporate, business, or new business development.

Strategic planners are often viewed as internal company consultants because (like external consultants, but unlike most management personnel) they make recommendations, but typically do not have responsibility for implementing the tactics driven by those recommendations. The work of strategic planners is project-driven, and uses processes similar to those used by external consultants.

Recommendations made by both strategic planners and external consultants are typically a result of analyzing internal and external data. Given confidentiality concerns, strategic planners may have greater access to internal data than external consultants do; however, external consultants may access larger amounts of external industry data—partly to compensate for their lack of internal data. And finally, strategic planners tend to incorporate more of an organization's cultural and organizational context into an analysis than external consultants do.

# THE PURPOSE OF STRATEGIC PLANNING GROUPS

Organizations—or parts of organizations—can conduct project work by "hiring" internal strategic planners, external consultants, or a combination of internal and external resources. Since all three options are viable, a company must decide which approach is most valuable. Most companies maintain an internal group, whose size and skills are determined by objectives defined by senior management. The organizational objectives for these internal groups are driven by:

- The dynamics and complexity of the business in which the company competes.
- The cultural preference for using internal versus external resources.
- The scope of responsibility of senior managers and other employees.
- The staffing philosophy regarding fixed and variable resources.

Regardless of the industry, business demands produce needs that can most easily be met by strategic planners. If management requires analysis and recommendations on specific business issues, their strategic planners can provide this analysis. Using internal resources over external consultants provides access to resources without going through a proposal process. Additionally, recommendations for highly confidential matters can be kept within the organization by using strategic planners.

The name "strategic planners" suggests that a primary objective of the group is to establish direction or strategies for the organization. The time period for these strategies may be short, medium, or long, depending on the company's needs. The company's organizational culture usually determines whether the process for developing strategies involves all levels of the organization or only top management.

Because strategies may involve new ideas or imperatives, these groups often have the responsibility for motivating change or paradigm shifts throughout the company. This may also be required in developing the strategy. Strategic planners are expected to motivate other employees to think "outside the box" to develop creative strategies, including "stretch goals" that enable the organization to seek a higher level of performance. Stretch goals will need to be adopted in the areas of an organization that will be held accountable for those goals. Strategic planners may find themselves operating as champions of these goals or other strategic ideas and directives to ensure their success.

Strategic planners are often given projects that require either a solution or a set of possible solutions. These solutions require "think tank" processes, whereby recommendations are supported by sound business data and cutting edge analysis. Intellectual capital tools may be developed to support this and other responsibilities of strategic planners, such as the analysis of relevant strategic business information. Table 3.1 shows typical organizational objectives for a strategic planning group.

# PROFESSIONAL AND PERSONAL CHALLENGES

The challenges faced by strategic planning groups are similar across different organizations, since these groups usually report to senior management, who, regardless of the industry, make comparable types of decisions (see Table 3.2). Individuals seeking employment in this environment will be expected to maintain a broad or "big picture" perspective, and a current understanding of organizational and business issues. Although strategic planners are expected to be more objective in developing organizational recommendations because they are hired by top management and line functions, they are expected to customize their work product to consider the culture and characteristics of the company.

Strategic planning groups must adopt a credible work style to gain clients' confidence. As would be expected of an external consultant, strategic planners should consistently display creativity and superior analytical skills in their project work. Many of these projects may also demand the support of various levels of the organization. Strategic planners should define situations that require the input and buy-in of other employees and secure it.

To obtain support, strategic planners must deliver analyses and recommendations in a concise and meaningful manner. They must effectively communicate their conclusions or recommendations,

**Table 3.1**
**Typical Organizational Objectives for Creating**
**an Internal Strategic Planning Group**

| Strategic Planning Objectives | Descriptions |
| --- | --- |
| Make recommendations | Advise senior management of recommended next steps resulting from detailed analyses. |
| Establish direction | Facilitate the development of long-, medium-, and/or short-term strategies through the collection and synthesis of organizational ideas based on a competitive assessment. This is accomplished using one of three interactive approaches: top-down, bottom-up, hybrid. |
| Motivate change and/or paradigm shifts | Stimulate and/or propose provocative and possibly controversial business ideas or analyses that encourage managers to think of nonconventional strategies and/or tactics. |
| | Motivate others to implement organizational change through education and presentation of business concepts and strategy. |
| Analyze relevant strategic business information | Evaluate business situations and data for use by senior management. |
| "Champion" Ideas and/or "spread the word" | Encourage or convince relevant groups within the organization to adopt and integrate strategic direction and/or business ideas into their area of responsibility. |
| Provide intellectual capital for confidential and other business decisions | Create and maintain data sources and analyses to support senior management's knowledge and decision making, typically for a restricted pool of managers and for the most sensitive business decisions (e.g., mergers and acquisitions, etc.) |
| Serve as a "think tank" | Develop cutting-edge analyses and positions to resolve business issues and to support longer-term strategic planning. |

especially when their ideas are to be delivered throughout a large part of the organization. Strategic planners may have to determine which processes best meet the needs of the specific situation, particularly when they are held accountable for the execution of their plans.

While strategic planners and external consultants have similar professional challenges, the personal challenges they face tend to differ,

**Table 3.2**
**Professional Challenges of Strategic Planners**

| Challenges | Description |
| --- | --- |
| Maintain a broad perspective | Consider the organizational impact in all recommendations even if the specific project if fairly compartmentalized. |
| Remain current | Keep in touch with organizational and business issues and incorporate this knowledge into the output of the group. |
| Customize work product | Develop recommendations and analyses that consider the culture the characteristics of the organization. |
| Maintain objectivity | Assess the strengths, weaknesses, opportunities, and threats of the company within the competitive environment without bias. |
| Demonstrate creativity | Consider and offer novel ideas in all deliverables. |
| Display analytical competence | Ensure the use of cutting-edge analytical (financial, strategic, and marketing) approaches and industry knowledge. |
| Rally support | Determine the need for input and buy-in from various levels within the organization, the secure it. |
| | Define, then satisfy, the organizational expectations for problem-solving and decision-making processes, including the required supporting data and analysis. |
| Present findings in a concise and meaningful manner | Develop communication vehicles (e.g., presentations, reports, and talking points) that relay only points of interest and relevancy, and maximize the audience's understanding. |
| Ensure plans are executed | Assure recommendations are implemented through the appropriate assignment of responsibility and the use of optimal processes. |
| Establish an effective means to communicate to the organization | Define and utilize processes to ensure the communication of strategy and other findings/recommendations developed by the group and approved by senior management. |
| Earn credibility | Exhibit a work style and provide deliverables that result in an organizational confidence enabling the group to meet its defined objectives. |

most importantly with respect to lifestyle, variability in the client, project work and career pathways. As for lifestyle, strategic planners tend to travel less frequently and more predictably than do external consultants. This may be an important consideration if personal commitments demand less travel and more advance notice. Because strategic planners remain in one organization rather than changing clients, they tend to identify organizational issues and develop a foundation of knowledge about the company's product line (strengths and weaknesses) that they can continually use in project work. External consultants must climb the learning curve for each of these dimensions for each new client.

Depending on the strategic planning group's scope of responsibility, the projects they work on may be fairly consistent with regard to the issues they address. Lastly, corporate culture may allow for more flexibility in defining future job paths than would be available in a consulting firm. A strategic planner may choose between climbing the corporate ladder or remaining on a technical track. Planners can also move to another function within the corporation. In contrast, many consulting firms have an "up or out culture," meaning that you must continue to be promoted within the firm or be counseled out.

## REQUIRED SKILLS

People interested in working as strategic planners must have certain skills for meeting both the challenges described in Table 3.2 and the project demands. Strong project management and interpersonal skills are a must. Because these projects are directed by top management, work plans must be completed on time and to specifications. Strategic Planning Managers must be able to collect and provide information throughout all levels of the organization using verbal and nonverbal communication techniques. To assure the most effective outcome, they must also feel comfortable challenging conventional thinking up through the highest level of management.

In addition to project management and interpersonal skills, well-rounded functional skills are needed. Almost all the business disciplines are used to some degree—finance, marketing, and strategy most frequently. The ability to exercise leadership supports the motivation of others toward project goals. Management experience lends an appreciation for the complexities involved in selecting and defending a recommendation among many alternatives. Finally, experience within the industry in which the organization competes is likely to increase an individual's opportunity to contribute quickly to the goals of a strategic planning group.

The rewards and challenges of a career as a strategic planner and an external consultant are similar, yet the intricacies of the job can differ significantly. You should contemplate these similarities and differences as you consider a job as a strategic planner, or as a management consultant.

— • • • —

# Consulting to the Financial Services Industry

STEVEN E. RUNIN
MITCHELL MADISON GROUP

Consulting to a specific industry requires not only a knowledge of that industry, but also an expertise in specific functional disciplines (e.g., strategy, technology management, organizational effectiveness) that will improve client performance. It is the rare individual that can combine both a broad understanding of an industry with the necessary range of functional expertise. As a result, consulting firms have a limited number of approaches for serving industry sectors. Firms that serve single industries tend to be small and may not have the range of functional specialties or cross-industry knowledge to serve clients well. Some may offer lots of functional knowledge but lack the industry understanding for the effective application of generic solutions to specific situations. Still others may achieve the scale necessary to do both—balance a knowledge of a group of interrelated industries with a command of multiple functional specialties. At Mitchell Madison Group, we have chosen the third course.

Over the past three years, my colleagues and I have expanded our capabilities beyond our original financial services core—not just because we wanted to, but because our clients demanded a perspective that extended beyond their own industry to address their problems. Furthermore, the functional disciplines we have developed apply equally to industries other than financial services, such as technology, telecommunications, healthcare, and media. Thus, we have broadened our perspectives as well as our opportunities.

## EMERGING CHALLENGES IN THE FINANCIAL SERVICES INDUSTRY

Among the many challenges confronting financial services companies, perhaps the gravest are those posed by interpenetration. Major market participants, once ensconced in the soft plush of environments insulated by custom and regulation, have been crowding into each other's territories, chasing somewhat reluctant customers with stale and homogenized product offerings. Thus, banks are poaching on the preserves of brokers and insurers; brokers are offering transaction accounts and mezzanine commercial loans; and thrifts are discarding the image of simple providers of retail mortgage finance. At the extreme, several institutions have responded to this challenge by embarking on some of the largest mergers in history.

By and large, most customers have too many financial supplier and product options from which to choose. In an oversupplied industry characterized by mature products, producers must gravitate from a mass-marketing to a segmented-market approach. Yet, the majority of financial service providers, while acknowledging the need for segmentation, either cannot or will not customize their products. Thus, there is a basic disconnect between the reality of the financial marketplace and the outlook of financial services suppliers.

Much of Mitchell Madison Group's work in the industry is aimed at addressing this disconnect. We believe that suppliers are in dire need of a Bill of Rights—the capacity to find the "right" customer with the "right" product, price, and delivery mechanism at the "right" time. Our efforts are aimed at developing a database-driven approach to marketing that emphasizes the accumulation and integration of internally and externally available information. Our goal is to identify the "value propositions"—once again, product, price, and delivery options—with the greatest appeal to targeted subsets of customers, and even discrete individuals and companies.

This strategy represents a radical shift from the past. Formerly, the typical financial service provider said: "Here is what I have to sell and the price I need to get. Now let's see who I can sell to." The new strategy is interactive, allowing the customer to help determine the product and its features. The supplier now says: "Here are the customer segments that the database suggests will provide the greatest number of profitable customers. Now let's use what we know or can learn about and from these customers to vary the components of the value proposition in a way that will best serve their needs and still guarantee acceptable returns."

At Mitchell Madison, we call this "strategic customer targeting." It is rooted in six propositions, two of which relate to targeting, two more to the customer, and a final two to strategy. The two targeting propositions are:

1. Advances in computer technology have enabled efficient manipulation of data on a scale not imaginable a few years ago.
2. New statistical techniques developed in manufacturing and medical research represent significant improvements in the ability to model complex customer behavior with necessarily incomplete data.

The two customer propositions are:

1. The preceding tools and techniques are generic and should be applied in an integrated way to the prediction of customer behavior in its many forms: purchasing, transactional, and the

propensity to remain loyal. Thus, the techniques can be used to gauge origination and cross-sell potential, cost-cutting possibilities, and retention likelihood.

2. The goal is to manage customer relationships at the individual retail or corporate level in order to maximize the expected present value of the lifetime relationship, which is often different in both size and sign (positive or negative) from the picture presented by an accounting analysis of the customer's "contribution."

The two strategic propositions are:

1. Successful application of customer modeling requires a corollary redesign of business processes and organizations.
2. Institutions that master the skills of customer modeling and develop the corollary new processes and organizations will have a decisive competition advantage over those that do not.

If strategic customer targeting is to be successful, the consulting effort must extend beyond mere database marketing. Indeed, such engagements will generally fail unless they evolve into exercises in change management. This is because most traditional financial services firms are not organizationally or culturally prepared to assimilate and internalize a data-driven marketing effort. No matter how skilled staff marketers may be, their skills will be irrelevant unless line personnel can be persuaded to understand and work with the approach they are designing. The client's task, with the help of the consultant, is to find a way to change the behavior of line personnel, many of whom are reluctant even to be guided, much less driven, by the data and those who are massaging it. Such a change may require the organization to change its structure from the prevailing silo structure to one that is cross-functional.

It is sometimes said that financial services have become marketing. That may be true in essence (after all, as formulated some years ago, marketing was to be the function that provided the economic conception of the firm). But the statement is obviously wrong in detail. And bankers, brokers, and insurers must keep their eyes on the details—one of which is the pressing need to pare outsize expense bases.

To be sure, a good marketer can reduce costs, for example, by using conjoint analysis to determine the relative importance different customers ascribe to product features, and eliminating features with the lowest utilities. We have found, however, that cost reduction can be achieved not just through marketing, but also through "antimarketing." That is, by increasing the effort needed to out-think those selling to it, a company can often reduce purchasing bills by 10 to 15 percent without adversely affecting the quality or functionality of what it is buying. And for many financial services companies, a 15 percent reduction in the cost of indirect purchases (e.g., advertising, technology, overhead, and human resources) can lead to an improvement of between 33 and 50 percent in bottom-line returns. Mitchell Madison has developed a large presence in this practice area, helping many of the top 50 banks, insurers, and brokers to source far more efficiently than in the past.

Our initiatives in the strategic targeting and purchased expense management areas, among others, testify to Mitchell Madison Group's innovativeness. We have been able to bring together multidisciplinary teams to address some of the financial services sector's most vexing problems, and to deliberately challenge standard viewpoints by considering multiple perspectives. The financial services industry is changing at an ever-increasing rate, and consultants must anticipate this change. But consultants are expected to do even more: they need to become proactive agents of change itself.

# Consulting in the World of Electronic Commerce

JOSEPH B. FULLER
MONITOR COMPANY

Strategy consulting offers the best career option I know for pioneers and explorers, for people who like to operate on the frontier, for people who want an early look over the horizon at the big new issues facing global industry. A perfect case in point is the growing surge of interest in Electronic Commerce (E-Commerce)—that emerging arena of economic activity defined by the convergence of telecom, computer, communications, software, hardware, and other information-related businesses. By any relevant standard, this process of convergence is a major development in the business world, confronting managers with seminal choices about where, how, and over what to compete.

For consultants on such a frontier, the challenge, of course, is to learn how to get quickly beyond the hype to a robust understanding of the real choices managers face. Make no mistake, there is plenty of hype to get beyond. You probably recognize the rhetoric:

> Something important—something major—is happening. From whatever angle you look, it represents a paradigm shift in the world of business. And given the magnitude of this shift, the whole apparatus of established ideas, analytical frameworks, and consulting approaches is suddenly obsolete. Sweep it all into the trash. Here—and here only—is the one true road to competitive success in so brave a new world.

This is, of course, nonsense. The old rules and the old logic may no longer blindly apply to businesses engaged in E-Commerce, but that does not mean they do not apply at all. The task is to determine on a case-by-case basis how far to push the rules and where they are most likely to need amendment or qualification.

# MIGRATION TO AN ELECTRONIC ENVIRONMENT

For some companies migrating to E-Commerce, the process of transition is pretty much a question of using the Internet to reshape and reconfigure assets and processes that already exist for an electronic environment. If a PC manufacturer originally sold directly to end users through catalogs, advertisements, and a toll-free telephone number, for example, how should it supplement those efforts with, or migrate them to, a Web-based system for on-line sales? Or how might a pharmaceutical firm allow a potential customer to research—in private—basic information about drugs for a socially embarrassing condition such as incontinence, before talking about it with his or her doctor?

For other companies, the main question has to do with selecting features and prices for products designed to support Electronic Commerce: software for ordering over the Web, for example, or databases for recording Web-based purchases or prestructured information about potential customers to better target marketing initiatives.

For still others, the new technology enables a more thorough redefinition of key parts of the underlying business model. Consumers who used to purchase books and recordings only if they happened to be immediately available at a local bookstore or music store can now access a much wider inventory of titles through Web sites like Amazon.com, and CDNow. What are the likely economic effects of such changes? Do they provide a plausible foundation for building competitive advantage? Or for building a sustainable advantage?

All these examples are linked by a common theme: moving into the world of E-Commerce forces companies to make strategic choices about their primary mode of participation. Should they be a provider of content, or of the interface between Web and consumer, or of the means for product distribution? Or, finally, a provider of some combination of distribution, interface, and content? True, the specific business content of these choices, as well as the context in which they sit, may be novel, but the need to make such choices is a familiar part of what managers do when addressing basic issues of strategy.

# EROSION OF INDUSTRY BOUNDARIES

At the same time, however, our work on questions related to E-Commerce regularly leads us onto new theoretical ground. As the boundaries between previously distinct industries become ever more permeable, the range of expertise needed to frame effective choices, let alone implement them, expands geometrically. And as the intensity and complexity of competition heighten, it becomes increasingly difficult to act as if a one-dimensional relationship existed between our clients and other companies operating in the same general industry space—or to act as if the classical laws of economics have remained unchanged.

Because a single company might simultaneously be a competitor, a complementor, a partner, an informal collaborator, a supplier, a distributor, a licensee, a licensor, and/or a customer of our client, we have to bring to our industry analyses an understanding of the mechanics of what my friends Professors Barry Nalebuff and Adam Brandenburger call, "co-opetition." Moreover, because such multidimensional, fluid industry settings are best thought of as interdependent ecosystems—and not as traditional competitive environments populated by independent entities—we must be sensitive to the ways in which the various participants in an industry co-evolve. Further, because the ecosystem of E-Commerce is being shaped by the convergence of leading-edge technologies, we cannot assume that, other things being equal, a participant's economic returns will tend toward equilibrium. We must be alert to the possibility of what Professor Brian Arthur calls "lock-in" effects: an economics of increasing, not decreasing, returns, where early movers can lock in sources of advantage—new technical standards, for example—that become more valuable as well as more defensible over time.

# ENRICHMENT OF STRATEGIC ANALYSIS

Equally important, the new ground associated with work in the E-Commerce domain also extends and enriches the practical, hands-on analyses associated with strategy consulting. Of the many possible examples, I will briefly mention five. First, given both the speed with which E-Commerce-related markets develop and the degree of uncertainty associated with those developments, we have found it extremely important to help managers carefully frame the questions they ask. Quite often, they express concern about selecting the best set of features for a new product or service when they really should be asking—at that stage of the market's evolution—whether they should be in it at all. And if they should not be in it at the moment, the next question is how they might best reserve the option to participate later.

Second, given the capabilities inherent in E-Commerce-related technologies, it is now reasonable for companies to review the pockets of "trapped value" in their industries. The purpose is to see if those capabilities might provide a cost-effective means for unlocking the traps and capturing the hidden value. As a rule, value gets trapped when extant modes of communication and coordination lock clusters of economic activity into inefficient structures and processes. Think, for example, of the huge amounts of money spent on business travel or document delivery services or the processing of paper-based transactions that could be freed up through better application of network and information technologies. Or of the proliferation of safety stock in a multitiered distribution system.

Third, as the economics of E-Commerce businesses become more transparent and as comparative information about their products and services becomes more widely available, consumers will expect access to the best prices and deals. They will also begin to demand control of, as well as economic value in return for, information about themselves generated as part of Net-based transactions. The availability of information is starting to outrun traditional efforts to segment markets, to calculate the cost to serve each segment, and to decide both how and among whom the value generated by economic activity gets divided. How, then, should segmentation be approached in an information-rich environment? And which segments should a company aspire to serve?

Fourth, given how quickly things are moving—a doubling of Web pages every nine months, for example, or the coming explosion in transmission capacity through wave division multiplexing in long-haul transmission and broadband wireless for local connectivity—the state of the Net-based art changes faster than the adoption and decision cycles of most companies. How, then, should they choose in their business planning whether to aim at the current state of the art or out ahead of the target—and, if the latter, out ahead by how much?

And fifth, because the Net-related choices that companies make can significantly affect their relative competitive position over the long term, on what basis should they decide whether to make a large, upfront bet about the future (like Dell, say, in computers, or Fruit of the Loom with its new on-line ordering system), or buy "insurance" against the destabilizing effects of new technology (like Compaq making on-the-Web ordering available in response to Dell's success), or wait for things to become clearer?

## CONCLUSION

Our work in these areas leads us to wrestle with a host of other recurring problems, including the innovation of performance metrics for companies engaged in E-Commerce, the selection of infrastructure optimally suited to support them, and the design of policies and procedures to promote the development of effective leadership. We have found absolutely no merit in the common assertion that patterns of industry evolution and technological change in the rest of the economy have no light to shed on the world of E-Commerce. Our challenge, then, is to understand what lessons do apply, how they need to be amended or qualified, and what new lessons need to be added.

• • •

# Information Technology Consulting

RUDY PURYEAR
ANDERSEN CONSULTING

As a strategy consultant who has surveyed the business landscape for a number of years, I have seen the power of information technology (IT) increase exponentially, and the role of IT in setting business strategy change dramatically. As a result, strategic IT consulting is now playing a critical role in helping organizations maximize their performance and stake a claim in the emerging electronic economy, or eEconomy.

## THE CHANGING ROLE OF INFORMATION TECHNOLOGY

Information technology has become a critical business enabler that is at the heart of every form of business consulting today. But to fully understand and appreciate the importance of IT today, we need to look back at its evolution.

Over the past 30 years, as the global marketplace has shifted from an industrial economy to an eEconomy, IT has evolved through three fairly distinct periods: data processing, information systems, and knowledge management. Throughout each period, the role that IT has played in helping organizations develop and execute business strategy has changed too.

In the 1970s, data processing automated business tasks, streamlined operations, and made things more efficient. Mainframe computing provided useful data for transactions, but the technology and the IT consultants of that day generally sat in the back room. Their role was primarily to track and report on the business, and provide business managers with the information they needed to execute against an existing strategy. Their job was not to identify strategy, and therefore IT was not a critical element in business strategy in the 1970s.

In the 1980s, sophisticated information systems provided user-friendly software applications, and hardware advancements gave the business environment efficient facsimile machines, desktop computers, modems, cell phones, broadband cable, fiber optics, satellite communication channels, and wide and local area networks. All this enhanced our homes and workplaces because it gave us the power to do things faster and with more geographic reach. In the workplace, technology evolved from simply reporting on business to actively conducting business. As a result, business began to rely more heavily on IT, and became more mindful of it.

The primary goal of the IT consultant at this time was to transform data into useful market information that could be strategically capitalized on. This information and the IT that supported it still did not drive strategy, but it became a critical tool for implementing strategy, and as a result IT became more respected for its overall contribution to the business.

During the 1980s, the challenges associated with using new and unproven technologies, platforms, and communications protocols created barriers that often impeded rapid strategy implementation and restricted strategic options. I remember one telecommunications client in particular that was trying to launch a new service. They needed the service and the associated billing systems to be ready at the same time, but because their product development cycle was 90 days long and their systems development cycle was two years, they had to hold back. That kind of scenario was fairly common in those days, and it placed a strain on the relationship between technology and strategy. Consequentially, the business strategists of the 1980s respected the potential of IT, but they were frustrated by the time and effort required for solution implementation.

In the 1990s, the focus shifted from business information to market knowledge. Laptops, high-speed modems, and desktop processors can now manage data and information at speeds unimagined by the mainframe programmers of the 1970s. In just 30 years, we have seen over a 50-million-fold increase in the price-performance of technology. Had the same productivity been applied to the automotive industry, you would have been able to purchase a Rolls Royce for under 10 cents today.

With the performance and implementation challenges of the 1970s and 1980s behind us, businesses are now able to turn IT loose on the challenges of complex, rapidly changing global markets. In these markets, knowledge is power. Specifically, managing the intellectual assets of the organization to turn market information (today's trends) into market knowledge (knowing your customers and suppliers so well you can drive tomorrow's trends) has become a key strategic weapon.

# A CRITICAL DRIVER OF STRATEGY

Today, as we prepare to enter the twenty-first century, IT finally has the capability to create business strategy, not just support it. For example, a major auto manufacturer recently asked our consulting practice to study the effectiveness of their IT. Years ago, this request would likely have resulted in a detailed functional review that would have uncovered processing inefficiencies and cost overruns. But once executive management recognized that IT was a key business enabler and not just a tool to support their operations, the project quickly became an opportunity to envision how IT could help reshape their business. The results were exciting. We helped the client totally redefine their customer relationships and make the transition from being a mass-marketing organization to becoming a relationship-marketing organization. We did this by helping them focus on their customers as individuals. We used technology—such as new data mining techniques, and technologies that allow business to be conducted independent of time and location—to make it easy for the customer to do business with the company instead of the other way around. The impacts were dramatic.

Bottom line, it is no longer enough for companies to use IT simply to support business strategy. More and more, they must embrace IT as the means to create business change throughout all levels of their organizations. Today's successful enterprises use IT to enlighten their strategy process and determine their tactics. They rely on IT strategy to drive and enable successful business strategy and its implementation.

They also realize that IT must be considered during, rather than after, the strategy formulation process.

# CHANGING THE PRACTICE OF CONSULTING

IT strategy consultants are on the cutting edge. Now that IT has become so tightly interwoven with business strategy, individuals who truly respect and understand the power and potential of technology have become extremely valuable business strategists. Today, my colleagues in IT practices around the world work at the boardroom level with the most exciting and aggressive companies, assisting them in their quest to become market leaders in the new eEconomy. We are defining and implementing meaningful and distinctive Internet strategies; we are designing revolutionary technology-enabled delivery models that allow business to be conducted independent of time and location; and we are helping clients discover new methods of differentiation through creative deployment of technology. These are exciting times.

Working every day at the crossroads of information technology and strategy, IT strategists possess the essential knowledge and skills to lead the changes demanded by today's complex marketplace. From our vantage point, we anticipate and monitor technology innovations that shape market trends and redefine entire industries. We understand the vital role IT has in setting business trends. And, most importantly, we help our clients anticipate and manage for these trends.

IT strategy consulting is a rewarding path to long-term success and satisfaction in a volatile business world. If you can bring to bear a strategic perspective on IT as a business enabler, you will have the opportunity to create real change and value. Moreover, if you became a consultant because you wanted to make things happen, you should most definitely consider a career in IT strategy consulting.

—————— ● ● ● ——————

# Change Management Consulting

ARUN MAIRA

ARTHUR D. LITTLE

Change management is one of the most important, and one of the least understood, services provided by management consultancies. Almost everything that a consultant does for a client, whether creating a new strategy or reengineering a process, requires the client's organization to make some kind of change. I will illustrate what change management encompasses with two case studies.

## REACTIVE CHANGE

"Why does change have to take so long?" This question came from a chief executive of a successful company in North America that was faced with new, low-cost competition from international companies. He had sought help in improving his organization's production and distribution capabilities, and he had heard presentations by eight consulting companies. The consultants all agreed that trying to introduce new ways of working would inevitably meet with resistance to change. They said the culture of the company would have to be changed—a complex, time-consuming process.

They had all exhorted him, as chief executive, to take responsibility for bringing about this culture change and to be patient with the process. He responded to this suggestion:

> I am willing to give the process whatever time it takes, but I am afraid the world may not give my company the time you say the process needs. I want sustainable change—so that we do not have to keep turning to consultants to help solve our operating problems. And we need the change to happen fast. What is it about the approach to the process of transformational change that makes it take so long? Why can't we think about it as a process and improve it? After all, by thinking about our product creation activities as a process, we have been able to reduce the time

required from several years to a few months. So, what are the essential activities in a transformation process, and in what order and combinations should they be done? Where is the real leverage in the process?

A multifunctional team from Arthur D. Little helped this chief executive and his organization answer these questions. We worked with our client on the business challenge of improving operating performance and changing the culture. At the same time, we examined the change models of all the leading academics and consultants and delved into the experience of our own firm with clients all over the world. Together with our client, we developed new thinking, and we customized approaches for their organization. They achieved what they needed: faster change than they had imagined, and sustainable change. They have used their new knowledge about creating faster change to improve the performance of several companies they have acquired around the world. And they are taking the battle back to the home grounds of their competitors and are becoming a successful global company.

## ANTICIPATORY CHANGE

On the other side of the world, the chief executive of a high-performing Asian company sensed that the world around his company and his country was changing in fundamental ways. These changes required rethinking his company's business model and competencies. The company needed to be much more innovative—in its strategies and in its product and service offerings. At the same time, it had to maintain, and perhaps even improve, its operational efficiencies. There was no immediate threat, but the company wanted to be able to change quickly to avoid being blindsided or caught flat-footed as the environment around it changed.

So how could the company be more innovative and more efficient at the same time? And how could it be even more responsive to local customer needs while being more global in its perspectives? This chief executive asked:

What are the organizational competencies we need to manage these paradoxes of innovation-and-efficiency, local-and-global, change-and-stability? And how will we develop these competencies quickly and cost-effectively?

He had already heard from several consultancies and concluded:

The advice of all consultancies, after all the arm-waving, always seems to boil down to choosing one thing or the other, rather than having both. Their industry experts have their views about where the industry is heading. And their process of strategy-making is about choosing a particular path, for which the organization is then designed. But what if the environment changes and we have to change our path? What we need is a new model of organizing which gives us more flexibility while improving our current performance.

A multifunctional team of consultants from Arthur D. Little, as well as from Innovation Associates (the "Learning Organization" consultancy, which is now part of Arthur D. Little), worked with the client's organization on this issue. We looked for new principles for organizing businesses that would be more flexible and innovative and better tuned to their environment. We turned to the fields of complexity and biological evolution. And we examined business organizations around the world that have displayed, at some time in their histories, the qualities we were looking for. The client organization learned in action. They acquired the ideas, customized them, implemented them, observed results, and amended the solutions as required. They are becoming the innovative-cum-efficient, faster-learning organization they set out to be. Their multiple stakeholders have responded positively to the changes in the organization. Business analysts have talked up the stock price of the company. Market share is increasing. Employees at all levels are participating in the management of the paradoxes.

# NEED FOR
# CONTINUING INNOVATION

These two cases illustrate the two principal, interrelated thrusts of Arthur D. Little's Global Organization Practice: change management and organizational transformation. Our practice has been greatly enriched by the merger with Innovation Associates, which brought us valuable knowledge and consulting skills around issues of leadership development, systemic thinking, and team learning. These competencies are, invariably, key leverage points for change management and organizational transformation.

These three competencies, as well as the broader capabilities for change management and organizational transformation in our Organization Practice, are often combined with other functional strengths of Arthur D. Little. Thus, we can help clients effectively manage more focused business needs. For example, with our Strategy Practice, we can help clients to develop "ambition driven" strategies and to manage mergers and alliances. With the resources of our Technology Management and Information Management Practices, we can help clients improve their innovation and knowledge management processes. Our Practices are centers of excellence, which combine their competencies to address our clients' important business issues.

Our collective mission is to increase our clients' capabilities to produce results they have not produced before. To do this, we must continuously innovate, combining the world of ideas and the world of action. Our clients expect us to have our heads in the clouds and our feet on the ground. It is a challenge: sometimes we may appear too theoretical to the client, and sometimes we may seem like just an extra (and expensive) pair of hands. But when we get it right (which we generally do—or so our clients say) not only do we add great value to our clients, but we also learn and acquire new capabilities.

## CONCLUSION

I came to consulting with Arthur D. Little after a satisfying career as an executive with a large operating company, where I had successfully solved many strategy, organization, and operations problems. To paraphrase Robert Frost, a few years ago, I came to a fork in the road, and took the road "less traveled by." As a consultant, I now work with clients in many industries and in many parts of the world, helping them create the new knowledge and competencies they need and want. Not only do I get to take action with my clients, but I also have the satisfaction of seeing the results emerge. As a consultant, I am at the intersection between the world of ideas and the world of action, the space in which real innovation takes place. It is a place for great challenge and great satisfaction.

———•••———

# The Evolving Role of Health Benefits Consulting

BRUCE KELLEY
WATSON WYATT WORLDWIDE

The benefits industry has changed rapidly over the past few decades and, as a result, so has benefits consulting. New regulations, more complex plans, and increased technological capabilities are just a few of the factors affecting the way employee benefits are administered today. But, even though the emphasis and the means of performing tasks have changed, employers must still help their employees face the same contingencies—retirement, savings, medical expenses, and death and disability. And now, more than ever, to help attract and retain employees, companies must provide competitive but affordable benefits. The benefits consulting industry has evolved to help companies meet these basic objectives and prepare for the future.

## A BRIEF HISTORY OF BENEFITS CONSULTING

When the first major benefits consulting firms were founded in the 1930s and 1940s, all were rooted in the insurance industry, either through actuarial work or the sale of insurance products. Without the numerous laws and regulations that burden the industry today, life in the benefits consulting business in the post-World War II era was much simpler and proved to be a time of slow, steady growth. Benefit and contribution calculations required the work of actuaries and administrators, and the consulting profession was more than happy to help supply the expertise.

The state of the industry became more complex with the passage of the Employee Retirement Income Security Act (ERISA) in 1974, which ushered in an era of legislative activity in benefits. Over a dozen major pieces of legislation were issued during this time, including the Tax Equity and Fiscal Responsibility Act, the Deficit Reduction Act and the Retirement Equity Act. Because employers needed help in complying with these new regulations, consulting firms were hard-pressed just keeping up with the increased demand. By the late 1970s, more than half of all business conducted by the major consulting firms related to defined benefit plans. The rest of the consulting business comprised thrift plan and profit-sharing work, executive compensation, health and welfare plan design, and some human resources functions.

# HEALTH BENEFITS CONSULTING

Health benefits consulting has been driven—and is even more driven today—by employers' need to recruit and retain employees and to motivate them to higher levels of performance. At any point in time, the primary focus of health benefits consulting is influenced by the national economy and the economics of employers and health plans. When the economy is strong and the labor market is tight, plan sponsors tend to enhance health benefits. Periods of health benefits enhancement are followed by excessive escalation of the cost of health benefits. The focus of health benefits consulting then shifts to benefit cost management. These periodic shifts in the focus of health benefits tend to follow shifts in the business cycle, normally a six- to eight-year cycle, and the underwriting cycle, which, until 1990, was a six-year cycle.

The current health benefits consulting cycle began about 1990 with the beginning of the business cycle that continues today. At that time, businesses began to trim inventories, seek favorable financing of debt, shed obsolete assets and lay off nonproductive workers. By 1992, healthcare benefit costs had flattened for most plan sponsors. This was attributable mainly to the growing penetration of managed healthcare, which began with the prior cycle's focus on cost management. And it may also have been attributable to the fact that management did not offer—and workers did not demand—many health benefits enhancements during a time characterized by labor force reductions.

Wages have been rising since 1993. Unemployment has declined to levels below what economists define as full employment. Yet, inflation in the general economy has remained low; corporate revenue continues to increase; and profits remain strong. It has become obvious that increases in productivity are the engine driving the current stage of the business cycle. These factors drive the current health benefits consulting cycle, which will probably continue for at least several years.

Many health plan administrators and provider organizations are beginning to increase premiums and prices again. However, this may not immediately provoke employers and other plan sponsors to focus vigorously on cost management. Senior and operations managers appear to be pressuring human resource managers to focus more on contributing to the business goals of their firms. Thus, it appears that human resources and, therefore, health benefits consulting will attempt to influence both the cost and the contribution of labor, which will translate to improved productivity of labor.

## COST OF LABOR

The cost of health benefits plays a role in the cost of labor. However, in most industries, health benefit costs comprise less than 20 percent of the cost of labor. Other factors have a much more direct and significant impact. There are early signs that management of these factors will become more central to human resource management and, therefore, to health benefits consulting.

In a tight labor market, the costs of recruiting and of not retaining productive employees are substantial. Employers will likely examine how health benefits can contribute to recruitment and retention. They may respond sympathetically to the concerns of employees—and of providers and legislators—about managed healthcare. Thus, employers may ask consultants to help them remove some of the limitations on access and significant contribution or out-of-pocket expense differentials associated with managed care. As a result, employers may accept greater increases in health benefit expenses to achieve reductions in the cost of recruiting and retaining employees.

To offset employees' negative perception of managed care portions of the health benefits package, employers may also seek (relatively) low-cost benefit enhancements that employees perceive to have high value. These enhancements may take the form of nurse advice line services, health promotion programs, disease management services, coverage of alternative medicine, and so on. Employers may ask consultants to identify and develop a business case for such services.

# CONTRIBUTION OF LABOR

Continuing to increase the contribution of labor may become even more important to employers. By raising morale or creating a sense of greater security, health benefits may have an indirect effect on employees' productivity. However, health benefits can affect whether employees are present at work. Health benefits consultants may be called on to help workers maintain their health and slow the progression of disease. They may also help workers avoid taking time off from work for unnecessary visits—their own or their dependents'—to medical professionals. In these areas, consultants can either help clients directly or work with their health plans to: cover preventive medical procedures cost-effectively; take a risk management (instead of an entitlement) approach to health promotion programs; provide self-care/nurse advice line services; implement disease management programs; and put in place integrated disability management programs.

# CONCLUSION

As the benefits industry changes, so do the needs of employer and the role of benefits consultants. Health benefits consulting now encompasses much more than matchmaking between clients and vendors and supporting clients in plan administration. It also includes helping clients manage benefits while keeping an eye on the bottom line. Health benefits consulting is part of a broader approach to human resource consulting.

Health benefits consulting is changing because human resource management is changing. More and more, senior and operations managers are directing corporate benefits managers to make benefits contribute directly to productivity, profitability, and other fundamental business goals of firms.

In the future, employers may hire benefits consultants primarily to learn how to use benefits as tools that encourage employees to perform at higher levels. Employers will more likely want to focus on how benefits can fulfill employees' fundamental needs for security and quality of life, which will motivate them to achieve higher levels of productivity.

● ● ●

## Consulting to the Nonprofit Sector

LAURA FREEBAIRN-SMITH
GOOD WORK ASSOCIATES

To effectively help nonprofit organizations, we, as consultants, must have a strong understanding of the nonprofit sector and its typical organizational structures. We need to convince our nonprofit clients that we have strong functional and industry expertise. And we also have to prove that we understand the organizational behaviors arising out of the three economic sectors: private, pubic, and nonprofit. Since organizations tend to experience similar issues regardless of sector, the solution to a nonprofit's problem may be similar to those for the private or public sectors. As a result, we can ask the same question of any of the three sectors: How does being a nonprofit—or a for-profit, or a public—organization either affect or create the issues our client faces? Although this question applies to all three sectors, the context within which we ask it leads to very different answers.

# THE THREE SECTORS OF THE U.S. ECONOMY

Each sector has its own distinct relationship among owners, customers, decision makers, and other constituents. The nonprofit sector fills a critical market niche by providing services and products for subsets of the population—services and products that are not provided by the other two sectors. Nonprofits fill the gap between market-driven and publicly provided goods, as Figure 3.1 shows.

As a culture, we are willing to pay taxes for certain goods—protection, clean air, education—products that we believe all people should have and from which no one should profit. These are publicly provided goods. The private sector, on the other hand, provides goods that we all believe are profit-driven. Coca-Cola, for example, is not essential to a functional society (although the students in my early morning classes might disagree).

The nonprofit sector provides goods and services of two primary types. First are those that we, as a society, believe no individual organization should profit from, and only a subset of the population believes are important to society's well-being. It would be considered morally inappropriate, for instance, to profit from providing housing for the homeless or food for the hungry.

Second, the nonprofit sector provides goods and services that we feel the public sector is often not suited to provide. The bureaucracy of the public sector can inhibit its ability to respond to crises, except through public organizations specifically designed for that purpose, such as the military, police and fire departments, and emergency medical teams. For example, the Red Cross manages the national blood supply. We do not feel that the public sector is capable of managing this type of operation since the technical knowledge required to run a blood bank is not the same as the knowledge required to be a good soldier or fire fighter. We look to the nonprofit sector to provide specialized

**Figure 3.1**
**Sources of Capital by Sector**

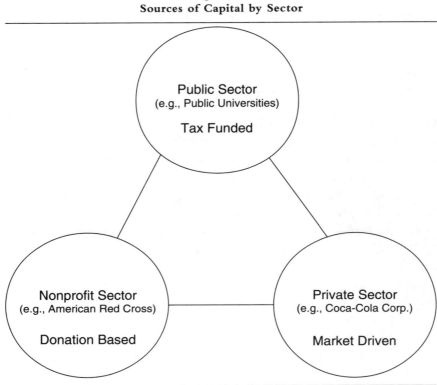

skills or services to fill just such gaps between the public and private sectors. Table 3.3 summarizes the key differentiating characteristics of each sector.

# THE NONDISTRIBUTION CONSTRAINT OF THE NONPROFIT SECTOR

The nonprofit sector involves three parties: the donor, the organization, and the recipient of the service or goods. That is, this sector is funded by donors, who pay for an organization to deliver a product to needy recipients.

Table 3.3
Key Characteristics of the Three Economic Sectors

| Sector | Goods and/or Services | Owners | Customers | Source of Funds | Customer's Recourse | Key Decision Makers | Managers |
|---|---|---|---|---|---|---|---|
| Private | Market-driven goods: (e.g., Coca-Cola houses) | Shareholders | Purchaser of good or service | Customer purchase; borrowing; equity offerings | Stop purchasing item | Board and top managers | Hired managers |
| Public | Public welfare goods (e.g., clean air, public education policing) | Unclear (Taxpayers? Voters? Citizens?) | Unclear (All citizens? Voters? Taxpayers? Users of the service?) | Taxes, fees, bonds | Withhold votes; lobby; run for office | Legislators | Government employees |
| Nonprofit | Gray market goods (e.g., some cancer research) | None; quasi-"owners" are members of the board of directors | User of good or service | Donations, grants, borrowing, fees (not commonly paid by users) | Limited; stop using good or service | Board of directors and executive director | Hired managers and executive director |

Unlike the private sector customers, the customer of a nonprofit may never have a financial transaction with the organization; the donor provides the funds that are transformed by the organization into goods or services for the "customer," without accruing a profit for the effort. Thus, nonprofits are subject to the "nondistribution constraint."

The nondistribution constraint provides the psychological trust donors need when giving money. The blood bank, the soup kitchen, and the homeless shelter are all examples of organizations that must not accrue a profit or, more accurately, must not distribute profit to any one individual or group. For example, the donor believes that when she gives her $1,000 to CARE (a worldwide agency working to eliminate hunger), most of the money will be used for the "consumer" or client, with some portion of the donation going to operating or fundraising expenses. She believes that no single person or group will reap personal wealth from her donation. Without this psychological contract, which is encoded in law, the nonprofit sector could not exist.

111

The nondistribution constraint, and the donors' trust it generates, is the primary differentiator of how nonprofits operate. Still, some 80 percent of the organizational issues occurring in nonprofit organizations are the same as in the private sector: teams still start, stop, succeed, and fail for many of the same reasons. And strategies are conceived and carried out for many of the same reasons.

The remaining 20 percent of the organizational issues are unique to the nonprofit sector because the nondistribution constraint drives nonprofits to pursue a mission—not a bottom line, as in the private sector. Nonprofits do not pursue missions such as "the best customer service in the world," or, "the largest bank in the universe." Rather, nonprofits must strive for missions that serve either the nonmonetary purposes of a group of people or the higher good of humankind.

# A CAREER IN CONSULTING TO NONPROFITS

What does this mean for a career in consulting to nonprofits? Primarily this: a "nonprofit" consulting focus works only to a certain extent—one also needs to acquire both industry (e.g., healthcare, transportation, education) and functional (e.g., human resources, marketing, finance) expertise. All too often, nonprofits are lumped together, and consultants assume they can provide services to any nonprofit. This may work for certain functional issues, but a consulting practice focused on nonprofits must be enhanced by elements other than a generic "nonprofit expertise." For example, a few areas of expertise are particular to consulting to nonprofits: developing a board of directors, managing endowments, and fund-raising. The following discussion is an example of one we frequently have with applicants:

A young, recent MBA graduate is sitting across from me at my desk. He eagerly asserts, "I want to be a consultant."

I look at him with curiosity, "Why?"

After a very brief pause, he responds, "I like to work on a variety of projects and I do not mind working long hours," having practiced his response in many interviews.

"Well, that tells me *how* you like to do your work, but it still does not answer why consulting? And why Good Work Associates?" I ask.

Earnestly, he replies, "I really care about the nonprofit sector—I want to help make the world a better place."

When we encounter such unbridled and idealistic enthusiasm, we are certainly pleased by the candidate's good intentions. But we are also concerned that the candidate has not seriously thought through his consulting interests. All candidates, before interviewing, should recognize three characteristics that are essential to success as a consultant, and determine the degree to which they possess each:

1. Consultants do not simply "want to be consultants." Consulting is the means to an end, a path to achieving some larger vision.

2. Good consultants not only have a passion for a topic or field, but they also have a strong liberal arts curiosity. Are you broadly trained? Are you fascinated by Plato, sundials, and the Aztecs? Do you write well? Are you reading *Harvard Business Review* as well as E. Annie Proulx's latest novel? Successful consultants can distill and integrate ideas from the past and from around the world and use those ideas for creative problem solving.

3. Consultants should have a sense of their path of personal development; they should seek to improve both themselves and the working world. And we believe consultants should aspire to balance the "three legs of life"—work, family, community—throughout the three concurrent phases of life—learning, earning, and returning.

Many of our young applicants see consulting as a way to make a lot of money or to build their resume. We believe that both goals are ultimately disappointing to everyone involved—the firm, the employee, and more importantly, our clients. We hope that our staff will see consulting as a means to several ends—an improved society, a meaningful career, and better workplaces for our clients.

# CHAPTER 4

## PLANNING YOUR
## CONSULTING CAREER

*Prestige may be the most important factor when it comes to recruiting. . . . Many students are heavily indebted upon graduation, and may migrate to prestigious firms in search of high compensation.*
Tim Bourgeois
Kennedy Information Research Group

**P**restige and compensation are powerful incentives for applying to consulting firms. In fact, many candidates base their entire job search on these two objectives. But such a shortsighted decision can lead to a mismatch between the individual and the firm. Choosing a firm is a much more complex decision than many applicants realize. Since more than half of your waking hours will be spent in the office, the right firm will offer not only adequate compensation and prestige, but also interesting work, an enjoyable office culture, and opportunity for career advancement. When consultants are professionally satisfied, they and their firms—as well as their clients—are likely to have a more productive and enjoyable relationship.

As stressed in Chapter 1, the complexity of the industry can make identifying and selecting the right firms a difficult task. And when it comes to applying, many candidates are so discouraged by the required preparation that they decide to avoid the profession altogether. Oddly enough, the application process itself is often one of the highest barriers to entering the profession.

This chapter will help you hurdle this barrier by providing a step-by-step way to pin down your own personal and professional interests, identify and select consulting firms that promise to meet these interests, and develop practical strategies for researching, contacting, and securing interviews at these firms. By the time you finish reading this chapter, you will have the tools you need to sell yourself on paper and get your foot in the door.

# FINDING YOUR NICHE IN CONSULTING

Before applying to a single firm, you should first reflect on your professional goals and personal interests, and then identify the types of consulting that best suit these interests. These initial steps are often overlooked or ignored by eager candidates who use simplistic criteria when pulling together their list of targeted firms. Rationales such as "I like strategy consulting," or, "I'm going to apply to all the big consulting firms," reveal a candidate's limited understanding of the need for serious research. These are the candidates who apply to as many firms as they can using a mail-merge, even though they know little to nothing about any individual firm. Casting a wide net over so many firms in the hope of catching the interest of a few is time- and resource-consuming, and it could possibly place you in an unsuitable position.

To find your niche, you need to invest time into the iterative process of continuous learning, as illustrated in Figure 4.1.

Whether applying for full-time or summer internship positions, you should choose a firm that suits all your needs, rather than a firm that would only strengthen your resume. Only if you understand your personal and professional objectives can you evaluate the opportunities afforded by different firms and their multitude of consulting practice areas. Then, as you learn more about the work and lifestyle of consulting, you will be able to clarify your objectives and, ultimately, distill your list of firms into the most attractive set.

Start your introspective learning by asking yourself forward-looking questions: Do you want a consulting job because you think it will help

**Figure 4.1**
**Finding Your Niche in Consulting**

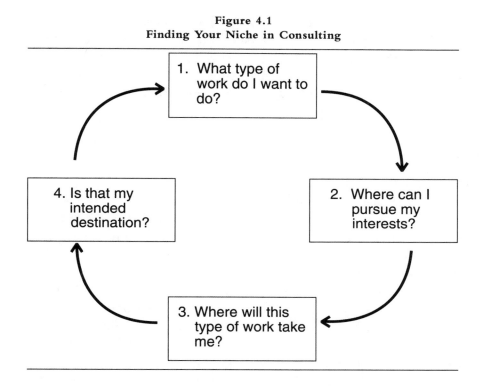

you get into graduate business school or, perhaps, into a law or doctoral program? Or, are you about to receive your MBA and believe that a consulting position will most rapidly accelerate your career? And how long do you envision yourself staying in consulting—only two or three years, or alternatively until you become a partner? These are the critical questions you must answer before you can identify firms that might be right for you. Ask yourself, "Where do I want to be in five years?" With this vision in mind, set some interim goals, and identify the consulting experience that will help you achieve these goals.

Once you have gained a basic understanding of your personal and professional goals, you are ready to begin researching the industry. Learn as much as you can about the different areas of consulting and its many firms, and try to envision yourself working at each. As you understand the industry better, you are likely to need to revise your initial self-assessment—after all, you are in a better position to know what you want to get out of consulting once you know more about the industry. So go back and reconsider your goals, and repeat the iterative process of comparing the industry's opportunities to your own personal aspirations until you find your proper niche.

# RESEARCHING THE INDUSTRY

With literally hundreds of firms in the industry, it is impossible to research all of them. But in Chapter 1, you learned how to efficiently sort through the mix of firms and focus on those that have the most to offer you. There, we introduced a technique for segmenting firms according to four dimensions: (1) the industries consulted, (2) the functional types of consulting performed, (3) the sectors from which clients are drawn (private, public, nonprofit), and (4) the firm's affiliation with its clients (external firms or internal corporate strategic planning units). By screening firms this way, you should be able to focus your research efforts and concentrate on only those firms that best match your personal and professional goals.

Are you attracted to a particular industry? Then you probably want to use the first segmentation dimension to eliminate firms that do not service companies in that industry. Or perhaps you have a background in engineering and want to leverage that experience by performing reengineering projects? Then rely on the second dimension to screen out firms that do not have reengineering practices. What if you want to develop growth strategies for a single company operating in the private sector? Then you should use a multidimensional screen to find strategic planning groups that belong to for-profit organizations.

You may understand the framework, but how do you locate the information you need? Although we live in the age of information, finding the right data to answer specific questions can be difficult. As the saying goes, you may be drowning in data, but starved of knowledge. Start your research by reading materials written by people who know the industry best: practicing consultants and leading strategy thinkers. By reading the personal essays in Chapter 3, you have already begun to learn about some of the latest thinking on the industry, and should have a sense of the kind of consulting you find attractive. Other useful resources include the recruiting and promotional brochures of each firm, consultants' speeches from forums sponsored by organizations like The Conference Board, and consultants' articles published in periodicals such as *Harvard Business Review, McKinsey Quarterly,* and *Strategy & Business.*

If you are an undergraduate or graduate student with access to a career planning office, finding primary research may be easier. You are likely to find a tremendous amount of information at on-campus events, delivered right to you by the consultants themselves. Firms that formally recruit new graduates will hold presentations so that you can meet them—and so they can meet you. These events give you a unique opportunity to ask targeted questions and to have short, one-on-one conversations with consultants in a relatively nonthreatening setting. Just be aware that not all firms can afford the time and money required to visit campuses. If you limit your primary research to on-campus events, your picture of the industry will be incomplete, and you may overlook a potentially attractive position at a smaller, non-visiting firm.

Those of you who are particularly interested in strategic planning may find that few, if any, corporations recruit on campus for their internal consulting positions. Because strategic planning groups tend to be smaller, they often expect candidates to approach them. Your primary research strategy will, therefore, have to be proactive. A proven, though time-consuming, method of finding strategic planning groups is to simply compile a list of companies you might want to work for, and then call their corporate switchboards to ask if they have strategic planning or business development groups. When organizations do not actively seek you out, you need to be creative.

If you are in graduate business school, many of your classmates may have worked at the very firms and companies you are researching. Ask them for their perspectives on their former employers, and collect contact names of consultants at those firms to talk to later. On rare occasions, having an insider contact can actually swing a candidacy from a "ding" to an "accept." And if you are a first-year MBA

**Table 4.1**
**Assorted Research Sources**

| Directories and Industry Guides | Organization |
|---|---|
| Ace Your Case! The Essential Management Consulting Case Workbook | Wet Feet Press |
| An Overview of Management Consulting in North America | Kennedy Information Research Group |
| Consultants and Consulting Organizations Directory | Gale Research, Inc. |
| Directory of Canadian Management Consultants | Department of Regional Industrial Expansion, Ottawa |
| Directory of Management Consultants | Kennedy Information Research Group |
| Directory of Members—Institute of Management Consultants | Institute of Management Consultants (IMC) |
| Directory of Members (Association of Management Consulting Firms) | The Association of Management Consulting Firms (ACME) |
| Dun's Consultants Directory | Dun's Marketing Services |
| European Consultants Directory | Gale Research, Inc. |
| Harvard Business School Career Guide: Management Consulting | Harvard Business School Press |
| So You Want to Be a Management Consultant | Wet Feet Press |

| Periodicals | Organization |
|---|---|
| Consultants News | Kennedy Information Research Group |
| Harvard Business Review | Harvard Business Review |
| Journal of Management Consulting | Institute of Management Consultants |
| The McKinsey Quarterly | McKinsey & Company |
| Strategy & Business | Booz•Allen & Hamilton |

| Electronic Sources | Organization |
|---|---|
| Dow Jones Business Directory (http://bis.dowjones.com/djreviews/jobpost.html#3) | Dow Jones |
| Management Consulting: Exploring the Field, Finding the Right Job and Landing It! | Convergence Multimedia & Harvard Business School |
| Ohio State Consulting Directory (http://www.cob.ohio-state.edu/dept/fin/jobs/cons/consult.htm) | Ohio State University |

**Table 4.1   (Continued)**

| Electronic Sources | Organization | |
|---|---|---|
| Yahoo: Management Consulting Companies (http://www.yahoo/com/Business-and-Economy/Companies/Consulting/Management-Consulting) | Yahoo | |

| Books | Author | Publisher |
|---|---|---|
| Co-opetition | A. Brandenbrger & B. Nalebuff | New York: Doubleday, 1996 |
| Competing in the Information Age | J.M. Luftman | Oxford: Oxford University Press, 1996 |
| Competing for the Future | G. Hamel & C.K. Prahalad | Boston: HBS Press, 1994 |
| Competitive Strategy | M. Porter | New York: Free Press, 1980 |
| The Loyalty Effect | F. Reichheld | Boston: HBS Press, 1996 |
| The Mind of the Strategist | K. Ohmae | New York: McGraw-Hill, 1991 |
| Modern Competitive Analysis | S. Oster | Oxford: Oxford University Press, 1994 |
| People, Performance & Pay | T. Flannery | New York: Free Press, 1995 |
| The Profit Zone | A. Slywotsky & D. Morrison | New York: Random House, 1997 |
| Strategic Management of Non-profit Organizations | S. Oster | Oxford: Oxford University Press, 1995 |
| Taking Charge of Change | D. Smith | Reading, MA: Addison-Wesley, 1995 |
| Thinking Strategically: The Competitive Edge in Business, Politics, and Everyday Life | A. Dixit & B. Nalebuff | New York: Norton, 1991 |
| Value Migration | A. Slywotsky | Boston: HBS Press, 1996 |

student looking for a summer position, speak to your second-year classmates who just completed internships at consulting or strategic planning groups for even more contact information.

Widely used secondary sources are also available to further your research. You could start with Appendix III of this book, which provides a directory of 50 consulting firms. Table 4.1 provides a partial list of additional directories, industry guides, periodicals, and electronic sources that may help your research. Although this is only a partial list, it should get you well on your way to developing a more complete understanding of the industry, its strategic ideas, and its firms.

# NARROWING YOUR LIST OF FIRMS

As you learn more about the industry and begin to prioritize your interests, you may find your list of attractive firms becoming unreasonably lengthy. To narrow your list, select other dimensions for screening firms such as firm culture, firm prestige, anticipated lifestyle, number and locations of offices, and estimated starting salaries and signing bonuses. As you select the dimensions you find most important, rank them by degree of significance.

For example, if you dislike the rigors of extensive travel, but would love to join the Rolls Royce of consulting firms, then you will have to decide which of the two attributes—balanced lifestyle or prestige—you value more. Every firm offers a different mix of benefits and requires different sacrifices. Without some ranking of these preferences, your short list may not be very meaningful.

Attributes like firm culture, firm prestige, and balanced lifestyle are subjective and consequently difficult to research. Two consultants from the same firm may have completely different subjective opinions of their firm's culture. The main point is that as you research these attributes, you should use as many primary and secondary sources of information as you can find.

# PRIORITIZING SHORT-TERM VERSUS LONG-TERM INTERESTS

As you select your screening criteria, decide explicitly whether you are more interested in satisfying short-term or long-term interests. Short-term considerations, such as starting salaries and signing bonuses, start dates, and initial office or client assignments, often dominate because they provide immediate gratification. A gigantic signing bonus, after

all, can be very gratifying to one's financial health and may even eliminate a student loan in one fell swoop.

Consulting firms clearly recognize the importance of short-term
considerations when persuading an applicant to join the firm. In 1998,
average starting salaries for undergraduate recruits were $40,000 to
$45,000, with signing bonuses around $5,000; for top MBAs, the average base salary reached $92,500,[1] with signing bonuses as high as
$40,000. These big numbers can overshadow all other considerations,
to the detriment of both the firm and applicant. Once you experience
the day-to-day realities of being a consultant, the money may no
longer seem so attractive if, for example, you discover that you really
place greater importance on working at a 9-to-5 job.

Explicitly considering your long-term objectives will help you make
a more rational—rather than emotional—decision. Company A may
be offering a starting salary of $92,000, with a $35,000 signing bonus,
but how will an experience with Company A position you for future
professional endeavors? What skills will you add to your resume? Conversely, Company B, with an $80,000 starting salary and a signing
bonus of $10,000, may have a less attractive package, but it may also
offer far superior opportunities for professional growth. And some
firms with lower starting packages may offer more frequent and higher
raises than others, which, in the long run, may result in significantly
higher compensation. As all these considerations suggest, when you
are comparing firms and potential offers, it pays to think ahead and
weigh the relative importance of future rewards against immediate
rewards.

# GETTING YOUR FOOT IN
# THE DOOR OF A FIRM

Once you have selected a group of firms to contact, how do you get
them to recognize you? As shown in Figure 4.2, getting your foot in
the door involves a four-step process: (1) perform targeted research
on an individual firm; (2) adjust your resume to suit the firm; (3) speak
to individuals with direct exposure to the firm; and (4) write a cover

**Figure 4.2**
**Getting Your Foot in the Door**

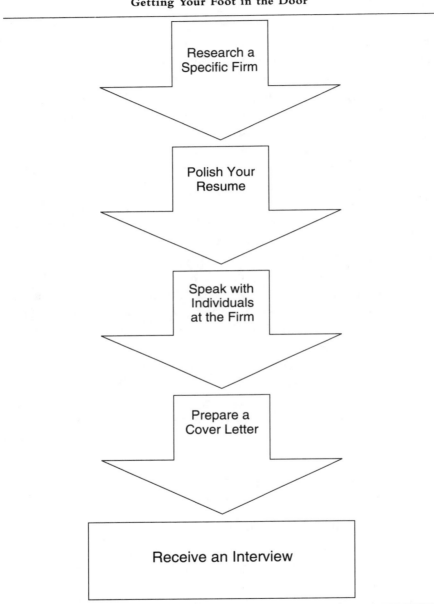

Research a Specific Firm

Polish Your Resume

Speak with Individuals at the Firm

Prepare a Cover Letter

Receive an Interview

letter that will capture the firm's interest. Although this may seem overly methodical, you should consider each step as a unique piece of the job-search puzzle, since a mistake at any one step can eliminate your candidacy altogether.

## Step 1. Performing Targeted Research

Although you have invested hours into your initial research on the industry and its firms, you probably will need to perform additional research on the firms you are targeting. You need very specific information to complete the next few steps: the exact title of the position you are applying for; the office location you prefer; the exact name of the practice area you seek to join; an accurate name and address of the recruiting coordinator; and other details that will give your application the polish it needs to impress. A small mistake, such as incorrectly referring to the position of "associate" as "research analyst" in a cover letter, has in the past been responsible for an immediate "ding" decision.

You should review all the firm's promotional materials, watch videotapes of on-campus presentations you might have missed, and perform targeted literature searches using search engines such as Lexus/Nexus to find the most current information available on a firm. If you are applying to an organization that does not participate in formal on-campus recruiting, you might even want to ask for an informational interview in the office. In addition to giving you direct access to a potential employer and enabling you to ask targeted questions, it will give you a chance to impress and establish a positive reputation with the firm even before submitting your application. Remember, targeted research can also have the proactive effect of promoting your candidacy.

## Step 2. Refining Your Resume

In the second step, you need to tailor your resume to the specific firm or company you are targeting. Your resume may be the most critical element of your application, since it usually carries more weight than your cover letter or, your (rarely requested) recommendations. As you may have guessed, a poorly written resume can ruin your chances of getting an interview. But what you may not realize is that a winning resume for a consulting application is slightly different from a resume that is appropriate for other jobs. When consultants review applications, they look for specific attributes that they see as critical to a successful consulting career. The most sought-after attributes are presented in Table 4.2.

A resume designed for a consulting firm must highlight a candidate's competencies. Each bullet point should begin with an action verb that emphasizes a critical skill area. Your goal is to prove to the reader that you have already developed, through your academic, professional, and extracurricular experiences, the minimum required skill set to become a consultant.

Each statement on a resume should also be results-oriented. For example, a candidate who analyzed the cost structure of a surgical procedure with the objective of reducing reimbursement claims for an insurance company could explain her experience in two different ways:

*Example: Cost Analysis for an Insurance Company*

Option 1:   Built an excel model to profile the cost distribution of stereotactic radiosurgery.

Option 2:   Led analysis to determine the cost distribution of stereotactic radiosurgery, resulting in an estimated savings of over $10,000 per patient treated.

Naturally, the second option is better because it goes beyond a simple description of the task and acknowledges the longer term impact.

Table 4.2
**Key Competencies of Qualified Candidates**

| | |
|---|---|
| • Academic achievement | • Extracurricular Involvement |
| • Analytical skills | • Leadership |
| • Communication skills | • Quantitative skills |
| • Creativity | • Results orientation |
| • Drive and commitment | • Team orientation |

But be careful: as you phrase your achievements and experiences according to the terminology consultants look for, do not stretch the truth. If you falsify any information on your resume—even unintentionally—and are discovered, you will likely lose your job and jeopardize the applications of all future candidates from your school.

A consulting resume is not carved in stone. Different firms may stress different competencies, and therefore should receive customized versions of your resume. You can expect to spend hours to review and revise your resume for each application. And consulting resumes need not be entirely formal—include some information about your personal interests at the end to show that you are a person who has a life too. A consultant reviewing your resume will want to know if you are someone who would be pleasant to work and travel with for long hours. Make sure you convey that you are an interesting, as well as bright, person.

The format of your resume should meet certain minimum standards. No resume should exceed a single page. If you need two pages, you need to be more selective with your bullet points and less verbose in your descriptions. Noting that you won your state's spelling bee, for example, is just not necessary once you have an MBA. The one-page limit forces you to judiciously choose the experiences you want to highlight, and the words you want to use. Avoid colored paper in favor of standard white and off-white stock. Likewise, avoid unusual fonts, and certainly never put graphic images on your resume. Always maintain a high degree of professionalism and let the content of your resume speak for itself. An extremely unconventional approach will draw attention to you for all the wrong reasons.

Finally, have others critique your resume before sending it off. Academic institutions often have dedicated resources to help students with their resumes, and your peers who are also going through the job search can offer additional perspectives. But the best proofreader may, in fact, be a consultant. If you have family, friends, or even willing alumni from your school who are consultants, ask them to read your resume as if you were applying to their firm. They will be able to provide current, relevant, and personal commentary on your resume. But never ask consultants at the firms to which you are applying to proofread your resume; they are likely to question your judgment—and with good reason!

## Step 3. Speak to Knowledgeable Individuals

Once you have the basic information about a firm and your resume is almost ready, you may want to compare notes with people who have had direct exposure to the firm. Family, friends, professors, and even "safe" consultants (e.g., individuals who have recently graduated from your school and are willing to speak with students in confidence) are all sources you might want to use. If you decide to contact safe consultants, select those who are close to the professional level that you plan to enter. For example, if you are about to graduate from college, speak to a research analyst at your targeted firm.

A more formal approach is to arrange an informational interview with a consultant at the targeted firm. As a proactive strategy, this may expose you to greater risk, but it may also let you leapfrog ahead of your competition if you make a good impression. In contacting these people, your objectives are to gain further insight into the firm and to demonstrate that you are serious about consulting and about that firm in particular. Ask questions that seek their opinions, rather than statistics that you could have looked up elsewhere. After all, that is why you wanted to speak with them instead of simply reading about the firm. What are the rewards of working for Mercer, and what are the sacrifices? What experience did they have before joining the firm? Which academic courses best helped them to prepare for consulting?

To arrange an informational interview, fax or mail your resume and a short letter to either a consultant or the recruiting coordinator, and then follow up with a call shortly thereafter. In the letter, explain how you got the person's name, who you are, and what your objective is for the interview. Close the letter with an action statement letting the addressee know that you will make a follow-up call on a specific date. Before you make that call, prepare your questions, since the individual may decide to use that moment to conduct a quick phone interview instead of arranging a later meeting. You may get only a few minutes of the person's time and should be respectful of his or her busy schedule. So do your research, prepare a list of questions in advance, and be ready to explain why you are interested in the firm, and even why they should hire you.

After the informational interview, close the loop by writing a thank-you letter. It should be short, but personal enough to remind the reader who you are and what you discussed. And since this was only an informational interview, do not conclude with a statement such as "I look forward to your response."

## Step 4. Write a Cover Letter

Here is where your research efforts really pay off. When writing your cover letter to formally apply for a position, you should address three essential topics in a single page. First, in the opening paragraph, state who you are and why you are writing: "I am a first-year graduate student at The Wharton School seeking a summer position at Hewitt Associates," or "I am a Vice President of Marketing at Procter & Gamble interested in transitioning to management consulting." Refer to the title of the position you are applying for, and identify the office location you prefer. This will demonstrate that you have done your homework. If you have spoken with anyone at the firm, mention that person as a point of contact who confirmed your interest in the firm.

Second, in the next paragraph or two, bring your resume to life by highlighting your skills. Explicitly connect your competencies to consulting, and convince the reader that you possess the necessary skills for the profession. If there are weaknesses on your resume, explain them here, and preferably describe a weakness in a way that makes it appear to be a strength. For example, if you worked at three companies in three years, explain how your apparent lack of commitment actually gave you a broader skill set by exposing you to a range of industries and responsibilities. Tell the reader why you would be a valuable professional addition, as well as a close personal fit with the firm culture. Although this is a lot of information to convey in a single page, the keys to an effective cover letter are directness and conciseness.

Third, end your letter with an action statement. Like the letter you wrote requesting an informational interview, your cover letter should include a request for an interview and state when you will call to follow up. Recruiters at large firms review literally hundreds of resumes and cover letters a day. Part of your objective, therefore, is to convince them to select yours from the pack and to meet with you.

The rules governing the format of your cover letters are the same as for your resume. Do not use paper of an unusual color, and make sure the cover letter paper exactly matches your resume paper. Avoid small or unusual fonts, and never use graphics. These comments should come as no surprise, but we mention them because we have seen far too many letters that violate these guidelines.

Be extremely careful to address the letter to the right recruiting co-ordinator, and at the right office address. Large consulting firms typically have multiple people in charge of different types of recruiting, such as an undergraduate recruiter, an MBA recruiter, an international office recruiter, and a professional hire recruiter who works with headhunters. Some firms may allocate their coordinators to specific schools, and in many cases, offices located in other countries have separate coordinators. Firms expect you to do your homework and find the right recruiter. If you make a mistake, your entire application could be sent to the wrong address and land in the trash.

Once you have completed all of these steps, you are ready to submit your application. Firms recruiting on campus often ask career planning offices to collect applications and mail them in all at once, rather than have students mail their applications directly to the firm. Pay close attention to submission deadlines: almost all firms stop accepting applications after a certain date, no matter who you are or what you say.

The competition for consulting positions is fierce, and little things can sway the end result. If you end up getting turned down, do not take it personally. You have to be thick-skinned during this process. "Ding" or "bullet" letters are so plentiful that many students wallpaper their dorm rooms with them. Once you get over the initial frustration of rejection, take a close look at the resume and cover letter you sent, and try to identify ways to improve them. With proper preparation next time, you can dramatically enhance your chances of securing an interview.

When your application is accepted and it is time to meet with the firm, the game changes entirely and presents a completely new set of challenges. In Chapter 5, we describe the process of case interviewing, and show you how to convert face-to-face meetings into a job offer.

# CHAPTER 5

## MASTERING THE CASE INTERVIEW

*You have been warned. The gentle job interview is dead. These days companies ask applicants to solve brainteasers and riddles, . . . act as managers of make-believe companies and solve complex business problems.*

Nina Munk and Suzanne Oliver
Forbes

**Y**ou have worked hard to secure an interview. You have diligently researched the firm's background, spoken with their consultants, polished your resume, and written a winning cover letter. Now, the only obstacles standing between you and the offer are the infamous rounds of case interviews. This chapter will help you hone your skills through practice and prepare you for successful case interviews. But your preparation cannot wait until the last minute. You should begin to practice immediately, and continue to do so throughout the entire application process.

Most candidates who fail the case interview do so because of inadequate preparation. They simply read through a list of sample case questions and think about how they would answer them. But when they are faced with the pressure of a face-to-face case interview, these candidates suddenly realize how inadequately prepared they are. Passive preparation is not enough; preparing for case interviews requires an active investment of time into practice.

This chapter begins by reviewing exactly what a case interview is, and then teaches you practical techniques for mastering each of the interview's component parts.

# THE PARTS OF A CASE INTERVIEW

A traditional interview includes three parts: an initial greeting, a discussion of the candidate's resume, and a final question-and-answer session. What, then, is a case interview? It is an expanded version of the traditional interview, which is uniquely characterized by its inclusion of a fourth part: a case question. These questions can ask you to discuss almost anything, from estimating the number of gas stations in the United States, to measuring the impact of El Niño on the world price of grapes. The case question is intended to test a candidate's ability to think and act like a consultant in an intense face-to-face situation. By simulating a client-consultant interaction, interviewers are able to observe firsthand how a candidate would manage a discussion with a client. Case questions are intentionally abstract, usually obscure and puzzling, and often technical. They are designed to test your ability to think creatively, make sense out of ambiguity, handle abstraction, and systematically derive an answer when an answer seems next to impossible.

Remember, though, that the case question is only one part—albeit the most important part—of the overall case interview. The case question will usually require 50 percent to 80 percent of the time allocated to a case interview, with the remainder of time allotted to the other three parts of the interview. Most case interviews follow this basic format, as presented in Figure 5.1.

Although the length of case interviews may vary between 30 and 45 minutes, they will typically proceed through each of the four parts. Rarely will an interviewer sacrifice a part. Each is deliberately designed to test for a different set of attributes. An interviewer who overlooks a part may have to base a decision on relatively incomplete information.

The following sections cover the four parts of a case interview. As we describe each part, try to internalize the process by envisioning yourself proceeding through it. Although no two interviews will be identical, the process outlined here will provide you with the tools to navigate through any case interview.

**Figure 5.1**
**The Four Parts of the Consulting Case Interview**

| Greetings | Resume Review | Case Question | Questions and Wrap-Up |
|---|---|---|---|

| Timing (minutes) | | | |
|---|---|---|---|
| 45-minute version | 1 | 10 | 30 | 4 |
| 30-minute version | 2 | 5 | 20 | 3 |

# PART I. GREETINGS

From the moment the interviewer extends her hand, she has begun to evaluate you—she is judging a book by its cover. Whether consciously or not, she notices the way you dress, the way you sit, and many other superficial elements of your appearance. If this first impression is positive, the interviewer is more likely to begin the interview with a favorable attitude toward you. Conversely, if the interviewer finds something odd or unexpected in your appearance, this negative perception of you may lead her to look for other reasons to not accept you. People have a tendency to be selectively rational—we register only those pieces of evidence that support our initial hypotheses. Perception, after all, largely forms our understanding of reality.

So to take control of the interviewer's first—albeit superficial—impression, pay close attention to the initial greetings. This is the time to put both yourself and the interviewer at ease, and to control her perception of you by building a positive rapport. This is also your chance to pass what is euphemistically known as the "airport test": If the interviewer were stranded with you at a snowed-in airport, would she enjoy your company? Practically all consulting firms emphasize this test. Since consultants tend to spend long hours together, and actually do get stranded in airports from time to time, it is best if they enjoy spending time together. You may be an outstanding candidate in all other respects, but unless you pass the airport test and make a social connection with your interviewer, chances are you will not be hired.

Experience has shown that interviewers typically prefer well-groomed candidates who give firm handshakes, look them directly in the eye, have a clear and confident voice, and show no signs of nervousness. Dress professionally and conservatively, regardless of the firm or company you are interviewing with. Women should wear either pant or skirt suits, preferably of a muted pastel or dark color, with limited jewelry and perfume. Men should likewise wear muted or dark suits, a tie, and polished shoes. Arrive early enough to prevent appearing harassed, and to have enough time to acclimate yourself to your surroundings.

What should you bring to an interview? The short answer is: as little as possible. You are likely to need a pad and pen to work through case questions, and you may want to carry them in a small portfolio. To refresh your memory just prior to the interview, bring a few notes on the firm or company and a list of questions you would like to ask. But do not carry books or volumes of information on the company or firm; instead, memorize anything you think you may need to know. Business cards, if you have them, are useful but not necessary, and a poorly prepared interviewer may ask for copies of your resume. Do not, under any circumstances, bring a calculator to an interview. In fact, you are likely to be tested for your ability to manipulate numbers in your head. Finally, do not chew gum or eat candy or other food during an interview; but if you are offered a drink, it is usually alright to accept.

How should you use the things you bring to an interview? Sparingly. Present your resume only if the interviewer asks for it or has not seen it before. Use your pad and pen only to jot down some simple notes during the case question. Too many candidates become dependent on their pads and write continuously during an interview. Before they know it, they are speaking into the pad, and forgetting to look up and make eye contact with the interviewer. Reference your notes on the firm and look at your list of questions before, not during, an interview. Memorize everything you may need to know.

After the interviewer leads you into a private meeting room, select a high-sitting chair, if possible, rather than a soft couch; your physical stature will undoubtedly have a direct impact on your level of confidence. Although case interviews can be stressful, try to remain relaxed. Smile, be enthusiastic, and do not be afraid to laugh, even if the interviewer seems stern. The best and easiest advice to follow is to be yourself. Remember: if the interviewer does not like who you are when you are yourself, chances are you would not want to work with that person, either. These simple, commonsense tips will give you a polished presence and increase the interviewer's confidence in your candidacy.

# PART II. THE RESUME REVIEW

After greeting you, the interviewer will typically launch into a 5- to 10-minute discussion of topics drawn from your resume. Work experience, academics, extracurricular pursuits and interests, and even hobbies are all fair game for this discussion. Interviewers use this opportunity to delve into your past and understand how you have grown from prior experiences. They hope to learn about your strengths and weaknesses, and to evaluate your professional and personal "fit" with their firm. Interviewers may even use this time to test your "business sense" (e.g., can you explain the business objectives of a former employer?) and to see if you keep up to date with your former employers (e.g., do you know what their current stock price is?).

Sounds simple enough, but you need to learn how to interpret their questions. When asking a question, interviewers tend to have a predetermined idea of a "good" answer, which rarely includes obvious responses. There is a difference between what the interviewer asks and what the interviewer means. For example, if an interviewer asks, "What did you do as an intern at IBM?" he is not looking for a list of tasks. Rather, he wants to see if you can take a broader perspective and articulate the competencies you developed and the impact that your work had on the company. His question should, therefore, be read as, "How did your position at IBM improve your professional skills?" Or better yet, "How did your position at IBM prepare you to join us?"

Similarly, if an interviewer asks, "How do you like Yale?" his true meaning is likely to be "Are you doing well at Yale?" or even "Are you a top performer at Yale?" Questions relating to hobbies or interests can be more difficult to interpret. For example, a question of "So, you like to ski?" is soliciting more than a confirmation from you. The interviewer wants to see if you can articulate the reasons why you like to ski and even convince him to try the sport himself.

To put it simply, you should use the Resume Review to sell yourself. Simple questions are actually invitations for you to provide a richer, more impressive description of your skills and abilities—and interviewers hope that you will use their questions to do just that. Although you can interpret a question in many ways, you should routinely try to take a step back from a simple answer, and instead offer a broader explanation of your skills to prove that you are an impressively competent candidate.

To prepare for the Resume Review, evaluate yourself introspectively, and identify the key skills you want to highlight. You actually began this process when you wrote your resume—a topic we covered in Chapter 4. By using action verbs such as "managed" and "supervised" to begin each bullet point on your resume, and by taking a results-oriented approach to describing the tasks you performed (e.g., ". . . resulting in an estimated savings of over $10,000 per patient treated"), you highlighted the evidence that proves you have certain skills. Then, when you wrote your cover letters—also covered in Chapter 4—you bundled the evidence into a smaller set of key skills and demonstrated that you have what it takes to be a management consultant.

Essentially the same process is required in the Resume Review: when an interviewer invites you to discuss a specific event on your resume, you have to demonstrate how that event taught you an essential skill for management consulting. And for each Resume Review question that an interviewer asks, you have the opportunity to highlight a different skill. You should thus be able to explain how any and all of the bullet points on your resume endowed you with a valuable competency.

So how should you characterize your competencies? If you recall, Table 4.2 provided a list of key competencies that interviewers want to see, and taught you to highlight as many of these skills as possible in your resume. This "core skill set" is what we call your "commercial": the summary of who you are and what you bring to the table. Although we would all like to think that we possess every skill listed in Table 4.2, in reality, we have different selling points, and hence, different commercials. Your commercial makes you unique, and tells the interviewer why he should hire you. Before an interview is over, you will want to talk about each and every one of your core skills. Practice answering Resume Review questions with these skills in mind, and, as explicitly as possible, link them to your academic, professional, and extracurricular experiences. When you can adeptly convert almost any set of Resume Review questions into a discussion of your entire commercial, you will be ready to conquer the Resume Review.

Successful candidates report that the best way to remember a commercial is to create a mnemonic. For example, a candidate who has Communication, Analytic, and Teamwork skills could think of herself as a "C.A.T." Add in Organizational skills, and she could then become a "T.A.C.O." Although you should not get carried away with this idea (we would hate to turn the consulting applicant pool into a zoo or restaurant), in the stressful atmosphere of an interview, it is much easier to think of your commercial as a single word than as a series of three to five words. Experiment with the skills of your commercial, and have some fun characterizing yourself.

Finally, prepare to answer open-ended questions, such as "Who are you?" or, "Why should I hire you?" A partial list of such questions is provided in Table 5.1.

By asking these questions, the interviewer is testing your reaction to an unexpected question. Your best bet is to fall back on your commercial, and use the open-ended question to sell yourself. For example, if your interviewer asks, "Who are you?" you have a perfect invitation to recite your commercial: your key skills, and the experiences that developed and demonstrate these skills. Or, if your interviewer asks, "What

139

**Table 5.1**
**Common Open-Ended Interview Questions**

What are your greatest strengths? Weaknesses?
Why should I hire you?
Tell me about yourself.
Who are you?
How do you like your school?
What is your favorite book and why?
What are your three greatest achievements?
What are your three greatest failures?
What three things must you do in your life?
What are your dreams?
Where do you see yourself in five years? Ten years?
What kind of people do you like? Dislike?
What would you like me to know that is not already in your resume?
How do you spend your free time?
Why are you here?
How would you describe your ideal job?
Which other companies are you interviewing with? Why?
What do you know about our firm?
How will an experience with us help your career?
Why did you choose to go to school A? Why not school B?
Why did you leave your last job?
Which courses have you liked the most? The least?
Do you like to travel?
What do you think of the stock market's performance?
What have you done with your life over the last few years?

is your greatest weakness?" you should think of a weakness that could also be considered a strength, such as paying meticulous attention to detail. Naturally, you can not anticipate and practice all the open-ended questions that you may get. But with some practice, you can avoid becoming flustered, and learn to deal with the tough questions by falling back on your commercial.

# PART III. THE CASE QUESTION

We finally come to the case question. You have had your chance to develop a rapport with the interviewer in the first few minutes, and explain why you possess the skills required to be a consultant in the subsequent 5 to 10 minutes. Over the next 20 to 30 minutes, you will have to prove that you can think "on-the-fly" and actually behave like the consultant you promise to be.

As mentioned, case questions are intentionally abstract, usually obscure and puzzling, and often technical. Their primary purpose is to test a candidate's ability to think and act like a consultant in a live simulation, and to verify whether a candidate truly has the skills claimed in the resume and cover letter. Case questions challenge you to discuss hypothetical situations using either information the interviewer provides, or assumptions you must make based on other, commonly known information. Even if you have no background to help you with the case, you will still be expected to address the question thoughtfully under pressure. Do not be surprised if the interviewer unexpectedly becomes impatient or irritable when discussing the case question. This may just be part of his strategy to test your ability to handle ambiguity in a pressured face-to-face interaction.

Case questions are infinitely variable. They can be based on any industry, company, or organization, and may be either reality based or entirely fictional. Although most deal with business situations, some cases may have to do with everyday life activities (e.g., "Why do the hands on a clock turn clockwise?"). Although cases vary greatly from requiring intense quantitative analysis to demanding purely abstract thinking, most case questions can be grouped into 10 broad types. Table 5.2 illustrates these types with a sample case question for each.

You will find a set of 100 case questions in Appendix II, along with 10 sample answers (one for each type). Remember that the type of question is more important than the actual question itself. The set we have provided in Appendix II is merely illustrative and by no means encompasses even the smallest portion of all the possible cases you may get. But if you learn how to recognize each of the types of cases, then you should be able to handle any variety of questions within that type.

Cases are not always clearly stated; interviewers occasionally turn a Resume Review question into a case without telling you. An interviewer may ask, "I see you worked at a bank last summer. Could you tell me about something that didn't work well at the bank and how you would have improved it?" This question may actually be a

**Table 5.2**
**Ten Types of Case Questions**

| Type | Example |
| --- | --- |
| 1. Brain teaser | Why are manhole covers round? |
| 2. Business strategy | Should an airline offer fee services, like travel insurance? |
| 3. Human resource management | What should banks do with their tellers as ATM networks expand? |
| 4. Market entry | How should a gourmet coffee chain locate its stores? |
| 5. Market sizing | How many people surf the Web in a single weekday? |
| 6. Mergers and acquisitions | Should a gin distillery buy a beer company, or chip dip company? |
| 7. New product introduction | Should a food canning company offer olives with pits, or without? |
| 8. Opportunity assessment | Should a soda bottler backward integrate into the manufacturing of syrup? |
| 9. Pricing | How does the U.S. Post Office price a first-class stamp? |
| 10. Profitability loss | A pharmaceutical company is losing money. What should it do? |

"business strategy" case rather than simple interviewer curiosity. Although most interviewers stick to more traditional case questions and make a clear transition from the Resume Review to the Case, you should pay close attention to questions that raise hypothetical situations, and be ready to treat scenarios arising from your own experience as case questions.

Even though cases come in many shapes and sizes, they are all designed with the same objective: to test your ability to rationally, methodically, and persuasively discuss the relevant issues of a question, and, ultimately, work your way toward a possible conclusion. Always remember: interviewers primarily want to see how you think—not whether you can get the right answer. In fact, many interviewers have no idea what the "right" answer is! Instead, most interviewers will grade your performance along the predetermined dimensions of an interview evaluation form, a version of which is presented in Figure 5.2. You will notice that getting the right answer is not one of the dimensions.

**Figure 5.2**
**Sample Interview Evaluation Form**

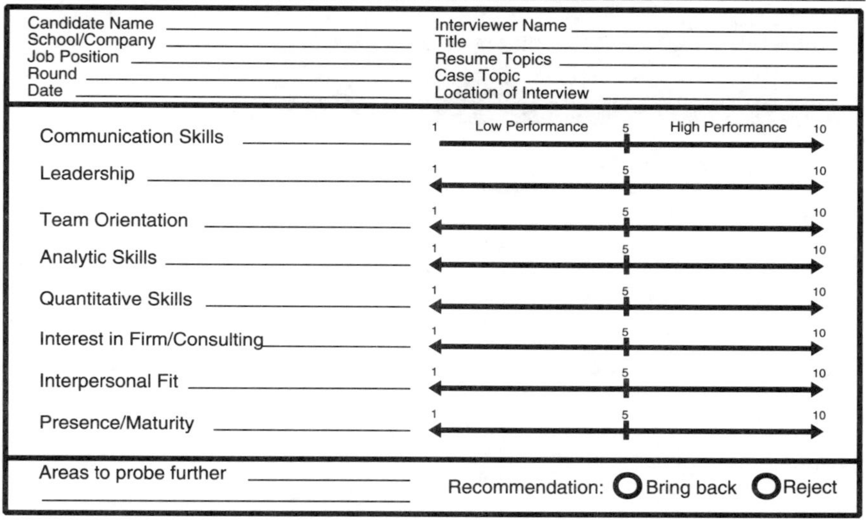

| | |
|---|---|
| Candidate Name _____ | Interviewer Name _____ |
| School/Company _____ | Title _____ |
| Job Position _____ | Resume Topics _____ |
| Round _____ | Case Topic _____ |
| Date _____ | Location of Interview _____ |

| | 1 Low Performance | 5 High Performance 10 |
|---|---|---|
| Communication Skills _____ | | |
| Leadership _____ | 1 | 5 10 |
| Team Orientation _____ | 1 | 5 10 |
| Analytic Skills _____ | 1 | 5 10 |
| Quantitative Skills _____ | 1 | 5 10 |
| Interest in Firm/Consulting _____ | 1 | 5 10 |
| Interpersonal Fit _____ | 1 | 5 10 |
| Presence/Maturity _____ | 1 | 5 10 |

| | |
|---|---|
| Areas to probe further _____ | Recommendation: ◯ Bring back ◯ Reject |

Now that you have an idea of what interviewers are looking for, how will you navigate your way through a case? Figure 5.3 outlines a proven five-step process to help you structure your thinking, and methodically work through a case from start to finish. Each step is reviewed in detail in the pages that follow.

# Case Step 1. Listen to the Question and Repeat

The first step in answering a case question involves careful, active listening. Too many candidates fall into the trap of misinterpreting the question and then talking on and on for 20 minutes about an entirely different subject. These candidates are doomed from the start, no matter how well they performed on the Resume Review. Interviewers may or may not be considerate enough to guide them back on track, and some interviewers are actually entertained by watching candidates crash and burn.

**Figure 5.3**
**The Five Steps of Answering a Case Question**

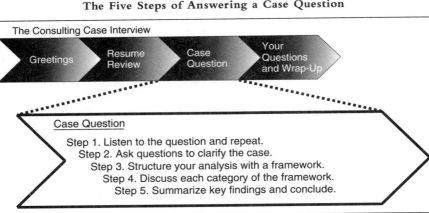

The Consulting Case Interview

Greetings — Resume Review — Case Question — Your Questions and Wrap-Up

Case Question
Step 1. Listen to the question and repeat.
Step 2. Ask questions to clarify the case.
Step 3. Structure your analysis with a framework.
Step 4. Discuss each category of the framework.
Step 5. Summarize key findings and conclude.

While the interviewer is explaining the question and providing some background information, you may want to take a few notes on your pad. Jot down the question at the top of the page and circle it for easier future reference. Record any numbers or figures you are given, and be sure to label them. On occasion, your interviewer will present you with a visual: a chart, graph, set of data points, and so on. Jot down any conclusions made by the interviewer when presenting the visuals, since these are the "so-what's" that the interviewer evidently finds most important. But remember: your pad is only a tool to help you recall crucial information; do not take too many notes, and be sure to look up and make eye contact with your interviewer. Once the interviewer has finished, you should mentally review the question and then repeat it to the interviewer for validation—we call this the "question check." Only after the interviewer agrees with your version of the question should you then proceed to the next step. We do have one caveat, however: if the question is simple enough to understand at first blush (e.g., "Tell me how many gas stations are in the United States."), then you probably should not embarrass yourself by mindlessly repeating the question.

## Case Step 2. Ask Clarifying Questions

Many case questions are abstract and ill-defined. This is intentional. The interviewer wants to see if you can organize your thoughts and structure a logical discussion. In these situations, you will need to ask some clarifying questions of the interviewer to solicit additional information. For example, a case simulation commonly places you in the consultant's seat and the interviewer in the client's, and requires you to interview the client as if you were in a real consulting engagement. Your client has a great deal of information but does not know which information you need until you ask for it.

Ask questions that will provide you with additional context and background. Take, for example, the following case question: "My company is losing money. What should I do?" You will want to find out what industry the company is in, how long the company has been losing money, and what products or services the company provides. Each of these clarifying questions will help you add structure and lucidity to an ambiguous case. Try to limit the amount of time you spend asking clarifying questions. The purpose here is simply to collect enough information to clarify the question, and be able to move on to the next step: structuring your intended path of analysis by developing a discussion framework.

## Case Step 3. Structure Your Analysis with a Framework

Before you jump into the discussion of a case, you should outline your intended path of analysis. Not only will this help you structure your thinking, it will also give your interviewer a road map for following the logic of your discussion. Consultants refer to this analytical outline as a "framework:" an intellectual tool that directs an analysis toward the critical issues of a case in a logical manner. Frameworks, such as Porter's Five Forces or BCG's Growth-Share Matrix, are frequently used in business strategy classes. Others, such as the 4-P's (Product, Price, Place, Promotion) and the 3-C's (Company, Competitors, Customers), are frequently used in marketing classes. These and many more are listed in Table 5.3 and are described in more detail in Appendix I.

You should use a framework as a mental checklist of the topics you intend to discuss. Frameworks will help you identify the critical issues logically and systematically, help you reorient your train of thought if you become confused or lost, and recharge your analytic creativity if you begin to run out of ideas. In themselves, frameworks will not give you answers; but they will orient you in the right direction and provide a structure for your thinking.

When selecting a framework for a case, you may want to look beyond the preceding list and develop your own. Use your imagination to build a framework that suits the unique needs of a case. If, for example, you believe that a discussion should revolve around only three of the four P's, then go ahead and use a "3-P's" framework and forget about the fourth. Or, if you believe that a situation is best analyzed by looking at customer fads, weather patterns, and the fuel efficiency of car engines, then offer these three categories as your framework. Do not be afraid to sketch out framework ideas on paper as they come to

**Table 5.3**
**15 Essential Frameworks**

1. 3-C's (Company, Competitors, Customers)
2. 4-P's (Product, Price, Place, Promotion)
3. The Boston Consulting Group Growth–Share Matrix
4. Breakeven
5. Cost-benefit analysis
6. Internal–external
7. Life cycle
8. McKinsey 7-S's (Style, Staff, Systems, Strategy, Structure, Skills, Shared Values)
9. Porter's Five Forces
10. Profits
11. Ratio analysis
12. Supply and demand
13. SWOT (Strengths, Weaknesses, Opportunities, Threats)
14. Value chain
15. Value net

mind—a visual image may actually make your task of developing a framework easier.

Many interviewers prefer to see candidates display their creativity and initiative by generating new frameworks, rather than using traditional ones. And some interviewers may even deduct points if a standard framework is inappropriately used, and most will cringe if Porter's Five Forces are mindlessly applied to an analysis. Under no circumstances should you force a case into a framework; rather, always build your framework around the case.

Do not be afraid to take a minute to think in silence when developing a framework. Most interviewers will understand your prudence and appreciate your desire to offer an intelligent—and intelligible—discussion. Even though silence may make you feel uncomfortable, it is well worth the effort to carefully plan the framework that will drive your ensuing analysis. But be aware of the interviewer's response: if he is visibly impatient, or if you take more than a minute out of an already short interview, you should immediately begin introducing your framework.

After you have outlined your intended path of analysis, ask the interviewer what he thinks: "Does this framework seem reasonable to you?" We call this question the "directional check": seeing whether the interviewer thinks your framework will lead you in the right direction to identify the relevant issues. If you receive agreement, then proceed with the next step. But if the interviewer attempts to direct you in a different direction—"You might want to consider the customers as well," for example—then be sensitive to her advice and adapt your framework accordingly.

## Case Step 4. Discuss Each Category of the Framework

Once you have outlined your framework and received agreement from your interviewer, you are ready to tackle the case. Steps 1 through 3 should have taken you no more than 5 minutes, leaving you with a residual 20 to 25 minutes. Pay close attention to the time: if you have a four-part framework such as the 4-P's, then you should allocate approximately 5 minutes to each part, keeping in mind that you will need a few minutes at the end to summarize your thoughts. Consulting interviews are hard to come by; you would not want to be eliminated from the running simply because you ran out of time.

Your discussion of the case should closely follow your framework. Cover one part of the framework at a time, moving sequentially through each of the parts within the allotted time. Try to discuss all the issues relevant to one part of the framework before moving on to the next. Do not jump back and forth from one part to another—after all, the ability to organize your thoughts into a structured analysis is one of the key skills being evaluated.

Be careful to explain each step in your discussion and avoid making logic jumps. Assume that the interviewer has little to no knowledge of the topic and needs a full explanation of your assumptions and conclusions—unless, of course, the interviewer instructs you otherwise. A good indicator of your performance is the interviewer's body language and facial expression. Does he look confused? Perhaps you are making leaps in your logic that he cannot follow. Is he bored? This is probably a sign that you are either belaboring a point or failing to hit the most important points. Not all interviewers will stop you when you are heading in the wrong direction, but many may reveal their thoughts through their demeanor.

As you work your way through your framework, be flexible enough to respond to the interviewer's comments. If you are redirected or instructed to look into a particular area in more detail, then do so. If you learn something new from the discussion and feel that an alternative framework would be more appropriate, then offer to adjust your approach, and have the interviewer approve your suggestion. Again, your primary objective is to prove to the interviewer that you are an active and structured thinker. By changing your mind and admitting a mistake, you are demonstrating your ability to self-improve.

When discussing highly quantitative cases, you want your numbers to be reasonably correct. To help you accurately approximate and calculate your numbers, Table 5.4 provides some useful statistics, many of which you may want to memorize.

Table 5.4
Useful Statistics

| U.S. Statistic | Figure | Year |
|---|---|---|
| Total population | 262.7 million | 1995 |
| Number of women | 134.4 million | 1995 |
| Number of men | 128.3 million | 1995 |
| Median age | 34.3 years | 1995 |
| People per household | 2.67 | 1994 |
| Number of households | 99 million | 1995 |
| Number of family households with children under 18 | 34 million | 1994 |
| People below poverty level | 38 million | 1994 |
| Total number of household vehicles | 151 million | 1991 |
| Median household income | $32,264 | 1994 |
| Median sales price of new privately owned one-family house | $130,000 | 1994 |
| People per square mile of land area | 70.3 | 1990 |
| Number of metropolitan areas (MSAs and CMSAs) | 269 | 1992 |
| Population of metropolitan areas (MSAs and CMSAs) | 203 million | 1992 |
| Percent of land in metropolitan areas (MSAs and CMSAs) | 19.1% | 1992 |
| Gross domestic product | $6.7 trillion | 1995 |
| Total number of revenue passengers boarding airplanes | 528 million | 1994 |
| Total number of farms | 2.1 million | 1995 |
| Total number of births per year | 3.99 million | 1994 |
| Total number of deaths per year | 2.29 million | 1994 |
| Total number of marriages per year | 2.36 million | 1994 |
| Total number of divorces per year | 1.19 million | 1994 |
| Total Bachelor degrees earned per year | 1.17 million | 1993 |
| Total Master degrees earned per year | 370,000 | 1993 |
| Total Doctorate degrees earned per year | 42,000 | 1993 |

Note: MSA = metropolitan statistical area; CMSA = consolidated metropolitan statistical area.
Source: Statistical Abstract of the United States: 1996, 116th Edition, U.S. Department of Commerce, Economics and Statistics Administration, Bureau of the Census.

Interviewers deliberately use quantitative cases to test your comfort with numbers and to see if your calculations are not only accurate, but also within a sensible range. You should get into the habit of subjecting your numbers to the "sanity test" by mentally checking them for reasonableness, and by comparing them with other numbers that you know.

For example, if you are calculating the number of gas stations in the United States and assume that a single station services 5,000 cars a day, you can subject the number to the sanity test by figuring out how many minutes per car this would equal. You probably know from your own experience that filling and paying for a tank of gas takes approximately five minutes. So, if your sanity test reveals that each of the 5,000 cars can be serviced by a station in five minutes, then the assumption is reasonable. Assume an average station has four pumps and is open from 6 A.M. to 9 P.M., or 15 hours a day: 4 pumps × 15 hours × 60 minutes = 3,600 pump-minutes. When 3,600 pump-minutes is divided by 5,000 cars, the answer tells us that each car is allotted less than a minute, which is ludicrously low. Thus, the assumption that a station can service 5,000 cars a day is over six times too high! A more reasonable assumption, therefore, would be about 700 cars per day instead of 5,000. By checking your numbers this way, you will end up with more accurate quantitative assessments, and you are even likely to earn points with your interviewer.

What should you do if your numbers are completely off? Or worse still, what if your entire analysis—both conceptual and quantitative—has gone awry in the middle of your discussion? First, do not panic. You may still be able to save your interview. Second, admit your mistakes rather than trying to hide them, and push on. Most interviewers have a strong familiarity with their cases and will not be easily distracted from noticing your mistakes. If you do not admit your error, your interviewer is likely to give you a low score for analytical thinking. On those occasions when you do have to admit a mistake, you should always identify where you made your error and how you would correct it—and then actually make the correction if you have time. This will show that in addition to having an analytical mind, you have the confidence to admit mistakes, and the drive to succeed.

## Case Step 5. Summarize and Conclude

As you approach the last few minutes of the case question, you should summarize your thoughts. This is your opportunity to give your discussion closure, to make sure it is not left dangling. Because many interviewers evaluate candidates by their ability to achieve results, they may evaluate your summary as an indication of your aptitude. Your summary should always refer back to the original question—the one that you circled at the top of your pad when you began the case—to ensure that you have directly answered it. Pull together all the conclusions you derived while proceeding through your framework, and summarize what you have learned. Then, offer the appropriate conclusion: a recommendation (e.g., the company should acquire its competitor), a decision (e.g., do not launch the product), or a number (e.g., there are *n*-number of gas stations in the United States).

If you have identified all the critical issues and made a convincing argument, you will probably receive an "ah-ha" reaction from the interviewer. He will be supportive of your effort and perhaps even smile with satisfaction. In most cases, you will know you performed well if your reasoning was structured, logical, and rational. And in the best scenario, you will have learned something, and maybe even have enjoyed the case.

# PART IV. QUESTIONS AND WRAP-UP

When you have completed the case, your interviewer will typically finish the interview by asking if you have any questions. Our advice here is simple: you should always come prepared with questions to ask. This is your last chance to show that you have a strong interest in the firm or company, and to prove that you are serious about joining. Last impressions count, and you should do your best to control how your interviewer perceives you. To the extent that your questions are insightful or unique, you may stand apart from the crowd. You can quickly generate a list of questions by reading through promotional materials, browsing Web sites, or reading annual reports, if available. The research you performed earlier when writing cover letters is useful here as well.

Examples of effective questions include: "A number of strategy firms are developing IT practices. Is yours planning to do the same?" or, "How will your firm respond to the unique needs of companies in emerging markets?" Conversely, any question that could have been answered by simply reading the firm's literature or browsing their Web site would be considered a "poor" question (e.g., "Do you have an office in Tokyo?" or, "Do you have a financial services practice?"). These questions signal poor preparation and a possible lack of interest in the firm.

Make sure your questions are appropriate to the interviewer's position. You probably will not want to ask a principal, for example, about the local night life in Chicago. Avoid questions about your interview performance or chances of getting an offer, which could be interpreted as symptoms of poor self-esteem or confidence as well as poor judgment. And never, under any circumstances, ask questions relating to starting pay or compensation packages until you are extended an offer.

When the interview is over and your interviewer stands to leave, extend a firm handshake, thank him for his time, and mention that you are looking forward to hearing from the firm. Just as first impressions counted when you met your interviewer, here, too, last impressions count as well. A confident and mature "good-bye" puts the final polish on your performance.

# PRACTICE MAKES PERFECT

Now that you understand the four parts of the typical case interview, you are ready to develop your case skills through practice. Get together with another person and alternate roles of interviewer and candidate. Or better yet, since it is admittedly difficult to think of interview questions while simultaneously evaluating a candidate's performance, grab a third person to play the role of an outside observer. You may want to photocopy the evaluation form in Figure 5.2, and fill one out for each practice interview.

Run through each of the steps of a case interview, including the greetings and good-byes—and try not to laugh! The closer your role-play replicates the intensity and pressure of an actual case interview, the more you will learn and the better prepared you will be. You should take time in advance to develop challenging "Resume Review" questions from the other person's resume to replicate the Resume Review, and draw case questions from those provided in Appendix II (you may want to start with the ones that have sample answers to get properly oriented). If the candidate is practicing for upcoming interviews at a particular firm, have the candidate bring questions to ask at the end of the interview that relate to that firm. If you know that an upcoming interview will last only 30 minutes, then practice within that time constraint, and cut the candidate off if he runs over. After a few rounds, you may want to change the members of your role-play group to get a diversity of opinions and see a variety of styles.

Do not underestimate the importance of role-playing; there is no better way to learn than through experience. Even if you feel confident after reading through this chapter, you may be caught off guard when it comes time to actually work through a case. Speaking about yourself is harder than you think, and dealing with ambiguous cases can be a nearly impossible task if the interviewer is particularly obnoxious. This process takes time, so you should set time aside to prepare in advance. It will pay off once your real interviews begin.

## POST-INTERVIEW FOLLOW-UP

After every round of interviews, mail a thank-you letter to each of your interviewers within a few days, regardless of whether you get called back or receive an offer. It is a polite gesture that has become an accepted practice. Your letters should be typed, written professionally, and as short as possible without seeming like a generic template. Avoid sending handwritten notes, cute cards, or e-mails; faxes may give the impression that you are overeager. If you are writing to multiple people at the same firm, send each person a different letter, since the letters will likely be entered into your personal file and may be compared. Try to personalize your letters by highlighting at least one element of each interview discussion. Reiterate your interest in the firm or company, and tell them you are looking forward to meeting with them again—assuming that you are, of course.

## RESPONDING TO REJECTION

What should you do if you are not invited back ("dinged")? You have invested hours in researching and applying, preparing for case interviews, and meeting with firms—but to no avail, right? Wrong. Being rejected is a natural part of the process of getting hired. Not every firm will like you. And the people around you who are getting offers are also likely to have ding letters wallpapering their rooms. Instead of giving up, use this occasion to learn from your mistakes by proactively requesting feedback from your interviewers.

Call your interviewers and ask for specific reasons for having been rejected. Did you inadequately convince them of your leadership abilities? Was your case performance subpar? Did you use an inappropriate framework? You might also ask for a relative scale ranking of your performance compared with other candidates: Were you a top runner-up, or toward the middle of the pack, or honestly at the bottom? Do not be afraid to push them for concrete answers. It is their responsibility to provide them. Unless you know the reasons for your rejection, you will have no way to improve. But try not to use this information to compare your personality or credentials with those of the candidates who were called back. Since you were not present during their interviews, you cannot judge from their resume and character alone why they were selected over you.

Just remember: you are not deficient if you get rejected. After all, the firm wanted to interview you, and you beat out the competition to get your foot in the door. Your resume was impressive enough to warrant the interview. What you need to do now is take your paper credentials and bring them to life in a face-to-face situation. Go back and practice your case interviews some more, paying particular attention to the improvement areas identified by your interviewers. This is a continuous learning process—think of how far you have come to get to this point.

# CHAPTER 6

## NEGOTIATING YOUR OFFER

**C**ongratulations! The many hours spent on researching your targeted firms, polishing your resume, and practicing cases have finally paid off with an offer. You have had your last interview, and all you have to do is sign on the dotted line. Right? Wrong. You are not done yet. An important phase of the interviewing process is still before you: negotiating the terms of your offer.

Although the importance of this phase may seem obvious, prospective consultants often find it intimidating and difficult to navigate. Dr. Keith Allred of the Kennedy School of Government at Harvard University has developed a framework for successfully negotiating the terms of an offer. This chapter presents his framework, which highlights the critical issues you will need to think through, and provides step-by-step guidance on how to succeed in the negotiation process.

155

# Negotiating the Terms of an Offer

KEITH G. ALLRED
HARVARD UNIVERSITY

Receiving an offer from a consulting firm can justifiably feel like the successful conclusion of the rather arduous interviewing process. But after taking much-deserved time to celebrate that success, you will want to think through the next brief, but important, step toward your management consulting career. If you are fortunate, this time will be complicated by the need to choose between multiple offers. In any event, it is time to negotiate the terms of the offer. One of the simplest, yet most important, points in this chapter is that the initial offer you receive from a firm is not necessarily final. Although this can vary widely, many firms expect some negotiation of the terms of the offer. In fact, many of the offers are carefully crafted to begin the negotiation process on terms favorable to the firm.

This chapter provides you with guidelines for succeeding in three critical dimensions of negotiation performance: claiming value, creating value, and maintaining relationships. First, it is important to note that you and the firm will inevitably share both compatible and incompatible interests. One compatible interest would be that the firm wants you to work for them, and you, presumably, also want to work for the firm. A competing interest might have to do with salary: you would rather earn a higher salary, but they would rather pay you a lower one. These are just two of the most obvious examples of many competing and compatible interests. The mix of interests you and the firm share gives rise to the first two dimensions of negotiating the terms of your employment: claiming and creating value.

The mutual interest shared by you and the firm creates a certain amount of mutual value. The firm can generate more revenue by hiring you, and you can generate income and valuable experience by working for them. Thus, the first dimension of negotiation relates to how well you can claim a portion of the value generated by joining the firm. This is the value-claiming, or distributive (i.e., how the available value is distributed), dimension of negotiation.

Beyond the mutual value you and the firm create by joining forces, however, there may be creative ways of integrating your interests with the firm's interests, thereby making your relationship even more mutually beneficial. The extent to which you and the firm realize such opportunities for further joint gain is the value-creating, or integrative, dimension of negotiation.

The third dimension of negotiation reflects that you are entering into an ongoing relationship with the consulting firm. If you are highly successful in obtaining favorable terms for yourself, but sour your relationship with the firm in the process, you will have been less successful than if you had managed the same deal for yourself while still maintaining a good relationship with the firm.

In this chapter, I offer strategies and tactics you can use to claim value, then to create value, and finally to maintain your relationship with the firm. Of course, it is not always easy to succeed in the three dimensions simultaneously.

# NEGOTIATING A FAVORABLE DEAL FOR YOURSELF: THE ART OF SUCCESSFULLY CLAIMING VALUE

Throughout this chapter, the fictional example of Ann and Enterprise Consulting Partners (ECP) will illustrate effective negotiation strategies. Ann is about to complete her MBA. After three rounds of interviews, ECP, a medium-size, rapidly growing management consulting firm offers her a position. ECP's package includes an annual base salary of $60,000, an offer Ann is thrilled to receive. She thinks ECP is an exciting and interesting firm, and the thought of $60,000 in annual salary is a relief as she contemplates her student loans that will soon be coming due. Yet she certainly would not mind earning more than this and actually has friends who have received higher base salaries at similar firms. She starts to consider how she might negotiate with ECP for a better salary.

A number of concepts are useful in thinking about how Ann might proceed. First and foremost, Ann needs to consider what her best option would be if she did not accept an offer from ECP. In *Getting to Yes*, Fisher, Ury, and Patton[1] refer to this point as one's "Best Alternative to a Negotiated Agreement" (BATNA). Second, Ann will want to estimate ECP's own BATNA, which is probably a function of the next most attractive candidate they have identified for hire. Assume that Ann's BATNA is defined by an offer she has from a different firm for $55,000. Aside from differences in salary, she finds this other firm similarly attractive. Assume further that Ann believes ECP has identified another graduating MBA who is as attractive as she is, and that ECP estimates this other candidate would agree to work for them for $75,000.

These two BATNAs—Ann's and ECP's—define what is called "the settlement range," as seen in Figure 6.1. At any offer below $55,000

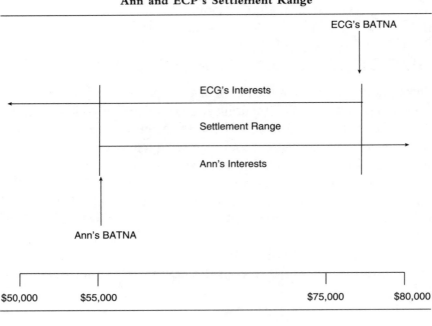

**Figure 6.1**
**Ann and ECP's Settlement Range**

from ECP, Ann would prefer to go work for the other firm. At any offer for Ann above $75,000, ECP would rather hire the other candidate. Within the settlement range from $55,000 to $75,000, both parties would prefer to conclude a deal with each other rather than go to their best alternative. This means that there is $20,000 ($75,000 – $55,000) worth of value to be claimed between Ann and ECP. The question is: how much of that $20,000 will each party get?

Because BATNAs define the settlement range, Ann's BATNA will be her primary source of leverage in the negotiation with ECP. If Ann had an offer from a similarly attractive consulting firm for $70,000, she would be able to negotiate a better deal for herself than with the offer for $55,000. This illustrates one of the most important points to be made. You should do everything you can to secure the best alternatives for yourself. Even if you have your eye on a particular firm, you need to seek out possibilities elsewhere. Furthermore, once you receive an offer from your preferred firm, you should not necessarily turn down other offers right away. Continuing to get as many offers as you can that are as attractive as possible is one of the best strategies for successfully claiming more value for yourself.

There is a deeper point to be made here: your BATNA will largely determine your negotiation leverage not only in your current negotiation, but also in negotiations throughout your career. The attractiveness of the alternatives available to you is a function of the skills, abilities, knowledge, experience, and contacts that you bring to your career. This suggests that jobs, particularly early in your career, that provide you with valuable opportunities to develop yourself are of great long-term value because they will allow you to generate future attractive alternatives. Although in the consulting industry there is likely to be a positive correlation between how developmentally beneficial a position is and the salary it offers, the correlation is far from perfect. If you have one offer that provides a lower salary but a better developmental opportunity, and another offer that provides a higher salary but a less interesting opportunity for development, there is much to be said for taking the greater developmental opportunity and accepting the lower salary. It is an investment you will be able to amortize over the entire length of your career.

Returning to the example of Ann, note that ECP's negotiation leverage is similarly a function of their best alternative to Ann. If they identify a candidate as attractive as Ann whom they could hire for $60,000, they should be able to negotiate a more favorable deal for themselves than if they could only hire a similarly attractive candidate for $75,000. Undergraduate and MBA students often feel that all the negotiation leverage is in the hands of the consulting firms. After all, the firms have jobs to offer or not offer. But the preceding analysis should help you realize that consulting firms do not necessarily have more leverage. Rather, their relative leverage is a function of how attractive their alternatives are (i.e., other candidates they can attract) relative to yours (i.e., other offers you can attract).

As the first chapter of this book indicated, management consulting has been growing at extraordinary rates. This means that the demand for management consultants has increased at a similarly extraordinary rate. While the supply of management consultants—people like yourself interested in going into management consulting—may have grown to a degree, it appears to have grown slower than demand over the past decade. This means that the BATNAs of candidates and, thus, their negotiation leverage, have improved relative to those of consulting firms in recent years. Take heart. You are not necessarily without alternatives!

It may be helpful to break down the negotiation process itself and see how the strength of one's BATNA plays out. In Ann's case, ECP offers her $60,000; she has an offer from a similarly attractive firm for $55,000; and she believes that ECP's best alternative is a candidate they could hire for $75,000. What should she do? If she is reasonably sure that she will not get additional offers, it would not be unreasonable, given that her next best alternative is a $55,000 offer, for her to accept the $60,000 offer from ECP. However, because she thinks ECP's best alternative is to hire someone else for $75,000, it would also be reasonable for her to seek a higher salary—up to the $75,000 limit.

When deciding how aggressively to pursue a higher salary, Ann faces a double-edged sword. The more aggressive she is, the greater potential she has to capture value. However, just as in financial investments, moves with higher potential gains also expose one to greater risk of loss. Specifically, research on the effects of the positions that negotiators take can be divided into opening positions or offers, intermediate positions or concessions, and final positions or final offers. The more extreme one's opening offers, the more stingy one's concession making. And the more aggressively one uses final offers, the more likely the negotiation will end in no agreement. But if an agreement is actually concluded, it will be all the more favorable.

Ann should take into account these potential benefits and risks when choosing her course of action. Two rules of thumb are helpful in thinking about an opening offer to make in response to the offer of $60,000. First, research suggests that negotiations typically settle at the mid-point between the two opening offers. So if she offers $70,000, chances are they will settle at $65,000. Second, Lax and Sebenius[2] suggest that Ann should make an opening offer that she is 90 percent to 95 percent certain is higher than the highest figure ECP is willing to pay.

Assume that Ann decides to ask for a salary of $75,000. Given that ECP has offered her $60,000, one or both sides will need to concede, or the negotiation will obviously end in no agreement since ECP could hire the other equally attractive recruit for $75,000. But if concessions are made, how large should they be? If it is likely that there will be a couple of rounds of counteroffers or concessions, it is generally wise to graduate the level of concessions. If Ann expects to make two more counteroffers before it is all concluded, she will want her second concession to be smaller than her first. Imagine that ECP counters her $75,000 with $65,000. She could now counter with $70,000, a concession of $5,000 over her prior offer. If ECP now counters with $67,000, she could counter that with $68,000, a concession of $2,000 over her last offer. By making a second concession that is substantially smaller than the first, Ann signals that she is approaching a point beyond which she will not go.

At some point in this process of concession and counterconcession, one of the parties may concede as far as it is willing and will then make a final offer. The implicit meaning of a final offer is that the party is willing to walk away from the deal rather than concede any further. In other words, the party is making a final commitment to that offer.

As mentioned, however, Ann faces a double-edged sword here. The more iron-clad she makes her commitment seem, the more likely it will be successful in inducing ECP to give her that salary amount. In the event that ECP is unwilling to settle at the point where Ann commits herself, however, this same appearance of commitment creates a situation from which it is difficult to extract herself. Either she must hold to the commitment and lose the job, or she must find a way to communicate that she was not committed to the offer after all, and is actually willing to concede. It is obviously more difficult for her to make a credible commitment after having a prior commitment unmasked as a bluff.

To summarize, when seeking to claim value, you must make a choice between more aggressive, higher risk, higher potential gain moves, and less aggressive, lower risk, lower gain moves. Two additional general points should be made about claiming value. First, firms vary widely in the extent to which they are willing to negotiate the terms of the offers they make. Some firms come in with their best offer up front and stick with it, refusing to negotiate with any recruit. Some firms make a policy decision that, because of the value they place on maintaining equity among members of the firm, or because of financial constraints, they will not offer different recruits different compensation packages. Of course, firms can also intimate that they have such policies as a negotiation ploy, when, in fact, they do negotiate.

It is difficult to get reliable information on how willing a firm is to negotiate, but you should learn what you can. Speak to consultants who have been recently hired by the firm. You will have to judge whether there are individuals with whom you feel comfortable discussing this topic. You might also try to identify friends or associates who have secondhand knowledge of your firm through acquaintances who have recently joined that firm. Or speak to pioneering classmates who have also received offers and have already attempted to negotiate. Not only do you want to find out whether the firm will negotiate the terms of the offer, but also the extent to which they will negotiate, and on which terms they are most willing to negotiate. In the Ann and ECP example, I have used base salary as the only issue under negotiation. This, in fact, is the one component that consulting firms are often least willing to negotiate. Frequently, firms are more flexible on issues such as the amount and timing of signing bonus, annual bonus, profit sharing, moving stipends, or tuition reimbursement.

When deciding whether to negotiate, it helps to know the typical range of consulting compensation packages. Although the figures are not the result of a scientific survey, I can provide a general sense of the range of recent compensation packages based on figures reported by Kennedy Research Group,[3] and by informal polling of recent recruits. The ranges can differ according to a number of factors, including prior experience, education, and the size of the consulting firm. In 1998, undergraduates taking entry-level consulting positions tended to earn an average annual salary of $40,000–$45,000, with some firms offering a modest signing bonus of around $5,000. For MBAs from top schools, average starting salaries were approximately $92,500, with signing bonuses ranging from $30,000 to $40,000. At most firms, year-end bonuses ranged from 10 percent to 25 percent of salary.

In addition to annual salary, signing bonuses, and year-end bonuses, candidates often receive some financial support for their relocation. Sometimes this comes in the form of a cash amount, but more often it is provided as a reimbursement for moving costs actually accrued, up to a predetermined limit. The moving reimbursement or stipend may range from $0 to $20,000. And candidates are sometimes offered, or negotiate for themselves, reimbursement for costs incurred during a housing search (e.g., realtor fees, travel, and hotel charges).

# ENLARGING THE PIE: THE ART OF CREATING VALUE

Now you know that negotiation is a win-lose proposition. A gain in salary for you represents an equal financial loss for the firm and vice versa. However, favorable changes in the terms must not necessarily come at the expense of the consulting firm. In other words, besides claiming a portion of the value pie for oneself, it is often possible to increase the overall size of the pie by dovetailing the two parties' interests in creative ways. The most common method of creating value can be illustrated by introducing the issue of a signing bonus into the negotiation between Ann and ECP.

Imagine that as Ann nears the end of business school, having had two years of very little income and high expenses, she is in a cash crunch. She is near her credit limits on her credit cards, and she knows that she will have considerable expenses over the next few months before starting her full-time job. Her old, unreliable car will no longer suffice, and she will have to trade it in for a new one. She needs a serious wardrobe upgrade to be ready for her new job. And, if at all possible, she would like to go to Europe with several business school friends after graduation. They will all be starting jobs with enormously demanding schedules, and this will be their last real opportunity for some recreation.

Imagine, also, that Ann spoke with another recent hire at ECP and discovered that ECP will negotiate salary, but only within a restricted range. The firm hesitates to bring in new recruits at different salaries due to equity concerns. Moreover, ECP would prefer to keep the monthly fixed cost of paying Ann's salary to a minimum. However, ECP is willing to negotiate the signing bonus since it is a one-time variable cost. This situation could be represented by the payoff schedules in Table 6.1. The numbers in parentheses indicate the relative value to each negotiator of concluding a particular issue at a particular level.

The point values in this case reflect Ann's preference for a higher salary and signing bonus (i.e., the greater the salary and the greater the signing bonus, the more points she gains) and ECP's preference to give her a lower annual salary and signing bonus (i.e., the lower the

**Table 6.1**
**Payoff Schedule**

| Ann's Payoff Schedule | | ECP's Payoff Schedule | |
|---|---|---|---|
| Annual Salary | Signing Bonus | Annual Salary | Signing Bonus |
| $69,000 (100) | $13,000 (250) | $69,000 (50) | $13,000 (20) |
| 68,000 (80) | 11,000 (200) | 68,000 (100) | 11,000 (40) |
| 67,000 (60) | 9,000 (150) | 67,000 (150) | 9,000 (60) |
| 66,000 (40) | 7,000 (100) | 66,000 (200) | 7,000 (80) |
| 65,000 (20) | 5,000 (50) | 65,000 (250) | 5,000 (100) |

salary and the lower the signing bonus, the more points they gain). However, salary and signing bonus are not of equal importance to the two parties. Because of her current cash crunch, Ann is more interested in the signing bonus than in the salary amount within the range under consideration.

This difference in relative weight is reflected in the greater points allocated to the signing bonus figures (i.e., an additional 50 points for each additional increment of signing bonus versus an additional 20 points for each additional increment of salary). In contrast, ECP's point allocation reflects the importance the firm places on salary level due to internal equity issues and a desire to limit fixed monthly costs relative to the less important one-time cost of a signing bonus (i.e., an additional 50 points for each lower increment of salary versus an additional 20 points for each lower increment of signing bonus).

Ann and ECP have offsetting priorities on these two issues. This creates integrative potential or the potential to increase the size of the pie that will be divided between them. Imagine that Ann responds to ECP's opening offer by saying, "I would prefer to receive a salary of $69,000 and a $13,000 signing bonus." ECP responds with a counteroffer of $66,000 and a $7,000 signing bonus. Through this typical dance of counteroffers, Ann and ECP haggle to the midpoint of the ranges for both issues, coming to an agreement in which Ann receives a salary of $67,000 and a signing bonus of $9,000. That agreement would be worth 210 "points" to each of them, for a total pie worth 420 points.

Now assume that Ann follows a different strategy. Drawing on the information from the recent hire at ECP, she responds to ECP's initial offer by saying, "I understand that you are particularly concerned with the salary amounts you offer because of fixed-cost and equity issues. Since I have some pressing financial needs at the present time, I'm willing to concede to a salary of $67,000, if you will give me a $13,000 signing bonus." Recognizing the opportunity for joint gain, ECP responds by saying, "We will come up to $13,000 on the signing bonus, if you'll agree to a salary of $65,000." Ann accepts, resulting in an agreement that is at the lowest end of the range on salary and at the highest end of the range for signing bonus. This agreement yields 270 points to each, for a total pie of 540—120 points more than the prior agreement in which they haggled to the middle on both issues.

This strategy, in which each party concedes on their issue of lesser importance to gain on their issue of greater importance, is known as "logrolling." You can use this strategy to create value anytime you and the firm attach offsetting values to different issues. The logrolling approach to creating value suggests a deeper point: it is critical to think through the relative importance of various issues in advance of your negotiation. Since it is unlikely you will be able to get everything you want, you need to focus on getting what is most important to you.

Once you clarify the relative importance of different issues for yourself, you face another dilemma in choosing how forthcoming and explicit to be in communicating those relative preferences to the firm. By telling ECP that she cares more about the signing bonus than about salary, Ann makes it more likely that she and ECP will discover a mutually beneficial trade-off. However, she also exposes herself to possible exploitation.

Imagine that ECP is actually willing, if necessary, to pay Ann both a $75,000 annual salary and a $13,000 signing bonus, and that their initial offer was just a way of trying to start the negotiation on terms favorable to the firm. Upon hearing that Ann has a preference for an increase in signing bonus over an increase in salary, the firm may respond opportunistically. They may disingenuously say, "Since the signing bonus represents an out-of-pocket expense long before you begin to really contribute to the firm's profitably, it is a particularly important issue to us as well. But we want to be responsive to your wishes, so we would be willing to give you a $10,000 signing bonus if you are willing to recognize the up-front cost we have to take and accept a salary of $62,000."

As you decide how forthcoming to be with information about the relative weights you attach to different issues, you will want to consider both the potential for discovering mutually beneficial trade-offs and the risk of exploitation. At a minimum, if you come to feel that you will have to make concessions to reach agreement, be sure to concede on issues of less importance to you before conceding on issues of greater importance.

## MAKING ALLIES OUT OF YOUR NEW COLLEAGUES: THE ART OF MAINTAINING AND ENHANCING RELATIONSHIPS

As you negotiate the terms of your offer, remember that you may eventually work with these same people. On occasion, an aggressive recruit can take advantage of an excess demand for consultants in a limited supply market to negotiate an extraordinary deal for herself. While a firm may agree to an unusually generous package to win an attractive prospect away from competing firms, the firm can end up begrudging it after the fact, and resenting the recruit who extracted the generous offer. This can make working relationships difficult once the new employee starts. Besides being the object of resentment, the unusually well-compensated recruit may become subject to extremely high work load and performance demands from the firm. This much you can usually count on—your firm will make every effort to get the full dollar's worth out of you.

Research indicates that ill will related to job offer negotiations is only partly a result of the firm resenting the recruit's success in negotiating a favorable offer. The resentment can be even greater if the firm feels as though the negotiation *process,* rather than the outcome, was unfair or unsavory. If the members of the firm involved in the negotiation come to feel like victims of extreme gamesmanship, or if they believe that the recruit exhibited an arrogant or disrespectful attitude, then the candidate will later pay for the lucrative package through the ill will it generated.

The same principles apply to you. If both the process and outcome of the negotiation leave you feeling exploited, you may want to reconsider whether these are the people with whom you want to spend the lion's share of your waking hours. Generally, consulting firms try to put their warmest and friendliest face forward during the recruiting process. But in the negotiating process, you may find the firm less friendly—and you will rarely find it more friendly.

## CONCLUSION

You would be well advised to do as much planning and preparation as you can prior to negotiating the terms of your offer. As mentioned, try to generate as attractive a set of alternatives as you can, and try to gather as much information as you can about how firms tend to negotiate with recruits. With that information in mind, plan your approach. Use the strategies in this chapter to achieve the goals of claiming value for yourself, creating value where possible, and maintaining a good working relationship with the firm. While planning is extremely helpful, you must also be ready to change your plan as new information comes to light during the negotiation.

Finally, remember that what you offer the firm is as valuable to them as what they offer is to you. The fact that they have made you an offer in the first place is evidence of this. Moreover, the current situation of demand for new recruits exceeding supply should give you a heightened sense of confidence as you enter your negotiations.

# EPILOGUE

**N**ow, armed with a powerful set of negotiating techniques, you have all the tools you need to jump into the consulting career search. The process is challenging, but you have already separated yourself from the pack by reading this book. You have overcome the first challenge of understanding the process. We have covered a great deal of material, detailing each of the steps you will have to go through to rightfully be able to say, "I am a consultant." At this point, you should have a realistic understanding of what consultants do, how you can successfully gain entrance to the industry, and finally, how you might negotiate the best offer for yourself.

The second challenge in the job search is execution. Understanding the consulting industry helps, but it does not get you through rounds of interviews. You should now move on to the appendixes, which have been carefully designed to jump-start your research and to sharpen your case interviewing skills. If you use these appendixes properly, you should be able to hurdle the challenge of execution, and develop consistently dependable and impressive interviewing skills. Remember: the more you know about the industry and its entrance requirements, the more confident and relaxed you will be when working your way to an offer. And the more you practice case interviews, the more enjoyable you will ultimately find them to be.

We are confident that you will learn a great deal about yourself through this process, and are even likely to surprise yourself with newfound analytical prowess. By practicing case questions, you will learn how to think in an entirely new way, and to apply common sense and rational insight to questions where you might previously have had no idea where to begin.

Getting a job in consulting is challenging, but you have the tools to succeed. It is now time to sharpen your tools, and to convince your interviewers that you are the candidate they want. We wish you the best as you work your way toward your new position.

# APPENDIX I

## FIFTEEN ESSENTIAL FRAMEWORKS

**B**efore you begin to practice case questions, you should familiarize yourself with the most common business frameworks. This section will provide you with a basic understanding of the 15 frameworks most often used to answer case questions. Although many may seem familiar, you should use the frameworks as you practice answering case questions to truly become comfortable with them. The descriptions that follow the frameworks are simplifications and are intended either to refresh your memory if you have had prior framework experience or to provide an introduction to the fundamentals if you have not. We highly recommend reading additional texts to fully capture the nuances of frameworks that are new or unfamiliar to you.

As you practice answering case questions, remember three things: First, well-prepared candidates will have learned to use frameworks as a mental checklist of topics to discuss. Some of the mnemonics used to name the frameworks (e.g., 3-C's, 4-P's, or 7-S's) may seem a bit foolish at first, but they are intentionally simplified to serve as memory hooks and to help you discipline your thinking as you answer case questions. In addition to helping you, frameworks also help interviewers follow your analysis. Second, the frameworks presented here are a mere subset of the limitless number you could generate. Feel free to use your creativity and generate your own. Recruiters appreciate creativity and may give you points for taking risks. Third, you should never try to squeeze a case into a framework; rather, the framework should be carefully selected or designed to suit the case. Only select or build a framework for a case once you have a clear understanding of the question and a good understanding of the relevant issues.

Please note that not all the frameworks are relevant to all case questions. Business school students will be expected to have a thorough understanding of all the frameworks and how to properly apply them. Other graduate school students, career-changing professionals, and undergraduate students are advised to be familiar with all the frameworks.

# 3-C'S (COMPANY, COMPETITORS, CUSTOMERS)

An effective marketing strategy leverages a company's relative competitive advantage (RCA): the degree to which a company possesses unique properties that enable it to outperform its competitors. The analytical model most commonly used to identify the sources and strength of a company's RCA is the "3-C's" framework depicted in Figure AI.1, which explores the interaction of a company with its competitors and customers.

## Company

The strength of a company's RCA is partially determined by the unique advantages the company possesses over the competition. Sources of advantage include distinguishing core competencies, such as product innovation, production efficiencies, responsiveness to changing customer needs, and ability to optimize market-entry timing. Proprietary corporate resources such as patents, established supplier and buyer networks, and exclusive technology capabilities may also provide competitive advantages to a company, as can structural arrangements such as joint ventures or strategic alliances.

**Figure AI.1**
**3-C's Framework**

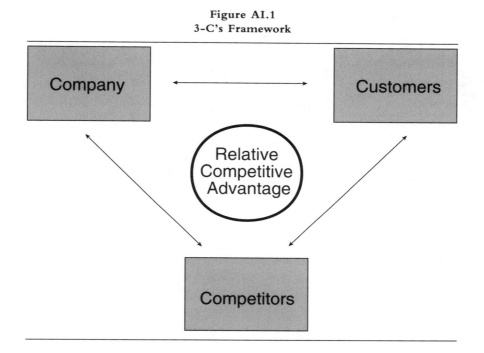

## Competitors

Similarly, the competition may possess unique core competencies that could weaken the company's RCA, such as superior production technologies or distribution networks, preferential sourcing relationships, or superior market positioning (i.e., the highest share of customer spending in a market). And the business strategies of the competition may impact the company's RCA over time: predatory strategies are likely to pose serious threats, whereas collaborative or complementary strategies may actually benefit the company by increasing overall industry profitability.

## Customers

As purchasers of products and services, customers are the final judges of a company's marketing strategy. Companies that understand the interests, needs, and behavior patterns of customers are able to produce superior goods, and thus strengthen their RCA. Persuasive marketing messages can be constructed around the behavior patterns of customers, and used to lure customers away from the competition. And companies can target emerging pockets of opportunity by monitoring changing customer needs and innovating their products or services accordingly.

An integrated analysis of the 3-C's enables a company to assess its relative competitive advantage in an industry, take the appropriate actions to either build or solidify its RCA, and ultimately generate a marketing strategy that captures optimal value from its RCA.

# 4-P'S (PRODUCT, PRICE, PLACE, PROMOTION)

The marketing strategy of a product must be sensitive to the interrelated forces operating within the market where the product will be sold. A 4-P's analysis will provide the necessary context, and will enable a company to generate a superior marketing strategy by evaluating the product, its pricing strategy, its place of sale, and its means of promotion, relative to the competition. A schematic of this framework is provided in Figure AI.2.

## Product

The attractiveness of a product to a customer is in part determined by its characteristics and features. Products that appear to offer greater value to a customer relative to competitor products, either through superior functionality, style, durability, or cost-effectiveness, may have the advantage of differentiation. However, products in commodity markets are perceived by customers to be similar if not identical in value regardless of feature or characteristic, and are typically only differentiated by low price. Over time, a product tends to pass through a series of "attractiveness" stages, depicted by the product life cycle curve (described later in this appendix): new products are developed

**Figure AI.2**
**4-P's Framework**

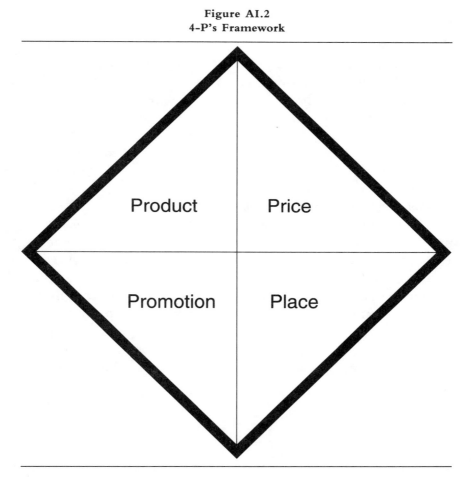

and introduced to the market; they then gain share and reach a natural maturity once sales plateau; thereafter, the product tends to decline in popularity due to either obsolescence or competitive substitution, and eventually production may be discontinued altogether. Understanding how customers perceive the value of a product with respect to substitutes is critical to the development of an effective marketing strategy.

# Price

The price of the product must be sensitive to customer perceptions, as well as to the product's features and characteristics. Products that are perceived to offer superior value relative to the competition merit premium prices, whereas products that are not differentiated will rarely sell at a premium, and must instead be priced below the market reservation price for the product. In a perfectly competitive market, the price of a product will over time equal the marginal cost of production. But in a monopoly, the market price will exceed the perfectly competitive price, and the quantity supplied will be less than the amount supplied in a perfectly competitive market, allowing the company to earn excess profits. But price-setting can be more than reactive—it can also be an active driver of a company's product strategy: a product's price can be set below market average to drive higher sales volume (a "volume-play" strategy), or it can be set high to maximize the unit margin (a "margin-optimization" strategy). Or the company may try to maximize profits by price discriminating (charging different customer segments different prices), or by extending special pricing offers such as volume discounts, rebates, limited-time promotions, or bundled prices (i.e., reduced price when purchased together with another product).

# Place

The place of sale, or sales channel, determines how a product will come in contact with customers. Alternative sales channels include retail, catalog, and door-to-door, and more recently e-commerce channels like the World Wide Web. Not all products are suited for all sales channels, and conversely not all sales channels can effectively sell all products. The choice of sales channel has a direct impact on sales volume and pricing: a broad retail network will likely drive high sales volume and a higher price to cover the costs of delivering the goods to market; conversely, a narrower direct sales channel such as mail-order catalogs may limit sales volume due to more limited customer exposure, and perhaps offer lower prices due to the absence of middlemen (e.g., third-party wholesale distributors) who tend to charge for additional services (e.g., storage, delivery, financing, payment processing, and promotion).

## Promotion

The promotion of a product is critical to raising customer awareness, and to inducing trial of the product through a purchase. Promotions can be broad-based, attempting to communicate a single message to multiple customer groups simultaneously, or it can be targeted, tailoring specific messages to different customer segments. A product's degree of differentiation will naturally make it more attractive to certain customer segments than others. Similarly, a product's price may attract only certain customer segments, and its primary sales channel may give it access to even fewer. Here, again, targeted promotions may be preferable.

The product, price, and place dimensions all have a direct impact on promotion, and collectively, the four dimensions characterize the environment to which product strategy must respond.

# THE BOSTON CONSULTING GROUP GROWTH-SHARE MATRIX

The growth-share matrix characterizes the relative attractiveness of a company within its industry according to two dimensions: relative market share, and rate of industry growth. All companies can be placed into one of the four quadrants displayed in Figure AI.3.

Companies that are considered to be worth starting, buying, or investing in lie within the upper right or "star" quadrant (high market share and high growth). These companies are expected to flourish because they are already the dominant players, and over time will become even more dominant in a high-growth market. Conversely, companies that should be sold, closed, or avoided as investments are situated in the lower left or "dog" quadrant (low market share and low growth).

**Figure AI.3**
**The Boston Consulting Group Growth-Share Matrix**

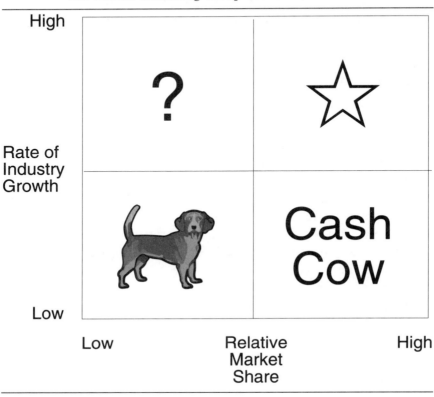

These companies are weak and relatively small, existing in stagnant markets. Lower right "cash cow" companies, due to their low growth and high market share, should be run with the primary purpose of capturing the maximum short-run value—or simply stated, milking the company for all its worth. These companies are worth a lot today, but may not continue to be so in the future. And lastly, companies in the upper left "question mark" quadrant have an uncertain future due to their low relative market share, and are not guaranteed to become attractive over time even though they operate in a high growth market. They may or may not be able to capture the value that is being generated by the market's growth, since their small size may make them vulnerable to the competition.

The growth-share matrix can also be used to discuss product differentiation: brand managers would be advised to focus marketing investments on products in either the star or cash cow quadrants (and arguably even the question mark quadrant), since their high relative market share is likely to secure a high return on marketing investment. New product developers would be wise to invest R&D dollars on products that are likely to lie in the "star" quadrant—high industry growth and high relative market share—since these promise to offer the longest-term profitability.

The matrix is versatile and can also be used to segment markets, or to discuss the evolution of a product over time from a question mark, to a star, to a cash cow, to eventually a dog (i.e., obsolescence).

# BREAKEVEN

The attractiveness of a new business venture or product introduction can be evaluated using a breakeven analysis, which determines the minimum profitability required for an operation to pay for its startup and operating costs without losing or making money. Figure AI.4

**Figure AI.4**
**Breakeven Equation**

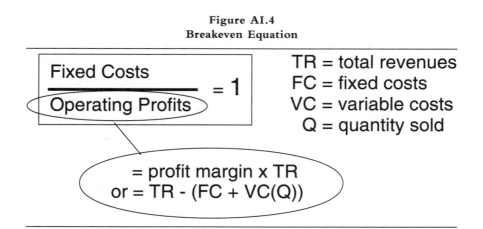

$$\frac{\text{Fixed Costs}}{\text{Operating Profits}} = 1$$

TR = total revenues
FC = fixed costs
VC = variable costs
Q = quantity sold

= profit margin x TR
or = TR - (FC + VC(Q))

details the required inputs into a breakeven equation, with fixed costs (e.g., start-up costs of purchasing equipment, technology, facilities, etc.) in the numerator and operating profits (e.g., the money left over from sales after the variable costs of production are deducted) in the denominator, all set equal to zero.

If, for example, you know the fixed costs of a new business venture and are trying to decide whether to launch the business, you can use the breakeven equation to determine the minimum sales the business will require to make zero profits. If the resulting sales figure seems reasonably attainable, then the business venture may be attractive; but if the required sales are ludicrously high, then the venture has little hope of succeeding. This same type of analysis can be performed if you know the operating margin of a business, for example, and need to determine the minimum number of product units sold to cover the fixed costs. Or if you know the total profits of the venture over a given period of time (e.g., have a contract to supply a certain amount of product to a single buyer with a predetermined price markup), then you can calculate the maximum amount of money the business can spend on start-up costs without losing money. So long as you have data for either the numerator or denominator of the equation, you should be able to calculate the other variables, and make a decision.

## COST-BENEFIT ANALYSIS

Cost-benefit analysis helps to determine whether the beneficial outcomes of a project are sufficient to justify the cost of undertaking the project. This approach is often used to assess capital expenditure projects. The strength of this framework is its simplicity and wide applicability. Simply stated, if the benefits of a project outweigh the associated costs, then the project should be adopted, as seen in Figure AI.5.

For example, assume that you are considering opening a lemonade stand. Assume that you can operate your lemonade business for only one day. Should you do it? Using a cost-benefit framework, you would

**Figure AI.5**
**Cost-Benefit Analysis**

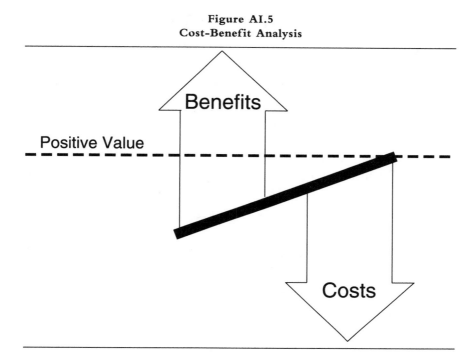

first look at all the potential cost drivers for your new project: ingredients, plastic cups, materials to construct an advertising sign and stand, and so on. Then you would compare these costs against the expected benefits (i.e., the number of cups of lemonade you expect to sell during a single day). If the difference is positive, then you should begin your business. In finance, net present value (NPV) analysis is a slightly more sophisticated version of this because it takes into consideration the impact of time, risk of failure and the cost of financing the project. Although a simple cost-benefit analysis alone will rarely get you through a complex case, it can help you structure your thinking in identifying all the drivers that need to be considered.

# INTERNAL-EXTERNAL ISSUES

The internal-external framework simply divides the analysis of a case into two parts, as seen in Figure AI.6: internal issues (e.g., within a company, an industry, a country), and external issues (e.g., outside the same company, industry, country).

Because of its simplicity and generic applicability, this framework can be helpful in starting an analysis to a case question, especially when you are flustered. For example, if an interviewer wanted you to determine why profits at a company had been steadily decreasing for the

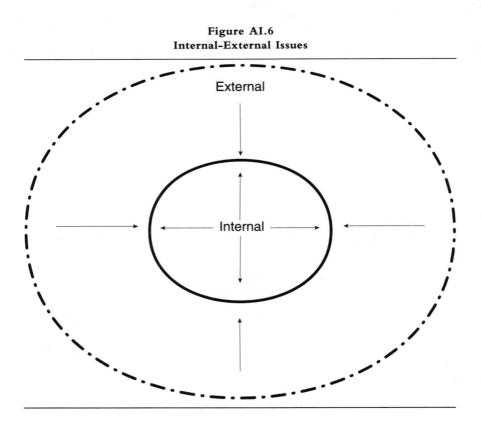

**Figure AI.6**
**Internal-External Issues**

last year, you would naturally want to use the profit equation (described later in this appendix). But what if you could not remember the profit equation? You could save yourself by using an internal-external framework to look for causes of declining profits first inside the company, and then outside the company.

Looking internally, you could discuss the elements of the balance sheet to determine whether the cause is hidden there. Perhaps a new factory was built recently that necessitated a rise in prices? This, in turn, might have negatively impacted sales because of a highly elastic consumer demand function, and therefore the decline in profits would likely be due to diminishing revenues. Notice that we took an internal diagnosis and moved our analysis to the external in this example. We started by evaluating the impact of a new fixed asset, and ended by linking the cause of the decline in profits to the elasticity of consumer demand.

## LIFE CYCLE

Although life cycles have multiple applications, they all have the unique feature of discussing business issues over a time-series. For example, a product life cycle is used to explain the evolution of product attractiveness over time, from the product's introduction, to growth, to maturity, to decline. As a product evolves through each of these stages, its sales will fluctuate, resulting in a slanted "S-shape" curve like the one displayed in Figure AI.7.

Similarly, a service life cycle can be used to describe the changing demand for a service over time, such as for travel agencies, which were once essential to the planning of almost all trips, but today are being replaced by direct-booking channels like the Web. Or a life cycle can be used to describe the spending patterns of an individual over the course of his life, from childhood, to having a family, to retiring.

In each of these cases, life cycles can be used to develop strategy. Brand managers, for example, will most likely want to introduce new products when their existing products approach the zero-growth stage,

**Figure AI.7**
**A Product Life Cycle**

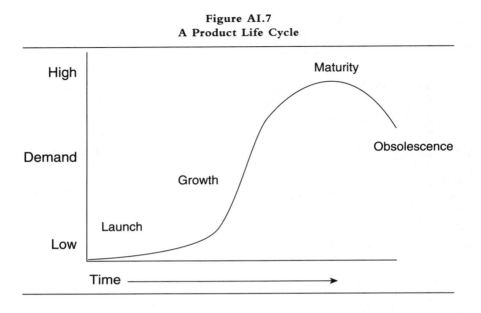

so that the sales growth of new products will compensate for the expected decline of existing products. Life cycles can also be used to describe seasonality (e.g., snowblowers sell more rapidly during winter months than summer), and as a result be schematically drawn as a series of cycles, or a wave.

# MCKINSEY 7-S's (STRATEGY, SKILLS, SHARED VALUES, STRUCTURE, STAFF, SYSTEMS, STYLE)

The McKinsey 7-S framework was developed to evaluate the effectiveness of an organization by explicitly considering seven critical elements of a firm: strategy, institutional skills, shared values (firm culture), structure, staff (people), systems, and style. As Figure AI.8 shows, the key elements of a company are interdependent, and thus, must work together to produce an effective organization.

**Figure AI.8**
**7-S Framework**

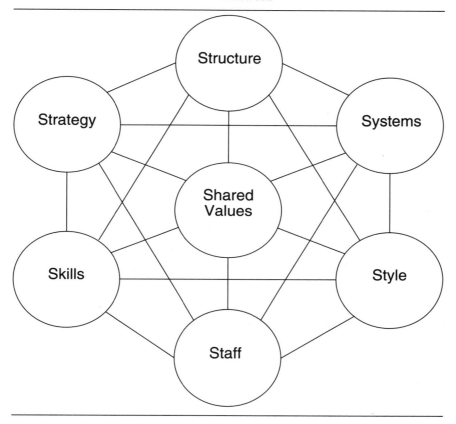

*Source:* Peters, T.J. & Waterman, R.H. *In Search of Excellence* (New York: Warner Books, 1983).

## Strategy

A strategy is a map or a plan of an integrated set of actions designed to achieve specific corporate objectives (e.g., operational efficiency, growth, shareholder value). The strategy is important because it gives direction and purpose to the company, sorts and identifies key

185

organizational needs, and provides a benchmark for measuring the company's success.

## Institutional Skills

Institutional skills refer to an organization's capabilities as well as the abilities of its managers and staff. Institutional skills drive organizational design. That is, other organizational elements must be designed to either build needed skills or properly exploit existing skills. Strategy development is incomplete without explicit consideration of the institutional skills necessary to execute the strategy.

## Shared Values

Shared values refers to the culture of the company. Although it is difficult to objectively evaluate company culture, shared value attributes include attitude toward work, competitive/cooperative nature among colleagues, and communication with corporate leadership. Although this is the most difficult "S-dimension" to influence, it may be shaped by frequent, and consistent communication from top management.

## Structure

Structure refers to the organization of the company: who reports to whom, and how tasks are divided up and integrated. The structure of the organization should be designed to facilitate coordination and integration between the layers of management and staff and focus the organization's attention. The structure should be consistent with the company's culture and skills. The type of structure (e.g., degree of centralization) is one of the key considerations of this dimension.

## Staff

This refers to the company's people in terms of their capabilities, experience, and potential. A company's staff ultimately determines whether the company is able to deliver superior products or service value. Staff composition and productivity are important determinants of present and future strategic success. Key issues include where to look for new hires, who to hire, how to train, and how to properly structure incentives.

## Systems

Systems refers to the processes and procedures that facilitate daily activities. Some important systems include management information systems, incentive systems, and communication. When evaluating the systems of a company, it is important to consider formal or institutionalized systems, and informal or ad hoc systems.

## Style

This refers to leadership style (e.g., supportive, argumentative): how the leaders spend time, what questions they ask, and what settings they appear in. Style can dramatically shape values and reinforce strategy. Although it is difficult to change a leader's personal tone, leadership style may be modified by changing how the leadership spends its time, the questions it asks, and the setting it appears in.

# PORTER'S FIVE FORCES

Michael Porter's Five Force model characterizes the dynamics of competitive rivalry within an industry. Figure AI.9 schematically illustrates the set of players that collectively shape an industry, and depicts the competitive forces that determine an industry's overall profitability.

The five forces interact as follows: (1) Within an industry, *companies* compete for market share by attempting to win customers and capture business from rivals. An activity of one company is likely to be met with a competitive reaction from another company, which in turn is likely to generate other competitive activities from other companies. Industries that have a high number of competitors are likely to face more intense competitive rivalry, and as a result the overall profitability of the industry will tend to be lower.

187

---

$$\text{Profits} = \text{Total Revenues} - \text{Total Costs}$$
$$\text{or}$$
$$\pi = (P \times Q) - (FC + VC(Q))$$

| | |
|---|---|
| $\pi$ = Profits | P = Price |
| TR = Total Revenues | FC = Fixed Costs |
| VC = Variable Costs | Q = Quantity Sold |

APPENDIX I

**Figure AI.9**
**Porter's Five Forces Industry Analysis**

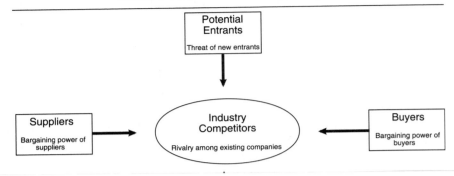

increase, profits should then decrease. The profit equation gives you a structure for remembering not only what the elements are, but also whether the elements cause profits to increase or decrease. For example, an interviewer may ask you the following question:

> Company A makes one variety of widgets. The widget market is currently booming. Company A is selling everything they can make. The huge demand for widgets has even caused the price to rise slightly. But despite all this good news, their profits have been falling. In fact, the more they sell, the worse their profits become. Why?

Using the profit equation, you can quickly highlight a potential cause of diminishing profits: variable cost. As quantity rises, so too might the variable costs of overtime wages, which ultimately may exceed the profit margin on a widget.

## RATIO ANALYSIS[1]

Ratio analysis assesses a company's financial performance and health. This is achieved by evaluating the company's ability to execute the key drivers of profitability and growth: product market, and financial market strategies. As Figure AI.11 shows, these strategies are implemented through the four "levers" of operating management, investment management, financing policies, and dividend policy. Ratio analysis directly evaluates the general profitability of a firm, as well as management's ability to operate each of the four levers.

Ratio analysis can be used in three ways. First, the ratios of a company can be compared over time to determine relative performance improvement or decline. Second, ratios for one company may be compared against the aggregate ratios of other companies (which is a proxy for overall industry performance) to evaluate relative performance. Third, ratios may be compared with a benchmark value to evaluate performance to some predetermined standard (e.g., a financial performance goal). Table AI.1 presents a list of useful ratios and their definitions, which some case interviewers may expect you to be familiar with.

value. Staff composition and productivity are important determinants of present and future strategic success. Key issues include where to look for new hires, who to hire, how to train, and how to properly structure incentives.

## Systems

Systems refers to the processes and procedures that facilitate daily activities. Some important systems include management information systems, incentive systems, and communication. When evaluating the systems of a company, it is important to consider formal or institutionalized systems, and informal or ad hoc systems.

## Style

This refers to leadership style (e.g., supportive, argumentative): how the leaders spend time, what questions they ask, and what settings they appear in. Style can dramatically shape values and reinforce strategy. Although it is difficult to change a leader's personal tone, leadership style may be modified by changing how the leadership spends its time, the questions it asks, and the setting it appears in.

# PORTER'S FIVE FORCES

Michael Porter's Five Force model characterizes the dynamics of competitive rivalry within an industry. Figure AI.9 schematically illustrates the set of players that collectively shape an industry, and depicts the competitive forces that determine an industry's overall profitability.

The five forces interact as follows: (1) Within an industry, *companies* compete for market share by attempting to win customers and capture business from rivals. An activity of one company is likely to be met with a competitive reaction from another company, which in turn is likely to generate other competitive activities from other companies. Industries that have a high number of competitors are likely to face more intense competitive rivalry, and as a result the overall profitability of the industry will tend to be lower.

**Figure AI.9**
**Porter's Five Forces Industry Analysis**

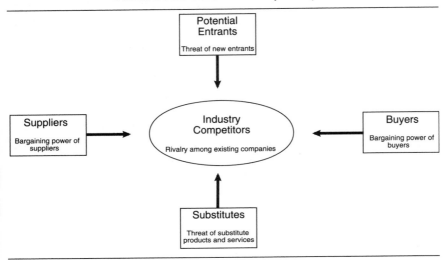

*Source:* Porter, M. *Competitive Strategy: Techniques for Analyzing Industries and Competitors* (Boston: Harvard Business School Press, 1980).

Influencing this cycle of rivalry are other competitive forces: (2) *Suppliers* (entities that provide necessary inputs to the production of the industry good) may be large enough to wield bargaining power over a company, or may band together to generate greater collective bargaining power. Powerful suppliers can increase the costs of inputs, and as a result reduce the profits of the input user. (3) Similarly, *buyers* (customers that purchase the good produced by the industry) may individually or collectively purchase enough quantity of the good to wield bargaining power over a company, and be able to drive prices down. (4) Potential *new entrants* into an industry may threaten to steal market share from existing industry competitors by offering unique customer benefits, for example, or by benefiting from preferential agreements with buyers or suppliers. (5) The industry's product may be threatened with replacement by *substitutes* from other industries.

The collective activity of all five forces produces a competitive environment in which each rival company must respond to, and better yet anticipate, each other's competitive actions, to protect their own interests.

## PROFITS

The profit equation is a function of two drivers, as seen in Figure AI.10: revenue and cost. Two versions of the equation can be written to encompass different levels of detail.

The profit equation can be used as a guide to step through most profit-related case questions, such as companies losing money, or incurring significant costs, or encountering sudden sales declines. To use the equation, look at each of the two drivers separately, breaking each down into its component parts. As the second, more detailed version of the equation shows, there are essentially four inputs that affect profit: price, fixed costs, variable costs, and quantity sold. If price increases, profits should increase. Likewise, if quantity increases, so too should profits increase. However, if either fixed costs or variable costs

**Figure AI.10**
**Profit Equation**

$$\text{Profits} = \text{Total Revenues} - \text{Total Costs}$$
$$\text{or}$$
$$\pi = (P \times Q) - (FC + VC(Q))$$

| | |
|---|---|
| $\pi$ = Profits | P = Price |
| TR = Total Revenues | FC = Fixed Costs |
| VC = Variable Costs | Q = Quantity Sold |

increase, profits should then decrease. The profit equation gives you a structure for remembering not only what the elements are, but also whether the elements cause profits to increase or decrease. For example, an interviewer may ask you the following question:

> Company A makes one variety of widgets. The widget market is currently booming. Company A is selling everything they can make. The huge demand for widgets has even caused the price to rise slightly. But despite all this good news, their profits have been falling. In fact, the more they sell, the worse their profits become. Why?

Using the profit equation, you can quickly highlight a potential cause of diminishing profits: variable cost. As quantity rises, so too might the variable costs of overtime wages, which ultimately may exceed the profit margin on a widget.

## RATIO ANALYSIS[1]

Ratio analysis assesses a company's financial performance and health. This is achieved by evaluating the company's ability to execute the key drivers of profitability and growth: product market, and financial market strategies. As Figure AI.11 shows, these strategies are implemented through the four "levers" of operating management, investment management, financing policies, and dividend policy. Ratio analysis directly evaluates the general profitability of a firm, as well as management's ability to operate each of the four levers.

Ratio analysis can be used in three ways. First, the ratios of a company can be compared over time to determine relative performance improvement or decline. Second, ratios for one company may be compared against the aggregate ratios of other companies (which is a proxy for overall industry performance) to evaluate relative performance. Third, ratios may be compared with a benchmark value to evaluate performance to some predetermined standard (e.g., a financial performance goal). Table AI.1 presents a list of useful ratios and their definitions, which some case interviewers may expect you to be familiar with.

**Figure AI.11**
**The Components of Profitability and Growth**

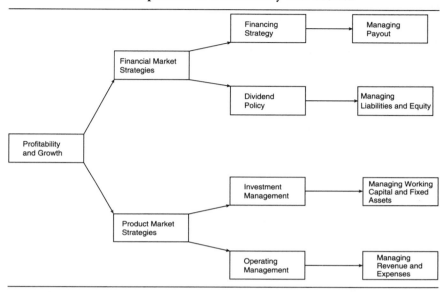

*Source:* Palepo, K.G., Bernard, V.I., & Healy, P.M. *Business Analysis & Evaluation: Using Financial Statements* (Cincinnati: Southwestern Publishing, 1996).

Return on Equity (ROE) is a good indicator of a company's general profitability because it indicates how well the company is using the capital invested by its shareholders (equity) to generate returns. As Table AI.1 shows, there are many ways to measure ROE. Another method of calculating ROE is to use return on assets (ROA) and financial leverage. ROA indicates how much profit a company is able to generate for each dollar invested (assets), and financial leverage indicates how many dollars of assets the firm is able to deploy for each dollar invested.

*Operating management* involves the management of a company's revenues and expenses. Net profit margin (NPM) indicates the residual portion of revenues that the company can keep as profits for each sales dollar. Thus, NPM shows the profitability of a company's operating activities.

**Table AI.1**
**Ratio Analysis**

| Category | Ratio | Definition |
|---|---|---|
| General profitability | Return on equity (ROE) | = NI/SE<br>= (NI/assets) × (assets/SE)<br>= ROA × financial leverage |
| Operating management | Net profit margin | = NI/sales |
| Investment management | Current asset turnover<br>Accounts receivable turnover<br>Days' receivable<br>PP&E turnover | = sales/CA<br><br>= sales/(CA − CL)<br>= AR/average sales per day<br>= sales/PP&E |
| Financing strategy | Current ratio<br>Quick ratio | = CA/CL<br>= (cash + short-term investments + AR)/CL |
| | Cash ratio<br>Operating cash flow ratio<br>Debt-to-equity ratio | = (cash + short-term investments)/CL<br><br>= cash flow from operations/CL<br>= total debt/(total debt + SE) |
| Dividend policies | Dividend payout ratio | = cash dividends paid/NI |

*Note:* AR = accounts receivable, CA = current assets, CL = current liabilities, NI = net income, PP&E = property, plant, and equipment, ROA = return on assets, SE = shareholder's equity.

*Investment management* involves managing a company's working capital and fixed assets. There are several good measures of investment management. Current asset turnover, accounts receivable turnover, and days' receivables are all helpful in analyzing a company's working capital management. Current asset turnover indicates how many dollars of sales a company is able to generate for each dollar invested in current assets. Accounts receivable turnover measures how productively accounts receivable is being used. And finally, days' receivables indicates the number of days of operating activity that are supported by the level of investment in the company's receivables. In terms of fixed asset management, property, plant, and equipment (PP&E) is the most important long-term asset on a company's balance sheet. Thus, PP&E turnover provides a metric for measuring fixed asset management because it shows the amount of sales generated by a dollar's investment in PP&E.

Analyzing a company's *financing strategy* involves evaluating its policies as they relate to their liabilities and equity. Analysis in this area may be divided into two broad categories: short-term liquidity, and long-term solvency. The following ratios are helpful in evaluating a company's ability to meet its short-term obligations: current ratio, quick ratio, cash ratio, and operating cash flow ratio. The first three focus on a company's short-term assets, which could be used to repay short-term liabilities. The fourth focuses on a company's ability to generate the resources to repay the short-term liabilities. In terms of long-term solvency, debt-to-equity ratio indicates how many dollars of debt financing a company is using for each dollar invested. This ratio, along with a few others, is helpful in evaluating how well a company is using debt.

Finally, a company's *dividend policy* can be measured by the dividend payout ratio, which has an inverse relationship with the company's sustainable growth rate. If the dividend payout ratio increases, the sustainable growth rate of the same company will decrease.

# SUPPLY AND DEMAND[2]

Supply and demand are the fundamental building blocks of economics, describing the market interaction between customers and producers. Although the framework is simple, it is a powerful tool that can help you perform three functions: (1) organize information, (2) gain insight into the effects of a change (e.g., increased government regulation, decrease in quantity supplied, etc.), and (3) develop strategies to achieve a given objective. The basic elements of this framework are a supply curve, a demand curve, an equilibrium price, an equilibrium quantity, consumer surplus, and producer surplus, all of which are related to each other in Figure AI.12.

First, the supply-and-demand framework is useful for organizing information. For example, suppose an interviewer asks you to determine the quantity of a good that will be sold, in the long run, given an equilibrium price of P* in a perfectly competitive market. To answer this

### Figure AI.12
### Supply and Demand

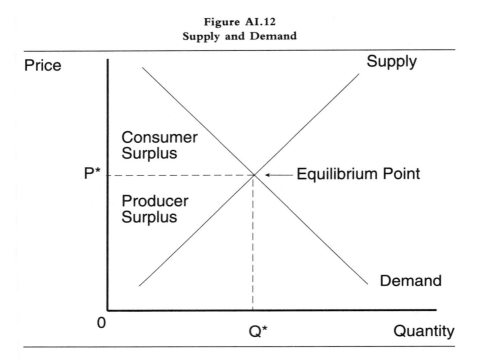

question, you could quickly sketch out the supply-and-demand chart presented in Figure AI.12 and indicate that supply equals demand at the price of P*, and therefore the quantity of the good that will be sold in the long run is Q*—the associated quantity equilibrium point. By using a graphic construct, you are able to convincingly argue your answer, as well as provide an analytical approach to your work.

Second, supply and demand can also be used to understand the effects of a change. For example, consider a technological breakthrough that enables an increase in the production of widgets. If we assume that all companies have this new technology, what would be the effect on the market? The new and more efficient production process would cause a shift in the supply curve outward, reflecting an increase in production. Holding all else constant, this outward shift would result in a decrease in price and an increase in quantity demanded. And the final effect on consumer and producer surplus will depend on the elasticity of the demand curve (i.e., the slope of the demand curve). Thus, by using the framework, you can provide a much more robust and analytical answer.

Third, supply and demand can also help you develop a strategy to achieve a given objective. For example, suppose a company set an objective for itself of increasing revenues. How would it do this? By using a supply-and-demand framework to map out the consumer surplus region, you can see that the company could increase revenues by capturing some of the consumer surplus value. This might be achieved by setting prices higher—but would this drive price-sensitive customers away from the product? Perhaps, so the best strategy would be to price discriminate—segment customers into different groups according to their sensitivity to price, and charge each group a different price. Hence, the supply-and-demand framework is a useful tool for strategy development.

# SWOT (STRENGTHS, WEAKNESSES, OPPORTUNITIES, THREATS)

Unlike Porter's Five Forces, which structures the analysis of industries around five distinct and well-defined dimensions, the SWOT framework, illustrated in Figure AI.13, offers a less restrained industry analysis framework by using four broad categories—strengths, weaknesses, opportunities, and threats—that have a great deal of definitional latitude.

You may be attracted to the framework because its flexibility enables it to be applied to a broad range of case questions. But you should recognize that the framework's flexibility requires greater effort on your part to clarify the key issues of the case before dropping them into the four buckets. And be careful before you pass judgment on what a strength is versus a weakness, or what an opportunity is versus a threat.

A company's strengths and weaknesses can, at times, be hard to define. What may be a strength to one company may actually be a weakness to another. And similarly, a company's strength today may

**Figure AI.13**
**SWOT Framework**

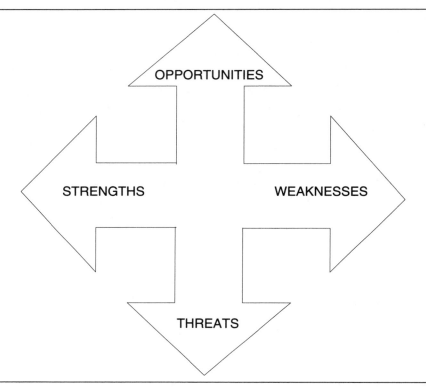

become a significant weakness tomorrow. For example, you might be told that a company enjoys dominant market share in an industry, and that the industry has high barriers to entry due to the high fixed cost of investing in production equipment. Here, you might immediately conclude that the company's dominant market position is a strength. But what if you were then told that the industry was actually doomed to become obsolete through technological innovation? Then, all of a sudden, today's apparent strength becomes an incredible weakness because the company's investment in the high fixed costs of production equipment now locks the company into a dying industry.

Likewise, a company's opportunities and threats may also be hard to define, since an opportunity may actually pose a threat, and a threat may conversely lead a company to discover a new opportunity. For example, the pursuit of an opportunity like a new product launch may actually threaten the core business of a company by diverting resources and funds toward a highly risky venture. And conversely, the threat posed by the entry of a new competitor into an industry may actually become an opportunity by scaring an established company into improving its product quality, production efficiencies, and so on—investments that in the long run may yield higher profitability for the company.

# VALUE CHAIN

A value chain, also known as a business system, is a descriptive framework used to detail a sequence of operational or functional events. The example in Figure AI.14 uses a value chain to describe the production stages of a product.

Value chains assume that the links are not in competition with each other but rather in collaboration, working toward the same collective end goal. Each link in a value chain represents an entity that adds value to the end product or service. Only when the final stage of the chain is reached will the product or service be considered complete. Value chains can also be used to describe other events, such as the process of bringing a finished product to market (e.g., from manufacturer, to shipper, to distributor, to another shipper, to retail store). And each link of a value chain most likely has its own underlying value chain (e.g., a raw material supplier must buy access to its product, perform

**Figure AI.14**
**Value Chain Example**

Raw Material Supplier | Distributor A | Manufacturer | Distributor B | Retailer extraction activities such as quarrying, and then process and refine the product for sale). Any individual link in a chain may seek to backward or forward integrate (i.e., assume responsibility for performing the tasks either ahead of or behind the initial link) to capture greater additional value. And if a single company performs the steps in all the links, it is said to be "fully integrated." Multiple value chains can be used to describe the same process, by breaking down the stages involved in bringing a product to market into discrete steps. As a result, two or more value chains can operate in parallel to achieve greater production efficiency.

# VALUE NET

The Brandenburger and Nalebuff Value Net characterizes all relationships among players in the game of business. Traditionally, a company produces a good using inputs from suppliers, and then competes with other producers to win the favor of customers. With the Value Net, Brandenburger and Nalebuff introduce a new dimension into the game of business: complementors—"those who provide complementary rather than competing products and services."[3] Figure AI.15 schematically describes this dynamic.

The Value Net emphasizes the element of symmetry in relationships. For example, there are competitors and complementors with respect to both customers and suppliers. A company's customers have other suppliers. If those other suppliers make the company's products or services more valuable to the customer, then these companies are complementors. If they make the products or services less valuable, then they are competitors. Similarly, a company's supplier has other customers. These other customers are either competitors or complementors depending on whether they make it more expensive or cheaper for the supplier to produce its products (or services) for the original company. Everything about customers applies to suppliers and everything about competitors applies in reverse to complementors.

It is important to remember that customer, supplier, competitor, or complementor is a role that companies play and the same company will often have multiple roles. To develop an effective strategy, a

**Figure AI.15**
**The Value Net**

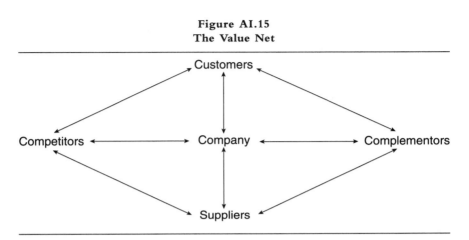

*Source:* Brandenburger, A., & Nalebuff, B. *Co-opetition* (New York: Doubleday, 1996).

company must understand the interests of all four roles each player might have.

While Michael Porter's Five Forces framework (described earlier in this Appendix) is typically associated with discussions of competition between the five types of players in an industry, Brandenburger and Nalebuff introduce a sixth force to the Porter model, namely complementors. This sixth force is not more important than the others, but it is as important and often less well understood.

Another difference between the Value Net and Five Forces is that Porter focuses on the division of the pie, while the Value Net emphasizes both the creation and division of value. Dividing the pie is a zero-sum game, and who does best is determined by the relative power of the players in the game. The Value Net emphasizes the dual aspect of competition and cooperation. Companies work with their customers, suppliers, and complementors to create value (win/win). At the same time, they are in a contest with their customers, suppliers, complementors, and competitors to capture portions of the pie (win/lose). This combination of competition and cooperation is called co-opetition.

# APPENDIX II

## ONE HUNDRED CASE QUESTIONS AND TEN SAMPLE ANSWERS

**Y**our key to successfully navigating the case interview is practice, practice, and more practice. We cannot overemphasize the value of role-playing when learning how to tackle ambiguous and almost certainly unfamiliar questions. Voluminous reading about cases cannot adequately prepare you for the intensity of an actual face-to-face interview.

As you will recall from Chapter 5, the questions asked by consulting firms can be grouped into 10 broad types, presented in Table AII.1. This appendix contains 10 questions from each category. Answers to the first question of each category are presented at the latter half of this appendix. As you begin your preparation for case interviewing, first, make sure that you practice every type of question. Avoiding questions that you find challenging will only hurt your overall preparation. By practicing a variety of question types, you will develop the confidence you need to succeed at any case interview.

Second, consider the relevance of the case questions to different business topics when formulating your answer to a case. If the question involves issues of organizational behavior, for example, it may not be appropriate to answer it using an economics framework (even though you may know economics very well).

Third, when practicing case questions, follow the steps detailed in Chapter 5: (1) listen to the question and repeat it, (2) ask clarifying questions, (3) structure your analysis with a framework, (4) discuss each category of the framework, and (5) summarize and conclude. The more you use this step-by-step approach, the better you will become at answering cases in a methodical, rational, and compelling manner.

Fourth, the cases provided here can be answered in many different ways, using a variety of frameworks and approaches. The sample answers provided are merely illustrative. They are not definitive examples of the "best" possible answers. Read through the sample answers within each type of case question, paying careful attention to recognizing patterns of structure and approach among the group, and then practice applying these patterns to the remaining 90 questions. Remember that the answer to a case is less important than the approach you use to work through the problem. Simply getting an answer right is not enough—interviewers are looking for discussions that are rational, systematic, and persuasive, and only after these three tests are passed will the answer or conclusion be important.

Fifth, work through these cases in role-playing groups of two to three people. Two people can exchange roles as interviewer and

#### Table AII.1
#### Ten Types of Case Questions

1. Brain teaser
2. Business strategy
3. Human resource management
4. Market entry
5. Market sizing
6. Mergers and acquisitions
7. New product introduction
8. Opportunity assessment
9. Pricing
10. Profitability loss

interviewee, and critique each other's performance (while also learning what it is like to be in the interviewer's shoes!). With three people, you can add the role of "observer" into the same exercise, which is often more instructive than the role of interviewer. You should also be careful to work with different people over time, since everyone has a different interviewing style, and you may find yourself becoming too accustomed to one.

Be sure to set time aside each day for practice. In time, you should not only find yourself excelling at cases, but also actually enjoying them.

## SAMPLE CASE QUESTIONS

### TYPE 1   BRAIN TEASER

**Case 1.1**        **Weight of a Boeing 747**
*Answer: p. 226* How much does a Boeing 747 jumbo jet weigh?

**Case 1.2**        **Manhole Covers**
Why are manhole covers round?

**Case 1.3**        **Golf Balls**
How many golf balls will fit into a 50-story skyscraper?

**Case 1.4**        **Bottle Tops**
Why do bottle tops unscrew counterclockwise?

**Case 1.5**        **Coffee Cans**
Why are coffee cans cylindrical in shape?

**Case 1.6**        **Concorde**
Why does the nose of a Concorde passenger jet move up and down?

**Case 1.7**        **House Construction**
In what ways does a house in New Hampshire differ in construction from a house in Florida?

**Case 1.8**        **Moving Mount Fuji**
How many truckloads of earth are required to move Mount Fuji?

**Case 1.9**        **CEO Office**
Why is the CEO's office often on the top floor of a corporate tower? Are there reasons why it should not be?

**Case 1.10**       **Clocks**
Why do the hands on a clock turn clockwise?

### TYPE 2   BUSINESS STRATEGY

**Case 2.1**        **Home Improvement Retailing**
*Answer: p. 227* A nationwide retail chain sells both soft (e.g., clothes) and hard (e.g., hardware) goods in each of its mall-based stores. Consumers, however, find this

mix odd, and the CEO has determined that shoppers of soft goods are very different from shoppers of hard. As a result, he decides to take the hard goods departments out of the stores and build a new chain of stores selling only hard goods, but does not know what format or size would be optimal. Given the information presented in the accompanying chart (Figure AII.1), what would you recommend he do?

**Case 2.2**    **Small Business School**
A small business school in southern Illinois wants to be recognized as a "top 20" business school in the next 10 years. How should the school do it?

**Case 2.3**    **Hollywood Film Production**
A Hollywood production company knows that only 1 movie out of every 20 is a blockbuster. How should the company decide which films to produce, and what should its marketing strategy be?

**Case 2.4**    **Pharmaceutical Patents**
A pharmaceutical company has 20 patented prescription drug products that all face patent expiration in two years or less. A generic brand drug manufacturer has offered to purchase 10 of the patents at a price to be negotiated. If the sale is approved, the pharmaceutical company would have to cede all production rights over the 10 drugs to the generic company for the remaining life of the patents. Should the company sell? If so, then for how much?

**Case 2.5**    **Entertainment Conglomerate**
An entertainment conglomerate in southern California owns an entertainment complex that consists of multiplex movie theaters, concert halls, restaurants, and theme parks. The facilities all share one parking complex, which was recently expanded

**Figure AII.1**
**Home Improvement Retail Industry Average Sales per Square Foot**

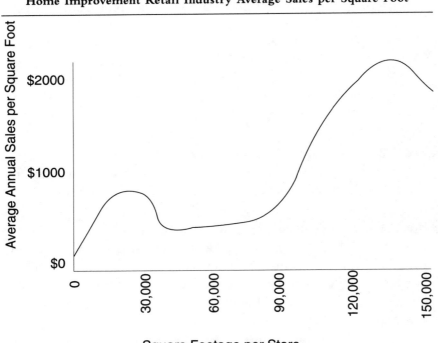

Square Footage per Store

using every available piece of remaining land. But customers are still being turned away due to a lack of parking space. What should the conglomerate do?

**Case 2.6**     **Consumer Products Competition**

A consumer products industry has three manufacturers that collectively own 100 percent of the market. Company 1 has 50 percent market share, company 2 has 40 percent market share, and company 3, your client, has the remaining 10 percent. Consumer research has found that your company's product is far superior in quality to those of the other two, but customers simply do not recognize your brand. Furthermore, your small share means that your company has higher distribution costs, higher manufacturing costs, lower manufacturing capacity, and poor negotiating power with stores for shelf space. What should your company do to increase market share?

**Case 2.7**  **Resuscitation Device**

You are developing a new resuscitation device which has two components: (1) a piece of permanent equipment, and (2) disposable attachments. You will be ready to sell the equipment next month, but the disposable attachments will not be ready for six months. Your competitor is developing the same device, and will be prepared to release both the equipment and the disposable attachments six months from now. What should you do?

**Case 2.8**  **Starting a Firm**

You and several close friends are considering leaving your consulting firm to start your own. Is this a good idea, and if so, what kind of firm should you open?

**Case 2.9**  **Wonder Drug**

On a recent trip to South America, you discovered the Salito flower. Locals claim that the petals from the Salito flower can help people lose weight. How can you make the Salito flower the next Echinacea, without scientific proof and with a very small advertising budget?

**Case 2.10**  **Advertising Strategy**

Your marketing strategy group has developed clever albeit childish advertisements attacking the number one and number two companies in your industry by exaggerating their weaknesses. You are concerned with the reaction to the ads, both by customers and competitors. Should you approve the ads?

## TYPE 3   HUMAN RESOURCE MANAGEMENT

**Case 3.1**       **Recruiting**

*Answer: p. 233* You are the recruiting director of a major consulting firm. Your firm has traditionally been known for very bright and innovative consultants. But what candidates do not know is that the office atmosphere is "cutthroat." Informally, you have been told by several senior partners that the atmosphere needs to change, but they fear that a selection bias in the recruiting process is perpetuating the cutthroat atmosphere. How would you begin to investigate this hypothesis?

**Case 3.2**       **High Tech Start-Up**

The CEO of a leading high tech start-up company is concerned by a recent exodus of nearly 50 percent (or 35 people) of his software engineers. During exit interviews with some of those who resigned, he learned that his company's compensation package of base pay, annual bonus, benefits, and stock options, is anywhere from 20 percent to 200 percent lower than those offered by the competition. However, as a start-up, his company is cash constrained and is resistant to putting additional stress on cash flow. How should he evaluate the situation, and what should he do to stop the exodus and ultimately revitalize his engineering staff?

**Case 3.3**       **Downsizing**

You are the CEO of a company that has just reported its third consecutive annual operating loss of over 100 million dollars. A consulting firm you hired to reengineer the company has recommended that you reduce operating costs by 40 percent through forced retirement or release of 2,000 middle management employees. How will you identify your targets, implement the decision, and position the downsizing effort to the company and investor community?

**Case 3.4**

## Leadership

You are the manager of a consulting team that has been helping a company develop a new electric automobile. Having successfully developed and tested a prototype, the company is ready to establish a new car division around the product and build 10,000 units for sale. But you have serious concerns about the leadership competencies of the individual nominated to head the division, even though she was working on the project since the beginning. On more than one occasion, you had to bail her out to avoid seriously embarrassing or disastrous consequences. What should you do?

**Case 3.5**

## Conflict Management

A real estate developer has had to stop construction of a 50-story luxury apartment building after its general contractor unexpectedly filed for bankruptcy. As a result, all the stakeholders in the project have threatened to file lawsuits against the developer to get their money back: investors, individuals who purchased apartments in advance, and the subcontractors who performed work and have yet to be paid by the general contractor. The developer wants to hold the project together, and needs one month to find additional project financing and a new contractor. How should she manage the impending conflict between the vested parties, and buy herself some time?

**Case 3.6**

## Profit Sharing

Cross Cultural Air (CCA) is an international airline with routes to various cities in the United States, Asia, Europe, and Africa. Five years ago, CCA was hailed as a cutting-edge airline when it instituted a generous profit sharing plan. The plan called for crews (pilots, flight attendants, etc.) to share profits based on the profitability of the route they serve. The idea was that crews who only flew short domestic flights should not get the same profits as those who served longer and more strenuous, international flights. In the five years since the plan was instituted, CCA noticed that morale has declined, and the recruiting and retention of new pilots has been more difficult. This is very surprising, considering that the plan was designed to specifically address these issues. What should CCA do?

**Case 3.7**

**Scapegoat**

You are the Senior Vice President at Brettenham Pharmaceuticals, the U.S. subsidiary of Brettenham Holding Group (BHG), a British holding company. Senior officials from BHG are planning a U.S. visit to inquire about the recent failure of Facor, a fat-reducing drug. You have been made aware of a plan to fire the product manager for Facor. You know BHG wants an explanation and action for the failure, but you feel that it is unfair to blame a single person. What should you do?

**Case 3.8**

**New Technology**

You are the new CEO of Winston Auto. Winston has a long tradition of building some of the finest automobiles in the world. Each model is hand-built requiring over two months and thousands of worker hours. Winston has two plants in the United States. Although Winston enjoys strong customer loyalty, growth has been stagnant for the past 10 years. It is your responsibility to increase either profits or revenues—or preferably both. You are considering automating a portion of the construction process, thereby reducing your costs and turning out more cars, but your employees are opposed to this. They have informed you of their intention to strike and begin a negative public relations campaign. Customer loyalty, as well as attracting new customers, is crucial for Winston's continued survival. What should you do?

**Case 3.9**

### Corporate Culture

You are the president of a large advertising firm. Several months ago, your company purchased a small PR firm. You thought that the merger was going well. However, it has come to your attention that the employees of the new firm are unhappy with the small kitchen that was installed in their new office space. You thought they would be delighted to have a kitchen at all because no other floor in the building has one. And now your employees are grumbling that the employees from the acquired company are being given too much. You want the merger to work, but you do not want to upset your existing employees. What options do you have?

**Case 3.10**

### Consulting Engagement

Your consulting team has been working diligently on a project for the past two months and is now nearing completion of the final presentation. But when you called one of the client team members this morning to verify some information, he unexpectedly told you that the vice president who hired your firm feels unacceptably distanced from your team's work, and is likely to reject all your firm's recommendations, believing that they are unfounded and inadequately researched. What should you do?

## Appendix II

### Type 4   Market Entry

**Case 4.1**   **Italian Pottery**

*Answer: p. 235* A family-owned pottery manufacturer in Assisi, Italy, has decided to export its handcrafted wares to the United States, but needs your help to determine how. The manufacturer is considering three options: (1) sell directly to stores; (2) sell to distributors, who then sell to individual stores; and (3) open its own chain of proprietary stores. What should the manufacturer do?

**Case 4.2**   **Consulting Firm**

A Boston-based start-up consulting firm has grown from 3 consultants to 100 in two years. It is now prepared to expand overseas and work with global clients. How would you help the firm develop a strategy, and what would you recommend?

**Case 4.3**   **Sports League Expansion**

You are the Commissioner of the NFL, and have learned that the League's profitability has leveled over the past 10 years. You are considering expanding the league to include teams in foreign countries to increase profits. Which countries should you enter, how, and when?

**Case 4.4**   **Auto Franchises**

A Korean auto manufacturer wants to enter the French market and is looking for franchise distributors. The company will supply 50,000 luxury cars per year at a wholesale price of $20,000 each, and suggests a retail price of $30,000. How many individual franchise distributors should the company establish in the first year?

**Case 4.5**   **Baby Clothes**

Your company is the number one manufacturer of baby clothes. Recently, a leading designer of women's apparel, Marie Briscoe, has launched its own line of baby clothes. What should your response be?

**Case 4.6**    **Electric Car**

You have just developed an electric car that has a top speed of 90 miles per hour, and a total battery operating time of six hours. Your production costs per car total $9,000, which is less than half of the cost of the closest competitor. Where should you first sell this car, and what would be your long-term strategy?

**Case 4.7**    **Water Filter**

Water filtration products have traditionally not sold well in rural U.S. communities because of the purity of local reservoirs. However, your boss believes that rural markets are the next growth area for water filtration devices, and has asked you to devise a rural market entry plan. What would you recommend?

**Case 4.8**    **Donut Chain**

A Texas-based chain of donut shops, A-Donut-A-Day, is considering nationwide expansion. How should the chain determine where to locate the first 100 company-owned shops?

**Case 4.9**    **Web Site**

A nonprofit environmental action group is considering building a Web site, since most of its peers have already done so. Why would the organization want to have a Web presence? What should be the content of the Web site?

**Case 4.10**    **Airport Gates**

A Midwest regional airline is prepared to expand its routes to the West Coast, but finds that all the gates at the San Francisco airport are rented to other airlines for at least five years. What should the regional airline do?

## Appendix II

### Type 5  Market Sizing

**Case 5.1**

*Answer: p. 239*

**Gourmet Coffee Shops**

**Part I:** A large coffee processing company has seen sales of its well-known supermarket brand coffee drop 15 percent per year over the past five years. As a result, manufacturing costs per pound of coffee are increasing, since 25 percent of the machines are no longer being used, and monthly production has dropped by 50,000 pounds. Meanwhile, gourmet coffee chains are growing rapidly across the United States. Should the company try to capture some of this growth by opening its own proprietary chain of gourmet coffee stores?"

**Part II:** How many individual coffee stores could the company supply, if it has 50,000 pounds of excess monthly production capacity? Assume one pound of coffee yields 10 cups of brewed coffee.

**Case 5.2**

**Gas Stations**

How many gas stations are in the United States?

**Case 5.3**

**Ridership of New York City Subways**

How many people ride the New York City subway during the morning rush hour?

**Case 5.4**

**College Pizza Consumption**

How many square feet of pizza are consumed on a college campus in a year?

**Case 5.5**

**Airplanes in Flight**

At noon on a typical weekday, how many airplanes are flying over the United States?

**Case 5.6**

**Diaper Demand**

Determine the annual demand for diapers in the United States.

**Case 5.7**

**Windshield Wipers**

How many pairs of windshield wipers are manufactured in the United States each year?

Case 5.8     **Fortune 500 Market Value**
What is the cumulative market value of the Fortune 500?

Case 5.9     **Lightbulb Sales**
How many lightbulbs were sold in the United States last year?

Case 5.10     **Tea in China**
Determine the annual demand for tea in China.

## TYPE 6   MERGERS AND ACQUISITIONS

Case 6.1     **HMO Acquisition**

*Answer: p. 244* A New York based health maintenance organization (HMO) is considering expanding its operations. They currently have the funds to purchase another HMO. Their internal M&A group has identified two possible targets: Allied HMO in Miami, and Washington Health in Seattle. Which should they purchase?

Case 6.2     **Merger Discontinuance**
Your company has been engaging in merger discussions with another company for the past year, and as a result the stock prices of both companies have risen by 30 percent. However, the two companies have come to a mutual realization that their businesses are not as compatible as previously thought. How should the companies announce their decision to remain independent, while still protecting their stock prices from sudden collapse?

Case 6.3     **Auto Parts Chain Acquisition**
A publicly held supermarket chain seeks profit-generating opportunities to increase its stock price and offer higher earnings per share. An undervalued auto parts chain has been identified, and evidently needs a cash infusion to pay off its mounting debt. Should the supermarket acquire the auto parts chain?

| | |
|---|---|
| **Case 6.4** | **Air Conditioner Company Acquisition** |

Our client is a conglomerate. One of its subsidiaries is a manufacturer of air conditioning systems that also performs the service of installing the sold units. In the past, there was a fierce price war between this conglomerate and an independent, family-owned air conditioning business. Recently, the family has approached the conglomerate and offered its company for sale. Should the conglomerate buy the family business? If so, what would the contractual and pricing arrangements be?

| | |
|---|---|
| **Case 6.5** | **Airline Synergies** |

Two major U.S. airlines have discussed the advantages of forming one airline and are now considering two scenarios: (1) One airline could simply purchase the other; or (2) the two airlines could merge under one name, and fully integrate their reservation systems, flight routes, and rewards programs into one. Which of the two options would be optimal for both airlines?

| | |
|---|---|
| **Case 6.6** | **Oil Exploration** |

A major U.S. oil company has been approached by an oil exploration company with a proposal to merge. Should the oil company agree, or instead continue to contract out all of its exploration?

| | |
|---|---|
| **Case 6.7** | **Cement Company** |

A cement company has just acquired another cement company that owns a 1,000 acre forest located 200 miles north of San Francisco. Our client would like to know what to do with the forest?

| | |
|---|---|
| **Case 6.8** | **Chemical Conglomerate** |

A holding company that owns 10 small chemical manufacturing companies has recently purchased an 11th one. Should the conglomerate operate all 11 companies under one consolidated name, or continue to operate them independently under their original names?

**Case 6.9**      **Company Valuation**

You are considering buying a start-up company that is trying to develop a new polymer but as of yet does not have a product to sell. How would you determine the value of the company?

**Case 6.10**      **Gin Distillery Acquisition Options**

Should a gin distillery expand by acquiring a beer company, a fruit juice company, or a chip dip company?

## TYPE 7    NEW PRODUCT INTRODUCTION

**Case 7.1**      **Cricket Ball Exports to the United States**

*Answer: p. 247* A U.K.-based cricket ball manufacturer seeks sales expansion opportunities in the United States. Current production is at full capacity, but US$500 million has been allocated to build additional capacity. Should the company introduce the product in the United States?

**Case 7.2**      **Nylons-R-US**

Nylons-R-US (NRU is a subsidiary of Athena Conglomerate) has developed a new hosiery that is 300 percent more durable than regular brands. The lifespan of the product is twice that of the old. Athena requires that all new projects show $100 million in U.S. revenues by the fifth year after launch. NRU is considering setting the price at $1.00 per unit. Should NRU go ahead with this project?

**Case 7.3**      **Olive Canning**

A food product canning company has decided to introduce a new canned olives product. Should the company offer prepitted olives, or olives with pits?

**Case 7.4**    **Hayatem**

Zorost Pharmaceuticals has been developing Hayatem, a revolutionary new weight-loss drug, for the past seven years. Clinical trials have shown that Hayatem, along with proper exercise and diet, can safely help individuals lose weight. Zorost has been simultaneously developing an over-the-counter version of the drug and a prescription version. Unfortunately, Brein, the leading weight loss drug, was linked to breast cancer and was hastily pulled from the market. The public seems to have a general distrust about weight loss drugs in general. Should Zorost introduce any of the drugs, and if so, how?

**Case 7.5**    **AME Biotech**

AME, a large, multinational biotech, is searching for new products to develop. You have a meeting with the CEO in a few hours. He wants three alternative methods for developing new products, and your recommendation of the one AME should pursue.

**Case 7.6**    **Cereal Manufacturer**

A major U.S. manufacturer of breakfast cereals currently produces 10 different brands, and collectively has a 30 percent market share. Five of the brands are positioned to attract children, while the other five tend to be purchased by health-conscious adults. Since the total U.S. cereal-eating population has remained relatively constant in size, the only way the company can increase market share is by taking sales away from the competition. To do so, the company seeks to develop five new cereals within the next year, and hopefully capture customers who previously did not buy the company's brands. What step-by-step strategy would you advise to help the company develop and introduce five new cereals?

**Case 7.7**     **Home Diagnostics**

Smith Labs, a diagnostics company, is seeking ways to expand its core competency: diagnostic services. It is currently completing the development of a multiuse home diagnostic kit, targeted to home-bound elderly patients who need diagnostic services. The kit's final design will depend on the marketing strategy for introducing this product. What should the strategy be, in terms of price, promotional strategy, and distribution channels?

**Case 7.8**     **Small Business**

Heartland Consulting Group is a small management consulting firm based in Columbus, Ohio. They specialize in small business consulting and are about to launch an Internet-based consulting tool for small businesses. The program will be able to help small business owners with basic management questions. How should the product be designed to add value to the customer without taking business away from Heartland?

**Case 7.9**     **Personal Computers**

A major manufacturer of personal computers is going to design a desktop model to suit the needs of a specific customer segment: homemakers. What design process would you recommend to ensure a close "fit" between the features of the model, and customer needs?

**Case 7.10**     **Rewards Program**

An Internet-access provider is considering offering a points-based rewards program to its subscribers. One point would be credited for every dollar spent by a subscriber, in any of the following activities: (1) paying the monthly membership fee of $19.95, (2) purchasing items through the provider's on-line shopping service, and (3) signing up additional members. How should the company decide whether to offer this rewards program?

## TYPE 8   OPPORTUNITY ASSESSMENT

**Case 8.1**       **On-line Bookstore**

*Answer: p. 251* If a book distributor were thinking about launching an on-line bookstore, what would be its estimated annual sales?

**Case 8.2**       **Light SUVs**

A small automobile company in Japan is considering developing a new lightweight sport utility vehicle (LSUV). The car is designed to attract women who want the size of an SUV, but also want a vehicle that drives like a car. The company has a $10 million R&D budget with a monthly burn rate of $200,000, and knows that development costs will be high. Venture capital funds are likely to be needed, but VC firms are only interested in projects that have a very high upside. The meeting with a potential VC investor is next week. What should the company tell the investor?

**Case 8.3**       **Profitability of Backward Integrating**

Could a juice manufacturer significantly increase its profitability by backward integrating?

**Case 8.4**       **Express Mail**

Could an overnight express mail company build a viable new business by introducing two- and three-day delivery service? If so, how would it differentiate itself from the competition, and by approximately how much would its revenues increase?

**Case 8.5**       **Microbrewery**

A restaurant-based microbrewery in Montana produces three types of beer: a dark stout, a medium amber beer, and a light pale ale. All three have been very popular among customers, and are often sold out. As entrepreneurs, the owners of the brewery have naturally thought about expansion, and now have dreams of selling their beers nationwide. How would you help them evaluate the idea? If it seems to be a viable business opportunity, what strategy would you suggest?

**Case 8.6**

**Pastry Shop**

A famous European pastry chef has for decades owned and operated a café in New York City. With a flair for the dramatic, the chef has become renowned for catering special occasions, such as weddings, New Year's parties, and black-tie dinners. He would now like to offer a new "breakfast in bed" service, where customers could arrange in advance for delivery of an elegant breakfast or brunch spread to their apartments, complete with flowers, chinaware, and fine linen. How many "breakfast in bed" customers would you expect the café to attract? With what pricing scheme? Could you improve on the business concept?

**Case 8.7**

**Device Manufacturer**

A venture capital firm is considering investing $5 million in a start-up device company that is developing a somewhat controversial method of storing blood products. The VC will be given a certain equity stake in the company for its investment. They have asked you to develop a model to determine how equity should be shared between the company and the VC firm.

*Case 8.8*

*Woman's Week*

*Woman's Week,* a newsstand magazine, is considering using the Internet to increase its readership. Would you recommend this strategy?

**Case 8.9**       **DLS Consulting Group**

DLS Consulting Group has a well established strategy-based consulting practice, and is considering offering information technology consulting services. The primary motivation of this interest is not to enter a new consulting field, but rather to increase the firm's profit margin. Is this a good way for the firm to improve its profitability?

**Case 8.10**      **Eye Care Center**

The Eye Care Center has developed a new technique for correcting nearsightedness. The technique involves using a microscalpel, and is considered a somewhat risky procedure. But if successful, the surgery permanently corrects the problem. What should their optimistic, pessimistic, and realistic market demand forecasts be?

## TYPE 9   PRICING

**Case 9.1**       **Amtrak Rail Ticket**

*Answer: p. 254* How does Amtrak price a rail ticket from Boston to Washington, DC?

**Case 9.2**       **Pharmacies**

You own a pharmacy that promises to meet or beat any competitor's prices. Your brother-in-law's pharmacy next door is exactly the same size, shares the same product mix as you, and advertises the same price guarantee. You both have the same volume of customers, but your brother-in-law's revenues are much higher. Why?

**Case 9.3**       **U.S. Post Office Stamps**

How does the U.S. Post Office price a first-class, 1-ounce letter stamp?

**Case 9.4**       **Stock Exchange**

How are the stock prices on the New York Stock Exchange determined?

| | |
|---|---|
| **Case 9.5** | **Flat Tax Rate** |
| | If the United States switched to a flat income tax, what percentage tax rate would enable the government to collect the same level of revenue as today? |
| **Case 9.6** | **Sports Car Development** |
| | An Italian car company wants to develop and introduce a new sports car in the United States. What considerations should be taken into account when determining the style, features, target customers, and ultimately the price of the car? |
| **Case 9.7** | **Airline Seat Pricing** |
| | Passengers on any given flight rarely pay the same price for seats in the same class. How do airlines determine the optimal mix of prices? |
| **Case 9.8** | **Red Wine** |
| | How is the retail price of a bottle of red wine determined? |
| **Case 9.9** | **Valentine's Day** |
| | On Valentine's Day, how should a florist price flowers other than roses? |
| **Case 9.10** | **Newspaper Pricing** |
| | The price of a one-year subscription to a newspaper is higher for the on-line version than the paper version. Does this make sense? |

## TYPE 10   PROFITABILITY LOSS

| | |
|---|---|
| **Case 10.1** | **Pharmaceutical Drugs** |
| *Answer: p. 257* | The CEO of a major pharmaceutical company wants to know why the profits of one of its leading over-the-counter drugs declined by 25 percent over the past year. |
| **Case 10.2** | **Blacksmith Shop** |
| | A blacksmith in Vermont owns and operates a custom wrought-iron shop, specializing in artistic gates and fencing. Over the past decade, the blacksmith |

has enjoyed steady business and has been able to develop a reputation of high quality and reliability. As a one-man shop, he has always had more work than he could handle, and could afford to be selective in the commissions he accepted. However, over the past two years, his annual income has dropped dramatically. Why?

**Case 10.3**     **TLJ Hot Dogs**

TLJ sells hots dogs from a small vending stand on the corner of 57th and Madison in New York City. TLJ actively price discriminates, by selling different hot dog combinations (i.e., toppings) for different prices at different times of day. Does this maximize his profits? Under what conditions would this approach fail? In answering this question, consider the practical barriers to perfect price discrimination.

**Case 10.4**     **Lumber Company Profit Loss**

A medium-size lumber milling company in Oregon has recently been experiencing a dramatic loss in profits. It owns and operates two mills located 25 miles apart, and also owns and operates a large tree farm. Approximately 50 percent of its wood is supplied from the farm, while the remaining 50 percent comes from sources in Canada. Should the company close one of its mills and consolidate operations? If not, what should it do?

**Case 10.5**     **Price Maintenance**

In the competitive game of airline pricing, airlines are encouraged to undercut their competitors to win customers. However, if prices continue to fall as competitors promote lower and lower prices, eventually zero if not negative profits will be made by all competitors. How can an airline attempt to control the pricing market, and not get trapped in a zero-profit price war?

**Case 10.6**  **Takamiya**

Takamiya Computers builds and sells hardware to Fortune 500 companies. However, they have noticed that their profits have leveled off over the past three years. How can they boost their profit margins?

**Case 10.7**  **Custom Windows and Doors**

A leading manufacturer of custom-made wood windows and doors located in Maine has developed a reputation for high quality, on-time, and competitively priced work. Over the past two years, however, the manufacturer has earned zero profit despite a backlog of work. Evidently, the costs of labor and wood materials have risen dramatically. What options does the company have, and what actions would you recommend to restore the company to profitability?

**Case 10.8**  **Deseret Printing Shop**

Deseret Printing Shop has been automating certain functions within their shops (6 sites across Utah, Colorado, and California), but they have not yet realized their expected profit increases. Why?

**Case 10.9**  **Outlet Malls**

The largest outlet mall in the United States is being developed outside Chicago. For the development group to maximize profits, how should it organize the mall, and which retailers should be invited to open stores in the mall?

**Case 10.10**  **Atlantic Daily**

Atlantic Daily is a newspaper with a circulation of 250,000 subscribers. After two other "specialized" newspapers came into the market, Atlantic saw its profits dwindle. Since a recent survey showed that people are reading more newspapers as the number of papers increase, why are profits for Atlantic going down? How should Atlantic respond?

# SOLUTIONS TO SELECTED CASE QUESTIONS

### TYPE 1   BRAIN TEASER

**Case 1.1   Weight of a Boeing 747**

How much does a Boeing 747 jumbo jet weigh?

*Elements of a Basic Answer*

*Framework:* Divide a 747 into variable and fixed-weight components, and calculate the weight of each.

1. Variable weights:
   - Passengers: A 747 can hold approximately 400 people. At 150 lbs. per person, the total weight of the passengers is $400 \times 150$ lbs. = 60,000 lbs.
   - Baggage: If each person carries two suitcases, weighing approximately 50 lbs. each, then the total baggage weight is $400 \times 50$ lbs. $\times$ 28 bags = 40,000 lbs.
   - Cargo: In addition to the baggage, a 747 can carry other cargo such as mail and overnight packages. To simplify the calculation, let's assume it is at least equal to the weight of the baggage: 40,000 lbs.
   - Supplies: Each of the passengers must be provided with meals, drinks, and other necessities. If we assume that each passenger accounts for 10 pounds of such supplies, we then have $400 \times 10$ lbs. = 4,000 lbs.
   - Fuel: A 747 can travel as far as New York City to Tokyo. Since a New York City to Tokyo round trip will usually provide a passenger with a free domestic US ticket on a frequent flyer program, we can assume the round-trip mileage to be 25,000 miles (the average required mileage for a free domestic ticket), and the one-way trip to be 12,500 miles. A 747 has four engines, each of which consumes much more fuel than a car engine; therefore, we know that each 747 engine must get far fewer than 25 miles to the gallon. To be conservative, we can assume that each engine gets 1 mile to the gallon. Thus, the total fuel consumed on the longest one-way trip is 12,500 miles $\times$ 1 mile/gal. $\times$ 4 engines = 50,000 gal. In terms of weight, we can assume 1 gallon equals 3 lbs., so 50,000 gal equals 150,000 lbs.

2. Fixed weights:
   - The structure: We can estimate the weight of a 747's fuselage, wings, engines, and all other component parts by comparing the size of a 747 to the size of another unit of machinery that we are more familiar with, such as a car. If we assume the weight of an average car is two tons, or 4,000 lbs., we can estimate the weight of a 747 by approximating the number of cars that will fit into a 747. A simple approach would divide the number of passengers that can ride a 747 (400 people) by the number of passengers that can ride in a car (5 people), thus approximating the number of cars that would fit in a plane: $400/5 = 80$ cars. The weight of these 80 cars is $80 \times 4,000$ lbs. $= 320,000$ lbs.

3. The total weight of a 747 is simply the sum of each of these component weights:

   | | |
   |---|---|
   | • People | 60,000 lbs. |
   | • Luggage | 40,000 lbs. |
   | • Cargo | 40,000 lbs. |
   | • Supplies | 4,000 lbs. |
   | • Fuel | 150,000 lbs. |
   | • Structure | 320,000 lbs. |
   | | 614,000 lbs. |

(Boeing reports that a 747 can weigh up to 875,000 lbs.)[1]

### *Elements of an Outstanding Answer*

An outstanding answer would refine the total weight figure through two additional steps:

1. Identify the weight components which could vary considerably according to the distance of the flight, such as fuel.

2. Dissect the fixed weights into their components (i.e., seats, overhead bins, toilets, steel body, and wings, etc.) to derive a more "accurate" calculation.

• • •

## TYPE 2   BUSINESS STRATEGY

**Case 2.1**   **Home Improvement Retailing**

A nationwide retail chain sells both soft (e.g., clothes) and hard (e.g., hardware) goods in each of its mall–based stores. Consumers, however, find this mix odd, and the CEO has determined that shoppers of soft goods are very different from shoppers of hard. As a result, he decides to take the hard goods departments out of the stores and build a new chain of stores selling only hard goods, but does not know what format or size would be optimal. Given the information presented in the accompanying chart (Figure A.II.1), what would you recommend he do?

## Elements of a Basic Answer

*Framework:* First interpret the chart to learn as much as possible about the retail environment, and then perform a 3-C's analysis: Company, Customers, and Competitors.

**1.** Chart interpretation:
- This chart displays the average sales per square foot of all retail home improvement stores in aggregate, including hardware stores, specialty home improvement stores (paint, carpet, etc.), and "big box" superstores.
- Evidently, sales per square foot increase dramatically as small stores increase in size, but then taper off again. Similarly, large stores also exhibit a rapid increase in sales per square foot as size increases, but then again show signs of diminishing returns as the square footage approaches 150,000. All the stores in between the two peaks appear to have nearly identical sales per square foot, regardless of size.
- Small stores are likely to be hardware stores, located within cities. Due to high city rents, hardware stores tend to be smaller than 5,000 square feet, and quite cramped. The merchandise offered will cater to the apartment dweller, who will usually only enter a hardware store to purchase items for a repair or small project. Similarly, contractors are likely to make only "convenience" or "emergency" purchases at a hardware store, and prefer larger non-city stores for significant purchases. As a result, customers shopping at city hardware stores will typically purchase only one or two small items. To compensate for low sales

volume and high rents, hardware stores charge much higher prices than other home improvement stores. Why do customers pay these higher prices? Simply for the convenience of only having to walk down the street. The chart supports this argument by showing that small stores typically have higher sales per square foot than medium–size stores.

- The medium–size stores are likely to be suburban specialty home improvement stores, such as paint stores, tile stores, or carpet stores. These stores sell only one (maybe two) home improvement categories, and serve as a destination for customers who have a specific project to perform. Although both consumers and contractors are likely to shop at a specialty store and purchase multiple items, these stores still display lower sales per square foot than either the small or large stores. Why? This is most likely due to a number of factors: a poor ability to encourage customers to purchase incidentals (e.g., batteries); an inability to benefit from customer cross-shopping (e.g., a customer who came to the store to buy paint also realizing that she needs plant food); and a weakened ability to serve as a one-stop shop for customers needing items in multiple product categories. As a result, the combination of larger stores and fewer customers is responsible for lower sales per square foot.

- Large stores capture the highest sales per square foot for two reasons: (1) they are one-stop shops, offering not only the greatest selection within a product category, but also the greatest number of categories; (2) a large percentage of sales come from contractors, who may purchase thousands if not millions of dollars of merchandise from a single superstore in one year. Customers who shop at superstores hardly ever "just drive by;" rather, they make a conscious decision to drive to the store and sacrifice time for the benefit of selection, lower prices, and ultimately the convenience of not having to make a second trip to another store.

Now that we have interpreted the chart and learned about the industry, we can return to the original question of what retail size and format our client should adopt.

229

**2.** Company:
- The size and format of the new store should be designed to maximize sales per square foot. But it would be hasty to immediately recommend a big box format due to its superior sales performance, since we do not know if the current home improvement section in the department store has enough product categories to fill a superstore.

**Q** What product categories do we currently sell?

**A** We sell hand and power tools, hardware, electrical, plumbing, appliances, and paint and wallpaper.

- With so few categories, we can see that a big box store would be hard to fill. We currently have no experience with lumber, roofing materials, building materials, and lawn and garden, to name a few. Suddenly, the superstore format seems less attractive. But should we alternatively recommend a medium-size specialty store, or a hardware store at this point? We first need to know more about the competitive advantages of the store's hard goods to decide.

**Q** What brands do we carry?

**A** Some of our categories carry all the major brands, such as power tools, but others only offer our own proprietary brands such as hand tools. In fact, our hand tools brand has been proven through customer research to have the strongest reputation of quality and reliability. In addition, we also have our own brands of paint, and appliances, but carry other brands as well.

- If we have a superior hand tool brand, perhaps we should open a specialty hand tool store. But then what should we do with the other categories? Eliminate them? We need to know more about our customers before we can make such a decision.

**3.** Customers:

**Q** Who are our primary customers?

**A** We currently attract both consumers and contractors. Hard goods consumers tend to shop for a collection of items, and never even enter the soft goods sections of the store. Most consumers come back again at a later date to do more shopping. Contractors, on the other hand, typically come in to buy our proprietary brand of hand tools, and occasionally buy from the other categories at the same time, but rarely frequent our stores.

- Based on this response, it appears that the store benefits from having multiple product categories. A hand-tools-only store might not offer a strong enough reason for a consumer to enter, and while it may be attractive to contractors, this format would not be able to cross-sell additional products to contractors.

**Q** Do our customers also shop at other home improvement stores?

**A** Yes. Consumer research shows that most of our customers also shop at hardware stores for convenience, and big box stores for variety. They shop with us when they either need one of our superior hand tools, or would like advice on an item or project from one of our respected associates, or want one of our brands of appliances or paint. In short, we represent reliability and trust to our customers—that's why they come back.

- We have now learned that the store offers other respected brands in addition to hand tools. A hand-tools-only store can now be rejected in addition to the big box format.

**4.** Competitors:
- With two of the three format options eliminated, we should now test the concept of a hardware store.

**Q** Since our customers shop at all three types of stores, I would assume that our competition includes all home improvement retailers. But to what extent do hardware stores steal our customers away from us?

**A** Hardware stores have only a small impact on our competitiveness, primarily because of their superior neighborhood convenience. Our customers are willing to drive the extra mile, however, just to purchase our brands and talk to our respected associates. Ironically, we lose more customers because we are located in malls, and because we also sell products like underwear and designer suits, than because of the home improvement competition.

- At this point, we have enough evidence to strongly support a "hybrid" store format, one that is large enough to offer each of our product categories, and is also located outside the high-rent cities (since our customers are evidently willing to drive to us). We could call this format a "large suburban hardware store," a format that is new to the industry. These stores would allow us to continue to offer our proprietary brands, which are critical to getting customers in the store, and at the same time satisfy their cross-shopping interests. We would not have to learn how to merchandise new product categories, and could operate stores similar in size to the current hard goods department. Finally, we would avoid direct competition with the city hardware stores, and offer an easier, more convenient shopping experience for consumers and contractors that do not have the time or energy to navigate voluminous superstores.

## Elements of an Outstanding Answer

Although no numbers were provided, an improved answer would include a brief quantitative analysis to determine if the hybrid format could break even.

**1.** Store revenues
- Approximate sales per square foot of a 5,000 square foot store (from chart): $200
- Expected sales of entire store: $5,000 \times \$200 = \$1,000,000$

**2.** Fixed store expenses
- Cost of constructing 5,000 square feet of converted warehouse space: assume $100 per square foot: $\$100 \times 5,000 = \$500,000$
- Assume cost of leasing land is $25 per square foot per year: $\$25 \times 5,000 = \$125,000$

**3.** Variable store expenses
- Make a conservative assumption that the average store margin is only 10 percent, after all variable costs are recognized.

**4.** Store profitability
- Sales of $1,000,000 with a 10 percent margin produces annual profits of $100,000. At this rate, the store would require approximately 6 years to cover the fixed cost of the building.

Since our margin estimate of 10 percent is conservative and the store, under the experienced management of the company, will likely earn a higher annual margin, we can assume that the breakeven point will arrive in less than six years. We will therefore still recommend that the store adopt a hybrid format.

• • •

## TYPE 3    HUMAN RESOURCE MANAGEMENT

**Case 3.1    Recruiting**

You are the recruiting director of a major consulting firm. Your firm has traditionally been known for having bright and innovative consultants, but what candidates do not know is that the office atmosphere is "cutthroat." Informally, you have been told by several senior partners that the atmosphere needs to change, but they fear that a selection bias in the recruiting process is perpetuating the cutthroat atmosphere. How would you begin to investigate this hypothesis?

### Elements of a Basic Answer

*Framework:*  Internal–External.

As mentioned earlier in this book, it is very important that you answer the question that is asked and not the one that is anticipated. This case is a good example of an unexpected question attached to the end of a normal case. The case is not asking you to find a way to make the office less competitive, or to find out all the reasons why the office is overly competitive. It is only asking you to investigate the possibility of selection bias.

The generic nature of the internal/external framework makes it very useful in this case. Selection bias may occur because of the internal process that the firm uses to determine the best candidates. Or it may occur externally by the type of individuals who are attracted to the traditional image of this firm.

1. Internal:
   - Internally, three key elements may drive selection bias: the firm's target schools, the interviewing process, and the interviewers themselves.
   - Students at some schools traditionally have been more competitively inclined than at others. Is there a procedural bias toward these schools? How does the firm decide which schools to target? Are these targeted schools known for their cooperative or competitive student body? Are target schools determined by size of the alumni base at the firm or some other method (e.g., geographic proximity, popular press rankings)?
   - The interviewing process may effectively be screening out those applicants who may potentially be more cooperative in their work. What criteria are used to screen candidates during the initial resume review? On what attributes are candidates judged during the interviewing process? Is this rigid or flexible? How involved are the partners in the interviewing process?
   - There is a great deal of subjectivity in the interviewing process. Consequently, the personalities of the interviewers may intentionally or unintentionally influence those candidates who are selected. What type of consultants are allowed to interview? Have they observed any difference in competitive behavior from consultants from different schools?

2. External:
   - Externally, self-selection bias may be driven primarily by perceptions of the firm. How is the firm perceived by the candidates, particularly, in terms of the office culture, and promotion policies? Is it considered a high-stress environment where only those individuals who are willing to work long, difficult hours survive? Do candidates believe that the firm has an up-or-out policy?
   - The firm may be projecting an image that it does not intend. How does the firm present itself to students?

*Elements of an Outstanding Answer*
- An outstanding answer would consider how indirect forces may be influencing selection bias. For example, the company's internal promotion policies may develop competitive attributes in its consultants, who in turn may unintentionally have a bias toward those candidates who are more competitive.

## TYPE 4   MARKET ENTRY

**Case 4.1**   **Italian Pottery**

A family-owned pottery manufacturer in Assisi, Italy, has decided to export its handcrafted wares to the United States, but needs your help to determine how. The manufacturer is considering three options: (1) sell directly to stores; (2) sell to distributors, who then sell to individual stores; and (3) open its own chain of proprietary stores. What should the manufacturer do?

*Elements of a Basic Answer*

*Framework:* Review the 4-P's (Product, Place, Price, Promotion), and then evaluate the three options.

**1.** Product:
- Italian pottery is typically produced in relatively small batches, and is glazed with unique patterns that are hand-painted by artisans.
- Complete sets of pottery can be obtained with the same glazing: serving platters and bowls, dishes, pitchers, mugs, storage containers, and even soap dishes and matching mirrors.
- Colorful glazes are typically painted on white backgrounds, and are organic in nature (vines, birds, and abstractions of other natural forms).
- Italian pottery has many substitutes, including all other types of dishes and serving platters.
- Still, Italian pottery is differentiated by its handcrafted artistic origin, and by unique patterns that are difficult to replicate.

**2.** Place:
  - Handcrafted artisan pottery is currently sold through only a few channels in the United States: upscale department stores, specialty home stores, and mail-order catalogs.
  - Occasionally, museum stores and even some gourmet coffee chains sell selected pieces.
  - Very few if any stores that are entirely devoted to the sale of artisan pottery exist, other than individual stores located at pottery manufacturing sites.
  - Stores that sell pottery typically offer a wide variety, imported from many different countries and regions.

**3.** Price:
  - European artisan pottery tends to be sold at a premium in the United States, due to its upscale image, its uniqueness, its fragility, and the middle and upper-class incomes of its primary customers.
  - Prices must be set high enough to cover the aggregate costs of manufacturing, distribution, financing, and allowances for loss/breakage, while still offering acceptable profit margins for all the players involved in the venture. The price and margin captured by the Italian manufacturer depends on the distribution channel selected.
  - Pricing decisions for the Italian pottery should also consider the price levels of substitutes. Consider the pricing decision of an Italian dining plate: if the closest substitutes (e.g., artisan dining plates imported from other countries) are priced at $10 each, then to remain competitive, the Italian plate should also be priced at $10. Only if customers perceive the manufacturing or artistic value of the Italian plate to be higher than that of the primary substitutes can the price exceed $10, at say $12 or even $15. Similarly, if either the manufacturing or artistic quality of the Italian plate is perceived to be subpar, then the price should be set below $10, say at $8.
  - If Italian pottery has had little exposure in the United States, or has had trouble capturing market share of the artisan pottery niche, then an alternative pricing scheme could be adopted

undercut the prices of substitutes to develop customer interest and to encourage a trial purchase of the product, which in the long run may lead to repeat sales.

- Finally, pricing schemes need to consider customer perceptions: lower prices may attribute lower quality and uniqueness to the pottery, while higher prices may be translated into higher quality. Similarly, bundling schemes that offer lower prices when multiple pieces are purchased together may also connote lower quality.

**4.** Promotion:

- Italian pottery is likely to be difficult to promote, given the unique nature of each piece sold and the relatively limited quantities manufactured.
- If the pottery is sold through upscale department stores or home stores, then most of the promotion will likely be performed by the stores themselves, rather than either the manufacturer or distributor.
- Customers typically purchase artisan pottery for the following reasons: to buy a unique item as a gift; to buy a set of serving and dining ware for special occasions; or simply to satisfy an impulse urge when browsing through a store. As a result, customers may or may not have a predetermined intention to purchase artisan pottery before entering a store.

Let us now evaluate our three options.

Option 1: Sell directly to stores:
- This strategy would allow the manufacturer to bypass all middlemen and as a result capture greater profit. The manufacturer would also be able to carefully select the stores, and reject those that either do not support the upscale image of the product, or carry too many substitute products, or are not committed to promoting the product.
- However, it may be difficult for an Italian-based manufacturer to identify American stores that may be interested in carrying the product. To be selective in its choice of stores, the manufacturer must have enough alternative stores to sell to.

Option 2: Sell to distributors:
- Given the difficulty of identifying American stores from Italy, the manufacturer may benefit from selling to distributors who already have store relationships. By working with multiple distributors, the manufacturer could indirectly increase sales by encouraging distributors to compete with each other and increase their sales efforts to stores.
- However, the profit earned will have to be shared with the distributor. Moreover, the distributor may not be as discriminating as the manufacturer when selecting stores.

Option 3: Open a chain of proprietary stores:
- This option might allow the manufacturer to capture the greatest profit from the venture, since it would be fully vertically integrated. The manufacturer would have full control of the display and design of the store, and would make all retail pricing decisions.
- On the other hand, the expense of opening retail stores may substantially reduce if not consume all the profit earned. The manufacturer has no experience with retailing, and is likely to have little knowledge of markets in the United States. Finally, there is little evidence that stores selling only artisan pottery could even survive.

The lowest-risk option is clearly number 2: sell to distributors. Other than building relationships with distributors, the manufacturer would not have to develop additional competencies. The cost of establishing retail outlets would be avoided, as would the cost of selling to stores. Although the manufacturer might not capture as much profit from each unit sold, the costs associated with this option are also the lowest.

### Elements of an Outstanding Answer
- This entire analysis was performed without even questioning the fundamental idea of selling Italian pottery in the United States. Perhaps alternative strategies would yield preferable results, such as selling pottery to stores in Italy or other parts of Europe, or teaming up with tour agencies to bring vacationers to the factory store.

- An outstanding answer might also propose additional U.S. distribution strategies, such as mail-order catalogs, or sales though the World Wide Web.

———— • • • ————

### TYPE 5   MARKET SIZING

**Case 5.1   Gourmet Coffee Shops**

**Part I:** A large coffee processing company has seen sales of its well-known supermarket brand coffee drop 15 percent per year over the past five years. As a result, manufacturing costs per pound of coffee are increasing, since 25 percent of the machines are no longer being used, and monthly production has dropped by 50,000 pounds. Meanwhile, gourmet coffee chains are growing rapidly across the United States. Should the company try to capture some of this growth by opening its own proprietary chain of gourmet coffee stores?

**Part II:** How many individual coffee stores could the company supply, if it has 50,000 pounds of excess monthly production capacity? Assume one pound of coffee yields 10 cups of brewed coffee.

### Elements of a Basic Answer

*Framework:* **Part I:** 3-C's: Company, Customers, Competitors.

**Part II:** Bottom-up breakeven: estimate the number of customers who visit a gourmet coffee shop in a month, then translate visits into the number of pounds of coffee required to brew the cups consumed. Divide 50,000 pounds of excess monthly capacity by the total pounds of coffee consumed at a single shop in a month, to determine the total number of shops the company could supply.

### Part I

1. Company:
- We should begin to answer the question by understanding whether the company needs to look outside its existing sales

channels at all. Although sales have been declining, the company may be able to fix its current core business before exploring alternative ones.

**Q** Does the company sell its coffee only through supermarkets, or are additional channels used?

**A** All the coffee is sold in pressure-sealed cans through supermarkets and general food stores. No other channels are used.

**Q** Have supermarket and general store sales of coffee dropped overall, or only for this company's brand?

**A** Market research indicates that all the brands sold through these channels have experienced the same rate of sales decline.

- It appears that the channel is driving the company's declining performance. Although the company could attempt to capture greater market share through aggressive pricing schemes, the channel appears to be losing attractiveness overall. An alternative channel may indeed be an attractive way to solve the excess capacity problem.

- We should now assess the competencies of the company, to determine how well positioned it is to open coffee shops.

**Q** How well known is the brand? Does the company have more than one brand?

**A** The company sells all its coffee under a single brand, but the brand has universal recognition in the United States. It has been around for nearly a century as a household name, and is currently supported through an extensive television and print advertising campaign.

**Q** How many different products are offered under the brand, and which are the best sellers?

**A** The company produces regular, decaffeinated, gourmet, and instant. Their best selling coffee is regular, and very little of the gourmet is sold.

- The company is an established brand, with a complete array of products. But a weak gourmet product does not support the idea of opening a chain of gourmet coffee shops. The brand name may have strong equity, but it appears to be associated with more generic coffee products.

**Q** Does the company have any retail experience?

**A** No. Sales have always been through the same supermarket and general store channels.

- Not having a competency in retail management could threaten the success of a gourmet coffee shop venture. The company will either have to slow the rate of opening stores to learn from mistakes and build expertise, or buy managers from another company at great expense.

2. Customers:

- The strength of the brand lies in the loyalty of its customers. We might argue that a chain of gourmet coffee shops operating under the same brand name as the supermarket coffee will attract people who already select the brand.

**Q** How would you define the primary customers of the brand?

**A** Most customers are located in suburban or rural areas, and are of lower- to middle-income levels.

- Already, the argument looks weak. Most gourmet coffee shops are located in urban centers, but evidently the company's primary customers live elsewhere.

**Q** Is it fair to assume that most purchase this company's coffee to brew at home?

**A** Yes, or at the office.

**Q** How brand-loyal are people who purchase the canned coffee?

**A** Hardly. Price seems to be the primary driver of a purchasing decision, although some people stick with certain brands, believing that they taste better.

- If customers who already purchase the company's canned coffee are only weakly loyal, then they are unlikely to be any more attracted to a gourmet coffee shop under the same brand name than anyone else would be.

- In fact, the high recognition of the company's brand may actually be a handicap. It is undeniably ironic for a gourmet store to be named after a supermarket brand of generic household coffee.

3. Competitors:
   - If the company were to open a chain of coffee stores, it would most likely be the third or fourth (or higher) entrant in any given market. The company would be fighting an uphill battle from the very start.
   - Many competitor chains have national coverage, and operate hundreds of stores in most major cities. They already have the exposure to build a strong gourmet brand identity, and have spent years building customer loyalty.
   - The competition has had years to test and refine their retail concept, and to work the operational kinks out of stores.
   - Most of the prime real estate in many key gourmet coffee cities, like Boston, New York, and San Francisco, is already owned by the competition.

The evidence stacks up against the idea, and the company should not open a chain of gourmet coffee shops.

**Part II**   Treat this part of the case as a market sizing calculation.

1. Estimate the number of customers who visit a gourmet coffee shop in a day:
   - Assumed number of cash registers in one shop: 2
   - Estimated time to service one customer: 1 minute
   - Number of customers serviced in one minute: 2 registers × 1 customer per minute = 2 customers per minute
   - Hours of store operation (assume 6 A.M. to 12 midnight): 18 hours
   - Number of daily hours that are "peak" (assume 7 A.M. to 10 A.M., 12 P.M. to 1 P.M., and 8 P.M. to 10 P.M.): 6 hours

- Number of customers serviced during "peak" (assume lines are long and the flow of customers is constant): 6 hours × 60 minutes × 2 customers per minute = 720 customers
- Number of customers serviced during "nonpeak" (assume traffic flow is half of peak levels): 12 hours × 60 minutes × 1 customer per minute = 720 customers
- Total number of customers serviced during hours of operation: 720 + 720 = 1,440 customers

2. Estimate the number of pounds of coffee required to service customers in one month
   - Number of customers visiting in one month: 1,440 customers × 30 days = 43,200 customers
   - Number of cups of coffee consumed (assume 1 house coffee per customer): 43,200 cups
   - Equivalent number of pounds of coffee: 43,200 cups/10 cups per pound = 4,320 pounds.

With 50,000 pounds of excess monthly production capacity, the company can service 50,000 pounds/4,320 pounds per shop = almost 12 shops. We now have yet another piece of evidence to argue against the gourmet coffee shop idea: to successfully compete against the established chains, the new chain needs a presence that is broader than 12 shops.

### Elements of an Outstanding Answer

Rather then opening a proprietary chain of coffee shops, the company should become a supplier of coffee to existing shops. This strategy would build on the strengths of the company (coffee processing and distribution), would eliminate the need to develop new competencies (gourmet brand identity, retail experience, loyal customer base), and would allow the company to sell its excess production capacity to exactly 12 shops. Since the primary objective of the company was to restore production to prior levels of efficiency, this solution will achieve the desired result without creating any new problems.

## TYPE 6   MERGERS AND ACQUISITIONS

### Case 6.1       HMO Acquisition

*Question:*    A New York based health maintenance organization (HMO) is considering expanding its operations. They currently have the funds to purchase another HMO. Their internal M&A group has identified two possible targets: Allied HMO in Miami, and Washington Health in Seattle. Which should they purchase?

### *Elements of a Basic Answer*

*Framework:*  3-C's: Company, Customers, Competitors

When considering M&A questions, it is very helpful to first identify the purpose of the merger or acquisition. Often, candidates assume that the intent of the merger is to have a positive impact on the company's balance sheet. However, the actual purpose could be to improve the strategic positioning of the company, send a signal to the market, or eliminate a competitor. A company could have many reasons for choosing to merge or acquire another company. Understanding the original intent will guide the rest of the answer. In this case, the intent is to improve the geographic coverage of the HMO.

**1.** Company:

- At a minimum, you will want to determine if there is a cultural fit between the two companies. Significant cultural fit issues have the potential to sour any M&A activity. Other issues to consider include a company's public image, and its relationship with its doctors. Questions may include the following:

**Q**   What is the leadership style at the New York HMO (NY HMO)? And how does this differ with the other two companies?

**A**   NY HMO's former CEO developed a strong hierarchy of leadership within the company. The President, CEO, and COO decide most management issues. By contrast, Washington Health gives its individual divisions a great deal of autonomy. They developed a Leadership Board composed of the vice presidents of all the divisions. This approach is mirrored at Allied HMO. Allied makes a conscious attempt to include a wide variety of people in its decision-making process, through its Leadership Board, employee suggestion box, and a strong open-door policy.

**Q** Does the new CEO adhere to the old hierarchical approach? How open is this person to change? How open is the company to change?

**A** NY HMO's new CEO was recruited from a manufacturing firm. Consequently, she has not been indoctrinated into the traditional approach. As the COO of the manufacturing firm, she instituted policies that essentially decentralized the manufacturing process. Because of high wages and generous benefits, turnover at NY HMO is very low.

- Although there may be a cultural fit problem with acquisition targets, the new CEO may be able to resolve them.

- We should determine whether the corporate reputation of NY HMO among patients and physicians fits with those of its acquisition targets. A mixed reputation could potentially have a severe impact on the ability for an HMO to function well.

**Q** How is NY HMO viewed by the public? Is it viewed as an HMO with cutting-edge technology and methodologies? Does it have the best doctors? How does this image differ with those of the two acquisition targets? What is the relationship between doctors and NY HMO? Is this relationship similar to the other two acquisition targets?

**A** NY HMO is seen as the premier HMO in the New York and northern New Jersey areas. It is not a staff model (i.e., the doctors who serve NY HMO patients are not employees of the company). They recruit only the best doctors, keep close track of their performance with frequent customer satisfaction surveys, and generously compensate them for their work. Despite some late reimbursements, doctors are generally very pleased with their relationship with the company. Washington Health follows a traditional staff model. The doctors are well paid for their geographic region. Their reputation is strong in the area they serve. Allied is not a staff model and is considered average. Allied generally promises to help any company reduce its healthcare costs within two years. Because of this approach, they keep very close track of their doctors, but some physicians resent this level of scrutiny.

- Based on reputation, there seems to be a better fit with Washington Health.

2. Customers:
   - If the intent of the merger is to expand geographic coverage, then the purpose of the merger is to better serve the customers. So first you need to understand their customer base.

   **Q** What type of customers does NY HMO serve?

   **A** The majority (75%) of NY HMO's customers are older patients, who are either on Medicare, or can pay for healthcare themselves.

   **Q** What is the customer composition at the other two HMOs?

   **A** Washington Health and Allied have a standard mix of customers.

   **Q** Are there any other important demographic characteristics by which we could segment each HMO's customer base?

   **A** Yes—money. NY HMO's customers are generally fairly well off.

   - Customer composition is critical. In this case, it suggests that there may be behavioral aspects that should be considered.

   **Q** If NY HMO's customers are relatively well off, do they travel frequently?

   **A** Yes. They frequently travel to Florida for the winter.

   - Since the intent is to expand geographic coverage, NY HMO should consider Allied despite the potential problems, given the travel patterns of its largest customer segment.

3. Competitors:
   - **Q** If NY HMO were to acquire Allied, what kind of competitive response could there be in the New York-New Jersey market and in the Florida market?

**A** The competitive response would be weak. Most HMOs are actively recruiting Medicare patients and are generally limited to a single state.

- In this case, competition is not a significant factor.

The evidence supports the acquisition objective, so NY HMO should acquire Allied.

### *Elements of an Outstanding Answer*

A more in-depth analysis would include an abbreviated cost-benefit analysis. The acquisition of Allied may be strategically sound, but how much would it cost? Is the acquisition a positive NPV project?

Is NY HMO a public company? How would an acquisition impact their leverage ratios (ratios that indicate the long-run solvency of a company)? What kind of information would be needed? How would stockholders respond? Would stockholder objectives be different from that of management?

## TYPE 7   NEW PRODUCT INTRODUCTION

**Case 7.1**   **Cricket Ball Exports to the United States**

A U.K.-based cricket ball manufacturer seeks sales expansion opportunities in the United States. Current production is at full capacity, but US$500 million has been allocated to build additional capacity. Should the company introduce the product in the United States?

### *Elements of a Basic Answer*

*Framework:* Consider three topics: (1) the size of the current U.S. cricket ball market, (2) initiatives the company might take to promote the sale of cricket balls in the United States, and (3) whether US$500 million is an adequate investment in production capacity to meet U.S. demand.

**1.** Size of the United States cricket ball market:
- Approximate population of the United States:  250 million
- Age bracket of people who may play cricket:  16 to 45

- Percentage of population represented by this bracket using the following assumption:

  Ages  0–15     20% of population
          16–30    20
          31–45    20 $\Big\} = 40$ percent
          46–60    20
          61–80    20
                  100%

- Number of people of age to play cricket: 250 million × 40% = 100 million

- Assumption: only those people who have heard of cricket may play.
  Estimate 1 in 5 people have heard of the game: 100 million × 20% = 20 million

- Of the people who may play, only a few will actually play. Base this assumption on personal experience, by assuming that 1 in 20 people who have heard of baseball, for example, actually play: 20 million × 5% = 1 million

- But baseball is a much more widely played game than cricket, so we should scale this number down, say by 50% = 500,000 people

- How many cricket balls will these people purchase? For baseball, only one ball is required for 15 to 30 people to play. So assume a similar ratio for cricket of 1 ball for 20 people: 500,000 × 5% = 25,000 people

- Would it be worth the manufacturer's effort to sell 25,000 balls per year in the United States? If each ball were priced at US$10.00, then the total revenue (assuming 100% market share) would be US$250,000. This could be worthwhile if the cost structure were low enough, but we do not have enough information to make a judgment.

**2.** The company could try to increase the market for cricket balls through a number of promotional initiatives:

- Sponsor broadcasts of live cricket games over United States television to improve public familiarity of the game and even generate sustainable interest. However, this would be very expensive, and only a few viewers would purchase a cricket ball in response to the shows.
- Sponsor cricket camps for children to encourage interest in the game at an early age. This would be less expensive, but the strategy has a number of problems: children do not purchase cricket balls, their parents do; and cricket camps can only attract children (and parents) who already have an interest or curiosity in the game.
- Give away free cricket balls at other sporting events. This would introduce the game to a population that already has sporting interests; however, this could be extremely costly (especially when only 25,000 balls are expected to be sold in year one), and although people may appreciate the gesture, few of the balls would actually be used to play a game of cricket.
- Promotional efforts are likely to face a number of hurdles: high cost of promotions, low public awareness, and a high degree of organization required to play game.

3. Assess the adequacy of US$500 million to cover the cost of adding additional manufacturing capacity.
   - To determine the marginal cost of adding a unit of production capacity, we need to understand the fixed costs associated with the existing facility. However, no information was provided. Instead, we can assume that the company would have to build additional production space, and possibly add a new warehouse. We can be generous and allocate US$10 million toward property enhancements. As for additional machinery, we now know that 25,000 balls must be manufactured each year, which when divided by 250 working days yields 100 balls per day, or 12.5 balls per hour of an 8-hour day. Need the company buy more than one machine to meet this demand? Probably not. In short, US$500 million is an extremely large amount, and will certainly cover the cost of adding the requisite capacity.

**4.** So should the company introduce cricket balls into the United States? At this point, everything we have learned would support an answer of no: the market is too small, it is far too costly and difficult to promote the game, and with a cash reserve of US$500 million the company could easily explore other ideas.

### Elements of an Outstanding Answer

Three other strategic options could be considered: (1) alternative markets, (2) alternative ball products, and (3) acquisition.

**1.** Now that we have rejected the U.S. market as too small, perhaps we could consider other markets, especially those in which cricket is already played. Australia, India, Pakistan, Hong Kong, South Africa, Ireland, and Scotland are but a few of the markets the company could consider. However, we do not know whether the company already sells to these markets.

**2.** Another option could be to manufacture other ball products, such as baseballs, soccer balls, and tennis balls. If the company adopted this strategy, then entry into the U.S. market could once again become a possibility. However, to be able to compete in the United States, the company's products have to be lower in cost, or superior in quality, or in some other way unique. Thus the market for these alternative products may be larger, but the company would have to learn the business dynamics of unfamiliar products.

**3.** If the learning curve of manufacturing new products is too steep, then the company could consider purchasing an established ball manufacturer, either within or without the United States. This way, the company could immediately acquire the sales volume of the other company, and expand without having to build a competency or production capability from scratch. Still, alternative investments of the US$500 million exist, and may offer a higher return at a lower risk (e.g., bonds).

Ultimately, the selection of a strategy depends on more than a simple interest in expanding sales. It is directly related to the interests of the company's constituents (e.g., shareholders), and the competencies and vision of management.

## TYPE 8   OPPORTUNITY ASSESSMENT

### Case 8.1   On-line Bookstore

*Question:*   If a book distributor were thinking about launching an on-line bookstore, what would be its estimated annual sales?

### *Elements of a Basic Answer*

*Framework:*   Estimate the annual sales of a Web-based bookstore using a top-down approach.

1. Number of Americans with Internet access:
   - Number of people in the United States: 250 million
   - Age bracket of primary Internet users: 16 to 45
   - Percentage of population represented by this bracket using the following assumption: 40%

   | Ages | | |
   |------|------|-----------------|
   | 0–15 | 20% of population | |
   | 16–30 | 20 | |
   | 31–45 | 20 | = 40 percent |
   | 46–60 | 20 | |
   | 61–80 | 20 | |
   | | 100% | |

   - Number of people within primary bracket: 250 million × 40% = 100 million
   - Percentage of people within bracket who own computers with modems using the following assumptions:
       Students (ages 16 to 21): 30% have computers at home
       Young Professionals (ages 22 to 45): 60% have computers at home or work
       Average: 50%
   - Number of Americans with Internet access: 100 million × 50% = 50 million

**2.** Size of World Wide Web browsing population:
- Number of Americans with Internet access who have visited the Web: assume 1 in 2 = 50 million × 50% = 25 million
- Number of Web visitors who regularly repeat-visit (assume only those people who are very familiar with the Web are willing to make an on-line book purchase): assume 1 in 5 = 25 million × 20% = 5 million

**3.** Book sales on the Web:
- Percentage of frequent Web users who read books: assume a low 30 percent, since reading and Web browsing are both leisure activities that can consume a great deal of time, and cannot be pursued simultaneously.
- Number of possible on-line purchasers of books: 5 million × 30% = 1.5 million
- Percentage of book purchases made on-line versus through a book store: assume 20 percent, since the primary reasons for purchasing on-line are either convenience or low price; most book purchasers, however, will prefer to read books immediately on purchase, and will therefore shop book stores more frequently.
- Number of books purchased per year per person: assume 5
- Number of books purchased on-line: 1.5 million people × 5 books × 20% = 1.5 million books
- Average price of book: $20.00
- Total on-line book purchases: $20.00 × 1.5 million = $30 million

### Elements of an Outstanding Answer

**1.** If the book distributor were the first to establish an on-line store, then in the absence of competition its annual sales could approach $30 million. Of course, first-year sales will be substantially lower, and will rise slowly year to year thereafter. As the popularity of the Web increases, and people become more accustomed to making on-line purchases, the $30 million estimate should likewise increase.

Sensitivity analysis:

| Market Share | Total Annual Sales |
|---|---|
| 100% | $30 million |
| 75% | $22.5 million |
| 50% | $15 million |
| 25% | $7.5 million |

2. Since many of the assumptions in the opportunity assessment were based on either personal experience or conservative attempts to parse populations into smaller subgroupings, the resulting estimated sales number should be checked for reasonableness.

- The distributor should launch the on-line business only if the economics of the venture are equally or more attractive than those of a retail book store.
- How could we quickly estimate the sales of a retail book store, for comparative purposes? Estimate the costs associated with operating a store, say of the newer big-box variety of 50,000 square feet in a shopping mall:

| Cost Item | Amount |
|---|---|
| Rent ($25 square foot/year) | $1,250,000 |
| Staff (20 people at $40,000/year fully-costed) | 800,000 |
| Inventory (assume 50 shelving units, 10 shelves per unit, 20 feet long each, 10 books per foot) $50 \times 10 \times 20 \times 10 = 100,000$ books $\times$ average wholesale price of $15 = | 1,500,000 |
| Operations (utilities, maintenance, phone, etc.) | 100,000 |
| Allowance for loss: inventory $\times 5\% =$ | 75,000 |
| Total Cost | $3,725,000 |

To turn a profit, sales of a large retail book store must exceed $3.725 million, so our estimated sales could be $5 million.

- Compared with $5 million, on-line sales of $30 million is certainly attractive. Still, the wide disparity may be an indication that our assumptions are somewhat flawed, and as a result our on-line sales estimate may be slightly exaggerated.

## TYPE 9    PRICING

**Case 9.1    Amtrak Rail Ticket**

How does Amtrak price a rail ticket from Boston to Washington, DC?

*Elements of a Basic Answer*

*Framework:*    Three C's: Customers, Company, Competitors

1. Customers—Amtrak may want to price discriminate among its customers:
   - Amtrak has essentially four customer sets: (1) vacationing travelers, (2) business travelers, (3) students, and (4) commuters. Each of these customers has unique travel patterns. Vacationers will most likely travel during the weekend, often in pairs or families, but may also be present during the week. Business travelers are most common on weekdays, typically during the morning and evening. Students travel most often before and after holidays, and at the beginning and end of semesters. Commuters tend to be most prevalent during the morning and evening hours, riding the train for relatively short distances. For the Boston to Washington route, however, we would only expect to find vacationing, business, and student travelers.
   - Passenger volume is directly correlated to the day of the week, the time of day, the season, and the calendar of holidays. Amtrak may want to consider each of these factors when determining promotional or discounted pricing schemes.
   - Each of the four customer sets is likely to have different price sensitivities: Vacationers may be highly price sensitive and seek family or advance-purchase discounts; business travelers are likely to be less price sensitive, since many of their tickets will be reimbursed by corporations; students and commuters are likely to be the most price sensitive, and may be attracted to age-based or volume discounts.
   - Service expectations also vary for each customer type. Business travelers and commuters are negatively affected by delays and slow service, and as a result may be willing to pay a premium to have guaranteed or faster service. Vacationers and students, on

the other hand, may care more about low price than fast service. Still, all four customer sets would surely like to have a seat, a food car, toilets, and maybe even telephones.

- Given such a variety of customer needs and interests, Amtrak could benefit from a pricing strategy that offers different prices to different customers on different days.

2. Company—Amtrak must cover its costs, and still earn a profit:
   - Amtrak should price the ticket to at least cover the variable costs and the portion of the fixed costs associated with a one-way trip from Boston to Washington, DC. Included within the variable costs of the train are labor (1 train conductor, 1 food car agent, 2 ticket collectors), electricity or fuel to operate the locomotive and power the train cabins, drinking water, and miscellaneous toilet items (paper, soap, etc.). Fixed costs include the track, the train locomotive and cars, rail yards, maintenance facilities, corporate offices, customer service facilities, Amtrak information systems and technology, and so on. Only a tiny portion of the total fixed costs, however, should be attributed to operating one train from Boston to Washington. In fact, some of these costs could be considered "sunk" costs (e.g., the track), and therefore should not be attributed to this run at all.
   - At a more macro level, a cost-based pricing strategy should also look beyond the simple Boston to Washington route, and consider the cost of operating the total nationwide Amtrak system. It is quite possible that a cost associated with constructing a new rail in California will have to be borne in part by the operation of a train in the Northeast Corridor. Only once these factors are considered can a profitable margin be determined.

3. Competitors—Amtrak must be careful to not price itself out of the market:
   - Each customer group mentioned earlier will certainly factor price into their transportation decision. Therefore, the pricing of a one-way Boston to Washington rail ticket must be competitive with alternative transportation methods, such as airplanes (approximately $150 one-way), buses ($45 one-way), rental cars

($50 per day plus gas, tolls and parking), and personal cars (gas, tolls, and parking, plus a portion of insurance, and depreciation of the automobile). To effectively attract each customer group, the basic price of a rail ticket needs to be lower than a flight. But given the greater comfort of a train and perhaps even the faster speed, a rail ticket can cost more than the bus or driving a car.

**4.** An effective price discriminating strategy would therefore be the following:

| | |
|---|---|
| Vacationers: | Offer family, group, and senior citizen discounts to attract highly price-sensitive, low time-constrained customers: $50 to $100 one way. |
| Business Travelers: | Run express trains with reserved seating and special amenities (telephones, laptop plugs, etc.) with higher priced tickets to satisfy time-constrained, price-insensitive travelers: $75 to $125 one way. |
| Students: | Offer age, multipack ticket, and holiday discounts to satisfy price-sensitive, frequent traveling, seasonal customers: $50 to $100 one way. |
| Commuters: | (not applicable to the Boston to Washington route) |

### Elements of an Outstanding Answer

An outstanding answer would graphically argue that the demand curves of the different customer segments are also important drivers of pricing. Take, for example, an illustrative demand curve for business travelers. Although we argued that they had inelastic demand curves, this may hold true for only a certain range of price changes. That is, their demand curve may be a step curve, as seen in Figure AII.2.

Note that raising the price from $P_1$ to $P_2$, does not affect the demand for tickets. However, raising the price (only slightly) again to $P_3$ drastically reduces the demand for tickets. Why? One answer may be that the existence of alternatives creates strong price sensitivities after a

**Figure AII.2**
**Step Function Demand Curve for Business Travelers**

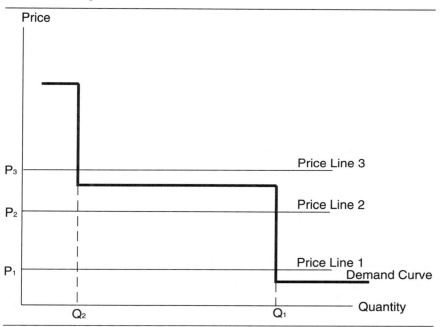

certain price range. Another may be corporate policy. Thus, the degree of price differentiation depends not only on price elasticity, but also on the nature of the demand function.

●  ●  ●

## TYPE 10   PROFITABILITY LOSS

### Case 10.1   Pharmaceutical Drugs

The CEO of a major pharmaceutical company wants to know why the profits of one of its leading over-the-counter drugs declined by 25% over the last year.

### Elements of a Basic Answer

*Framework:*  Profit = Total Revenues − Total Costs
Or Profit = (Price × Quantity) − (Fixed Costs + (Variable Costs × Quantity))

1. Total Costs: Understand if the product's costs have changed recently:
   - Total costs can be divided into fixed and variable costs. For this company, examples of fixed costs would include the machinery and equipment used to manufacture the drug, and the building within which the production equipment is housed.

   **Q** Have the fixed costs increased recently?

   **A** No, they have remained constant over time. The company has not had to increase the amount of space or the number of machines.

   - Evidently, fixed costs are not responsible for the profit loss. Let's turn to variable costs, which would include the materials used to manufacture the drug, shipping and distribution costs, and marketing and promotion of the product to doctors, hospitals, and the public.

   **Q** Are the drug's raw materials increasing in price?

   **A** No, they have remained constant.

   **Q** How about shipping costs? Do we have difficulty delivering the product to remote destinations?

   **A** No, we use third-party distributors who purchase the product in bulk from us and then deliver smaller quantities to the end users. We only have to carry the cost of shipping to these centralized distributors, which have not increased substantially over the past year.

   **Q** Have we changed our marketing efforts?

   **A** Yes, last year we increased our advertising and promotions budget 5 percent, since we are facing increasing competition.

   - Could this be the reason profits are declining? Only partially, since a 5 percent increase in spending does not necessarily equate to the 25 percent profitability decline. Something else must be responsible for our profit loss.

2. Total Revenues: Understand the sources of revenues for the product:
   - Since total revenues equals price x total quantity, we need to understand if these two inputs have changed.

**Q** Have you changed the price of the drug, or perhaps offered unusual discounts, in the past year?

**A** No, the price has remained the same, and we continue to offer the same volume discounts to our most important customers.

**Q** Then perhaps we have a problem collecting from our customers?

**A** We've always had approximately 5 percent loss from uncollected bills, but we price our product high enough to cover this loss.

• Next, consider sales volume.

**Q** Has the total quantity of the drug sold changed recently?

**A** Yes, it has decreased substantially in the last year.

• Finally, we have identified an element of the profitability equation that has significantly changed. But we cannot stop here—we still have to understand why volume has dropped. Could it be due to declining product quality? Or perhaps due to a declining rate of use among patients? Or even a recent customer preference for substitute products? To answer these questions, we need to better understand the product.

**Q** Is the drug unique, or are there other products that have the same or similar effects?

**A** We are currently the only branded product on the market, recognized by doctors, patients, and pharmacists as the leading brand. But dozens of almost identical generic products also exist.

• It would seem that the competition is responsible for our company's declining sales volume, but again we need to understand why. If the generics have always existed, then something else must be causing the sudden volume drop; but if the generics only recently entered the market, then perhaps their arrival has indeed caused the volume decline.

**Q** How recently have the generics become available?

**A** Only about a year ago—about the same time our drug patent expired.

• Now we have our answer: the expiration of the company's patent has allowed generics to invade the market, most likely at lower prices, but our company has evidently held the price of its drug constant. As a result, customers have switched to the generics, and our company has had to face lower revenues and hence lower profits.

### Elements of an Outstanding Answer

1. Take the case to the next level, by offering recommendations to remedy the situation:
   - The company should reconsider its pricing strategy. Several arguments favor holding the price constant: (a) to maintain an image of a superior, premium product; (b) to continue to extract as much value as possible out of an established brand ("milking" the product); and (c) to avoid the problem that once a price is dropped, it becomes extremely difficult to raise it later.
   - However, a number of different arguments favor a price reduction: (a) to compete with the generics, and perhaps even undercut them; (b) focus customer attention away from price and toward product reputation when deciding which product to buy; and (c) to increase sales volume and ultimately reap greater revenues and profits despite the lower price.

2. Based on these arguments, a final recommendation could be the following:
   - Lower the price only slightly, to reduce the price disparity with the generics and to restore sales with more price-sensitive customers; continue to lower the price until the share loss is stabilized, but be sure to maintain a slight price premium. As long as the generic products exist, our company is unlikely to restore its original 100 percent market share. The CEO will have to accept some profit loss from a year ago, but by following this strategy, the drug should be able to rely on its brand image to compete.

# APPENDIX III

## DIRECTORY OF
## FIFTY CONSULTING FIRMS

**T**o jump-start your research on consulting firms, we have provided a listing of fifty management consulting firms and corporate strategic planning units. Although many of the practices listed here are among the largest and best known in the industry, we did not simply select the top fifty firms. Rather, we deliberately provided a range of practices in terms of size, sector-focus (private, public, and nonprofit), and consulting practice area, to give you a sense of how diverse the opportunities are in the consulting industry. For specific information, contact the firms directly and supplement your research by browsing their Web sites, since recruiting and office information changes frequently and is sometimes specific to factors such as the geographic region or school of the candidate. Web sites, where available, appear at the end of each listing.

In the United States, the recruiting season runs from January to May for undergraduates, from January to May for first-year MBAs seeking summer internships, from September to January (although it may run through May for some firms) for graduating MBAs, and year-round for career-changing professionals.

261

**Abt Associates**
55 Wheeler Street
Cambridge, MA 02138-1168
(617) 492-7100
www.abtassoc.com

**American Express Strategic
Planning & Business
Development Group**
World Financial Center
200 Vesey Street, 38th Floor
New York, NY 10285-3809
(212) 640-7593
www.americanexpress.com

**American Management
Systems, Inc.**
4050 Legato Road
Fairfax, VA 22033
(703) 267-8000
www.amsinc.com

**Andersen Consulting**
33 West Monroe Street
Chicago, IL 60603
(312) 372-7100
www.ac.com

**Arthur D. Little, Inc.**
25 Acorn Park
Cambridge, MA 02140
(617) 498-5000
www.arthurdlittle.com

**A. T. Kearney, Inc. (division of
EDS)**
222 West Adams Street
Chicago, IL 60606
(312) 223-6030
www.atkearney.com

**Bain & Company, Inc.**
Two Copley Place
Boston, MA 02116
(617) 572-2000
www.bain.com

**Bankers Trust Management
Consulting Group**
One Bankers Trust Plaza
130 Liberty Street
New York, NY 10006
(212) 250-6019
www.bankerstrust.com

**Booz•Allen & Hamilton, Inc.**
Worldwide Commercial Business
101 Park Avenue
New York, NY 10178
(212) 551-6000
www.bah.com

**The Boston Consulting
Group, Inc.**
Exchange Place, 31st Floor
Boston, MA 02109
(617) 973-1200
www.bcg.com

**Braxton Associates**
Marketplace Center
200 State Street
Boston, MA 02109
(617) 697-0300
www.braxton.com

**Buck Consultants, Inc.**
One Pennsylvania Plaza
New York, NY 10119-4798
(212) 330-1000
www.buckconsultants.com

**Conflict Management Group**
20 University Road, 5th Floor
Cambridge, MA 02138
(617) 354-5444
www.cmgonline.org

**CSC**
2100 East Grand Avenue
El Segundo, CA 90245
(310) 615-0311
www.csc.com

**Deloitte & Touche Consulting Group**
1633 Broadway
New York, NY 10019-6754
(212) 489-1600
www.dtcg.com

**Delta Consulting Group, Inc.**
1177 Avenue of the Americas, 38th
  Floor
New York, NY 10036
(212) 403-7500
www.deltacg.com

**Dove Associates, Inc.**
75 Park Plaza
Boston, MA 02116
(617) 482-2100
www.doveassoc.com

**Easton Consultants, Inc.**
One Stamford Plaza
263 Tresser Boulevard
Stamford, CT 06901
(203) 348-8774
www.easton-consult.com

**EDS Management Consulting Services**
5400 Legacy Drive
Plano, TX 75024
(214) 605-8600
www.eds.com

**Ernst & Young Management Consulting**
787 Seventh Avenue
New York, NY 10019
(212) 773-1007
www.eyi.com

**First Annapolis**
900 Elkridge Landing Road,
  Suite 400
Linthicum, MD 21090
(410) 855-8500
www.1st-annapolis.com

**First Consulting Group**
100 East Wardlow Road
Long Beach, CA 90807
(310) 595-5291
kite.fcgnet.com

**First Manhattan Consulting Group**
90 Park Avenue, 19th Floor
New York, NY 10016
(212) 557-0500
www.fmcg.com

**The Futures Group, Inc.**
80 Glastonbury Boulevard
Glastonbury, CT 06033-4409
(860) 633-3501

**Gartner Group Consulting Services (division of Dun & Bradstreet)**
56 Top Gallant Road
Stamford, CT 06902
(203) 964-0096
www.gartner11.gartnerweb.com
/public/static/aboutgg/jobs
/consult.html

**Gemini Consulting**
25 Airport Road
Morristown, NJ 07960
(973) 285-9000
www.gemcon.com

**Good Work Associates**
85 Willow Street, Building #3
New Haven, CT 06511
(203) 773-3516

**Hay Group, Inc.**
The Wanamaker Building
100 Penn Square East
Philadelphia, PA 19107-3388
(215) 861-2000
www.haygroup.com

**Hewitt Associates, LLC**
100 Half Day Road
Lincolnshire, IL 60609
(847) 295-5000
www.hewittassoc.com

**HR Strategies, Inc.**
P.O. Box 36778
Grosse Pointe, MI 48236
(313) 881-8885

**IBM Consulting Group**
Route 9, Town of Mount Pleasant
North Tarrytown, NY 10591
(914) 332-3000
www.ibm.com/services/consulting

**KPMG Peat Marwick**
65 East 55th Street
New York, NY 10022
(212) 909-5000
www.us.kpmg.com

**Kurt Salmon Associates**
1355 Peachtree Street NE,
Suite 900
Atlanta, GA 30309
(404) 892-0321
www.kurtsalmon.com

**The LEK Partnership**
28 State Street, 16th Floor
Boston, MA 02110
(617) 951-9500
www.lekalcar.com

**Marakon Associates**
300 Atlantic Street
Stamford, CT 06901
(800) 695-4428
www.marakon.com

**Mars & Co.**
Mars Plaza
124 Mason Street
Greenwich, CT 06830
(203) 629-9292
www.marsandco.com

**McKinsey & Company, Inc.**
55 East 52nd, 21st Floor
New York, NY 10022
(212) 446-7000/(800) 221-1026
www.mckinsey.com

**Mercer Management
Consulting, Inc.**
33 Hayden Avenue
Lexington, MA 02173
(781) 861-7580
www.mercermc.com

**Mitchell Madison Group**
520 Madison Avenue
New York, NY 10022
(212) 372-9000
www.mmgnet.com

**Monitor Company**
25 First Street
Cambridge, MA 02141
(617) 252-2000
www.monitor.com

**National Economic Research
Associates, Inc.**
1 Main Street
Cambridge, MA 02142
(617) 621-0444

**Nickelodeon Strategy, Research
and Finance**
Corporate Headquarters
1515 Broadway
New York, NY 10036
(212) 258-6000

**PepsiCo, Inc. Corporate
Strategic Planning Group**
700 Anderson Hill Road
Purchase, NY 10577
(914) 253-2000
www.pepsico.com

**PricewaterhouseCoopers**
1251 Avenue of the Americas
New York, NY 10020
(212) 596-7000
www.pwcglobal.com

**Symmetrix, Inc.**
One Cranberry Hill
Lexington, MA 02173
(781) 862-3200
(781) 674-1300 (f)
www.symmetrix.com

**Theodore Barry & Associates**
515 South Figveroa Street,
Suite 1500
Los Angeles, CA 90071
(213) 689-0770
www.theodorebarry.com

**Towers Perrin**
335 Madison Avenue
New York, NY 10017
(212) 309-3400
www.towers.com

**Vertex Partners**
10 Post Office Square, Suite 700
Boston, MA 02109
(617) 292-0990
www.vpartners.com

**Watson Wyatt Worldwide**
6707 Democracy Boulevard,
    Suite 400
Bethesda, MD 20817
(301) 581–4600
www.watsonwyatt.com

**ZS Associates**
1800 Sherman Avenue, Suite 700
Evanston, IL 60201
(847) 492–3600
www.zsassociates.com

# NOTES

## Introduction

1. The answers to these case questions and more are provided in Appendix I.

## Chapter 1

1. *Consultant's News.* Kennedy Information Research Group, February 1998.

2. Corporate Decisions, Inc. (CDI) merged with Mercer Management Consulting in 1998.

3. Excluding Arthur Andersen, which had 4,200 consultants and $1.38 billion in revenues worldwide in 1996; *The Global Management Consulting Marketplace: Key Data, Forecasts & Trends 1997 Edition,* Kennedy Information Research Group, 1998.

4. *The Global Management Consulting Marketplace: Key Data, Forecasts & Trends 1997 Edition,* Kennedy Information Research Group, 1998.

5. Ibid.

6. Ibid.

7. "A Survey of Management Consultancy," *The Economist,* 1997.

8. *Management Consulting: Mergers and Acquisitions 1997 Edition,* Kennedy Information Research Group, 1998.

9. *The Global Management Consulting Marketplace: Key Data, Forecasts & Trends 1997 Edition,* Kennedy Information Research Group, 1998.

10. "A Survey of Management Consultancy, *The Economist,* 1997.

# NOTES

## Chapter 3

1. The added value of cars may be huge, but that does not mean Ford has a large added value. Without Ford, there is still GM, Toyota, and many others.

2. Donald A. Shön, *The Reflective Practitioner, How Professionals Think in Action,* (New York: Basic Books, 1982).

3. Ibid.

4. Ibid.

## Chapter 4

1. *Consultant's News,* Kennedy Information Research Group, February 1998; *The Global Management Consulting Marketplace; Key Data, Forecasts & Trends 1997 Edition,* Kennedy Information Research Group, 1998.

## Chapter 6

1. Fisher, R., Ury, W., & Patton, B. (1991). *Getting to Yes* (2nd ed.). New York: Penguin Books.

2. Lax, D. A., & Sebenius, J. K. (1986). *The Manager as Negotiator.* New York: The Free Press.

3. Kennedy Information Research Group, 1998. *The Global Management Consulting Marketplace: Key Data, Forecasts & Trends, 1997 Edition.*

## Appendix I

1. This discussion assumes a basic understanding of accounting. Reference: K. G. Palepu, V. L. Bernard, & P. M. Healy. 1996. *Business Analysis and Valuation: Using Financial Statements,* Cincinnati: South-Western College Publishing.

2. Assumes a basic understanding of economics.

3. A. Brandenburger and B. Nalebuff. 1996. *Co-opetition.* New York: Doubleday.

## Appendix II

1. Boeing Web site: http://www.boeing.com/commercial/747family/Boe747.html.

# CONTRIBUTORS

**Keith G. Allred** is an assistant professor at Harvard's Kennedy School of Government, where he teaches and conducts research on negotiations. He is also a member of the Negotiation Group and Negotiation Roundtable at Harvard Business School, and the Project on Negotiation at Harvard Law School. Before coming to Harvard, Dr. Allred was on the faculty at Columbia University. Dr. Allred has a Ph.D. in Organizational Behavior from UCLA's Anderson Graduate School of Management. Together with Sarah Sandberg, Dr. Allred founded Pioneer Negotiations, a firm that provides negotiation consulting services and training seminars to businesses, law firms, and government agencies. Dr. Allred can be reached at Pioneer Negotiations (Telephone: 500-449-5432. Fax: 500-449-5433. Web site: www.pioneernegotiations.com).

**Catherine Arnold** is an associate director with the Business Development and Strategic Planning Department of Hoffmann-La Roche Inc., a multinational pharmaceutical company. In this capacity, she has responsibility for the development of the U.S. Pharmaceutical Strategic Plan, identification and solicitation of pharmaceutical business development opportunities, and evaluation of merger and acquisition candidates. Prior to joining Hoffmann-La Roche, Ms. Arnold spent six years as a management consultant working for both Booz•Allen & Hamilton and Ernst & Young. Ms. Arnold also worked as a registered nurse and holds the degrees of Master of Business Administration, Master of Health Administration, and Bachelor of Science, all from the University of Pittsburgh.

**Laura Freebairn-Smith** is a partner at Good Work Associates, a consulting firm that specializes in the three areas of strategic planning, team development, and diversity development. Its primary mission is to help people understand and overcome obstacles to group effectiveness. After receiving her Bachelor of Arts in Philosophy and Political Science from the University of California at Berkeley, Ms. Freebairn-Smith moved to Asia. She spent four years on the Thai-Cambodian border serving as the Education Coordinator for the International Rescue Committee in Khao-I-Dang. This work sparked her interest in how organizations operate and how people within an organization work together. Ms. Freebairn-Smith earned her Master's in Public and Private Management (M.P.P.M.) from Yale School of Management in 1986. During the past 12 years, she was Chief Operating Officer for Jobs for the Future and Managing Director of the Gesell Institute of Human Development. She is an instructor at Yale University, and has taught at Central Connecticut State University and the University of New Haven. She also speaks at numerous workshops and seminars.

**Joseph B. Fuller** is a founder and director of Monitor Company. He joined Monitor Company at its inception and currently oversees its consulting operations globally. During his tenure at Monitor, Joe has worked with clients in many industries. His particular interest is in industries undergoing structural transition. This has led him to work in widely varied industries over the past 20 years including the automotive and consumer products sectors. He is an internationally recognized expert on telecommunications and has advised some of that industry's leading companies. In recent years, he has acted as an adviser to various governments on matters of privatization and deregulation in a range of industries. Mr. Fuller has contributed extensively to Monitor's conceptual work. In recent years, he has focused his attention on the interaction of market forces and companies' decision-making processes. He has recently published articles on the evolution of strategic planning for *Across the Board,* and on organization structure and strategy for the *Harvard Business Review.* His interest in research began during his collaboration with Professor Michael Porter of Harvard Business School on the development of the concepts presented in Porter's book, *Competitive Advantage: Creating and Sustaining Superior Performance* (New York: Free Press, 1985). His 1993 *Harvard Business Review* article, "Tailored Logistics," was among the most widely reprinted of that year. Mr. Fuller is a magna cum laude graduate of Harvard College, where he was a Charles Warren Fellow. He is a graduate of Harvard Business School, where he was an honors student, and serves as a director of the Phillips-Van Heusen Corporation.

**Charles P. Hoban** is a vice president at Mercer Management Consulting. Prior to joining Mercer, he was a partner of Corporate Decisions, Inc. (CDI), which was acquired by Mercer in the fall of 1997. In his nine years of strategy consulting, Mr. Hoban has consulted to clients in retailing, consumer products, chemicals, pharmaceuticals, computing, and telecommunications. As a founding member of CDI's European operation in 1991, Mr. Hoban has experience helping clients with growth strategy development in both U.S. and European markets. Mr. Hoban was a significant contributor to the development of the book *Value Migration* (Cambridge: HBS Press, 1996), leading the research team, managing the development of the manuscript, and articulating many of the book's basic frameworks. His ongoing work in understanding and quantifying shareholder value creation has been integral to the continued development of CDI's practice. Mr. Hoban holds an undergraduate degree from Dartmouth College and a Master of Management degree from Northwestern's Kellogg Graduate School of Management, where he graduated with distinction. Prior to joining CDI, he worked for Cargill, Inc., as an international copper and crude oil merchant.

**Bruce Kelley** is a senior consultant with Watson Wyatt Worldwide. He has more than 20 years of experience in the areas of health promotion, disease prevention, self-care, information-based benefits decision support, and managed healthcare. He has presented at many conferences, published extensively, and is frequently quoted in the professional and popular press. Previously, Dr. Kelley was a Principal and National Practice Leader for Health Management in William M. Mercer, Director of Client Services for the Central Region with the MEDSTAT Group in Ann Arbor, MI and Vice President of Analytical Services with Health Risk Management (HRM) in Minneapolis, MN. Dr. Kelley's undergraduate degree was a B.S. with a major in Economics and a minor in Human Resources Planning. He earned M.S. and Ph.D. degrees in Preventive Medicine from the College of Medicine at Ohio State University.

**Arun Maira** joined Arthur D. Little in 1989. He is leader of Arthur D. Little's Global Organization Practice and Managing Director of Innovation Associates Inc., an Arthur D. Little, Inc., subsidiary. Innovation Associates, cofounded by Dr. Peter Senge, author of *The Fifth Discipline: The Art and Practice of the Learning Organization* (New York: Doubleday, 1990), is the premier consulting company in the field of organizational learning. For over 30 years, Mr. Maira's work has focused on organization design and acceleration of change in large companies. He has worked as an executive at the board level of companies, and as a consultant to companies in many parts of the world and in many industries. This varied experience has given him practical insights into how to make change happen in large organizations. He is coauthor of a book, *The Accelerating Organization: Embracing the Human Face of Change,* (New York: McGraw-Hill, 1997). He has also written frequently for management journals and spoken at seminars for senior executives all over the world. Arun Maira was born in India in 1943. He holds an M.S. degree in Physics.

**Bill Matassoni** is McKinsey's Director of Communications. His responsibilities include both external and internal communications, including several of McKinsey's key systems for sharing knowledge among its consultants. He joined McKinsey in 1980 and was elected partner in 1982. He received a B.A. from Harvard College in 1968 and an M.B.A. from Harvard Business School in 1975.

**Ellen McGeeney** is a leader of the Communications and Technology practice at Vertex Partners. She draws on her experience in a variety of industries, including telecommunications, pharmaceuticals, consumer products, apparel, publishing, and specialty chemicals. She has addressed such problems as global organization structure and design, designing and managing a revenue turnaround, and improving the effectiveness of large sales forces. Ms. McGeeney has also coauthored "Looking Ahead, Looking Out," an article based on interviews with industry leaders. Prior to joining Vertex, Ms. McGeeney worked for Booz•Allen & Hamilton's consumer products practice. Before attending business school, she worked with the states of New York and Connecticut to implement a private-public partnership focused on reducing the welfare rolls. She received her B.A. with honors from Brown University in 1985, and her M.P.P.M. (Master's of Public and Private Management) from Yale School of Management in 1993.

**Barry Nalebuff** is the Milton Steinbach Professor at Yale School of Management. He graduated Phi Beta Kappa from the Massachusetts Institute of Technology in 1980, with degrees in Economics and Mathematics. A Rhodes Scholar, he received a doctorate in Economics from Oxford University two years later, and was awarded the George Webb Medley thesis prize. Before coming to Yale, he was a Junior Fellow at the Harvard Society of Fellows, and an Assistant Professor at Princeton University. Dr. Nalebuff is the author, with Princeton University Professor Avinash Dixit, of *Thinking Strategically: The Competitive Edge in Business, Politics, and Everyday Life,* and with Harvard Business School Professor Adam Brandenburger of *Co-opetition.*

**Gary Neilson** is a senior vice president of Booz•Allen & Hamilton and leader of the Transformation and Organization practice. During his nearly two decades with Booz•Allen, he has focused on organization and business process design, productivity improvement, and change management. Mr. Neilson has led the development of Booz•Allen's organization products—"Enterprise Value Engineering," "Creating High Performance Organizations . . . Making Strategy Work through Organization Capability," and "Theory P . . . Building Organization Capability through People and Business Processes." Prior to joining Booz•Allen, Mr. Neilson served on the financial staff of the IBM Corporation. He also served three years as a certified public accountant (C.P.A.) with Arthur Young & Company. Mr. Neilson received a B.S. in Accounting from King's College and an M.B.A. in finance from Columbia University's Graduate School of Business. At King's and Columbia, he graduated first in his class.

**Rudy Puryear** is the global managing partner for Electronic Commerce and Information Technology Strategy at Andersen Consulting. Based in Chicago, Mr. Puryear joined Andersen Consulting as a partner in 1991. He has over 25 years of experience in information technology, and has spent more than 20 years consulting to major organizations regarding IT strategy and planning. He routinely leads consulting assignments for large, complex multinational organizations addressing strategic technology issues. He frequently advises senior executives on critical IT issues and their relationship to business strategy. He is one of the firm's leading experts on Electronic Commerce and the implications of operating in the evolving Electronic Economy. His clients come from a broad cross-section of industries worldwide, and he regularly speaks before business audiences around the world. Prior to joining Andersen Consulting, Mr. Puryear was the managing director for Nolan, Norton & Co., an IT Strategy consulting firm. He did his graduate and undergraduate work in Computer Science at North Carolina State University.

**Steven E. Runin** is a partner and cofounder of Mitchell Madison Group and is based in the New York office. In his 14 years as a consultant, Mr. Runin has been involved in a variety of engagements, focusing primarily on the uses of technology within the banking and securities industries. In his work, Mr. Runin has counseled money center and superregional banks, securities firms, and insurers on operating cost improvement options including sourcing, outsourcing, business system redesign and consortia participation. In addition, he has developed financial services market entry strategies for institutions ranging from large European banks to telecommunications providers. Mr. Runin has also worked with a number of technology providers to help improve their marketing to financial institutions. Prior to establishing Mitchell Madison Group in 1994, Mr. Runin helped form the Financial Institutions/Services Practice of A.T. Kearney. Previously, Mr. Runin was a consultant with McKinsey & Company, where he was an active member of both McKinsey's Financial Institutions and Information Technology/Systems Practices. Mr. Runin received an M.B.A. from the Graduate School of Business of the University of Southern California and a B.A. in Film and Political Science from Syracuse University.

**Melissa Sabino** has been consulting in the medical products industry since 1979 and has been involved in well over 100 proprietary and multiclient studies. Since January 1995, she has been president of her own consulting firm, Wise Acres, Inc. Before forming her solo consulting practice, Ms. Sabino was a vice president at The Wilkerson Group, an IBM company, where she specialized in the medical device sector. She continues to work with TWG as a contract consultant. Before joining TWG, she served as a budget and policy analyst with the city of New York. Ms. Sabino has a M.S. in Public Finance and Budgeting from Harvard University and a B.S. degree from Bowling Green State University in Ohio with a concentration in Biology and Chemistry.

**Paul Smith** is a director and vice president in the Boston office of Bain & Company. He joined the firm in 1984 and was promoted to vice president in 1990. He specializes in the areas of high technology and telecommunications. In over 10 years of consulting, Mr. Smith has successfully led assignments in several industries, including telecommunications, information processing, high tech, healthcare, and technology. He has assisted clients in developing product technology, customer retention, reengineering and turnaround strategies. Prior to joining the consulting staff at Bain & Company, Mr. Smith was employed at Burroughs Corporation, where he was primary designer of a new-generation series of mainframe computer hardware and operating systems. He earned an M.B.A. from Harvard Business School with highest honors. Mr. Smith is a graduate of the University of California, where he received a B.S. in Mathematics and Computer Science with honors. In addition to his consulting activities, Mr. Smith has been actively engaged in the operations of Bain & Company's Boston office, heading the case assignment, evaluation, and compensation processes for Boston's consulting professionals for three years.

**George Stalk Jr.** joined The Boston Consulting Group (BCG) in 1978. He is a senior vice president and worldwide chair of BCG's Innovation, Marketing and Communications group. He focuses his professional practice on international and time-based competition. Now based in Toronto, Mr. Stalk has also worked in BCG's Boston, Chicago, and Tokyo offices. He is coauthor of *Competing against Time* (New York: Free Press, 1990), and of *Kaisha: The Japanese Corporation* (New York: Basic Books, 1987), Mr. Stalk has also been published in numerous business publications, including *Harvard Business Review,* and speaks regularly before prestigious business and industry associations. Mr. Stalk was recently identified by *Business-Week* as one among a new generation of leading management gurus. He holds a B.S. in Engineering Mechanics from the University of Michigan, an M.S. in Aeronautics and Astronautics from Massachusetts Institute of Technology, and an M.B.A. from Harvard Business School. He held previous positions with Applicon, Inc., and Exxon Research and Engineering.

**Harri V. Taranto** is a Managing Director of The Wilkerson Group. He maintains a special interest in corporate strategy development in the health care industry. Prior to joining the firm, he was a Senior Associate at McKinsey & Company, where he conducted corporate and divisional strategy studies. Mr. Taranto is an engineering graduate of Yale University, and holds an M.B.A. in Finance from Columbia Business School.

## Contributors

**L. John Wilkerson,** Chairman of The Wilkerson Group, an IBM company, combines extensive operating expertise in the healthcare industry with a background in healthcare securities and investment banking. Prior to joining the firm, Dr. Wilkerson headed marketing research and was in charge of corporate planning for Johnson & Johnson Company. He left Johnson & Johnson to accept a position in corporate finance at White Weld & Company, and later moved to Smith Barney, Harris Upham & Company to become a vice president, responsible for medical supply security analysis and research. He holds a Ph.D. from Cornell University, where he studied managerial economics and marketing research. In addition to his corporate activities, Dr. Wilkerson serves as a trustee for the Museum of American Folk Art and for Atlantic Health Systems.

# INDEX